April 2005

To Alan

and to ""
to build strong "
marriages in the
Jewish community.

Joel Crohn

# Beyond the Chuppah

Joel Crohn
Howard J. Markman
Susan L. Blumberg
Janice R. Levine


Foreword by Rabbi Harold M. Schulweis

Developed in collaboration with Jewish Family and Children's Services of San Francisco, the Peninsula, and Marin and Sonoma Counties.

# Beyond the Chuppah

## A Jewish Guide to
## Happy Marriages

JOSSEY-BASS
A Wiley Company
www.josseybass.com

Published by

 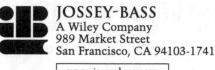

JOSSEY-BASS
A Wiley Company
989 Market Street
San Francisco, CA 94103-1741

www.josseybass.com

Jossey-Bass books and products are available through most bookstores. To contact Jossey-Bass directly, call (888) 378-2537, fax to (800) 605-2665, or visit our website at www.josseybass.com.

Substantial discounts on bulk quantities of Jossey-Bass books are available to corporations, professional associations, and other organizations. For details and discount information, contact the special sales department at Jossey-Bass.

We at Jossey-Bass strive to use the most environmentally sensitive paper stocks available to us. Our publications are printed on acid-free recycled stock whenever possible, and our paper always meets or exceeds minimum GPO and EPA requirements.

Library of Congress Cataloging-in-Publication Data
Crohn, Joel.
    A Jewish guide to happy marriages / Joel Crohn . . . [et al.].
      p.   cm.
    Includes bibliographical references.
    ISBN 0-7879-6042-X
    1. Marriage—Religious aspects—Judaism. 2, Communication in marriage. 3. Man-woman relationships. 4. Marriage—Psychological aspects. I. Title.
BM713. C76   2000
296.7'4—dc21                                                               2001005787

PB Printing   10 9 8 7 6 5 4 3 2                                    FIRST EDITION

# Contents

# Foreword

When I was ordained fifty years ago, one rarely heard of Jewish divorce in our community. We enjoyed the marvelous conceit that the Jewish family was healthy and that divorce, like alcoholism, was simply not the Jewish way.

This is regrettably no longer the Jewish condition. Divorce has become epidemic, and the bitter fruit of marital dissolution is publicly evident in the strained relations between family members at Bar and Bat Mitzvahs and at weddings. More often than not, young children are the innocent victims of marital struggles and the aftermath of divorce. I read with new pertinence the ancient rabbinic adage that when a divorce takes place, the very altar sheds tears.

Something must be done by the community to save the beleaguered family. This important book combines modern social-scientific research and traditional Jewish wisdom to help couples resurrect the buried promises of friendship, responsibility, and the joy of love. The old can be renewed, and the new can be hallowed.

Love in marriage is a gift, a potentiality to be cultivated. Marital love is a subtle art that calls for sustained and sensitive appreciation. This love is not blind. It reads between the lines. This love is not deaf. It hears what is not spoken. This love is not mute. It brings to articulation hidden emotions and concealed feelings. The art of loving relies on a conscious sensibility, an awareness of the other who is not a mere extension of the self. The other is not an ear into which the "I" can shout its wants and angers.

This book offers concrete ways for couples to create constructive and affirmative relations. It is rooted in a deep conviction that it is never too late to build again, to hope again, to love again.

April 2000                                Rabbi Harold M. Schulweis
                                          *Congregation Valley Beth Sholom*
                                          *Encino, California*

# Acknowledgments

Few books would ever be written without the support, friendship, and inspiration of many people. This book is certainly no exception. Those who helped us in so many ways over the years include Mindy Werner-Crohn, Irving M. Levine, Joseph Giordano, Monica McGoldrick, Esther Perel, James Levine, Fred Rosenbaum, Rosanne Levitt, Egon Mayer, Sylvia Weishaus, Dawn Kepler, Rachel Rosenfeld Harvey Shapiro, Leslie Goodman-Malamuth, and Jerry Barkan. The wisdom and humor of many rabbis contributed invaluably to this book as well. Rabbis Lavey Derby, Rachel Cowan, Michael Barenbaum, Isaiah Zeldin, Harold Schulweis, Helen Cohen, Alan Lew, Eli Herscher, David Wolfman, Sandy Seltzer, and Cary Yales all shared their time and insights generously. Judith Weinstein Klein's pioneering research was crucial to our work on Jewish identity and self-esteem.

The wise guidance of Anita Friedman, Amy Rassen, and Yael Moses of Jewish Family and Children's Services of San Francisco has been instrumental in the development of this book.

Over the years we have been assisted by a number of outstanding research assistants, consultants, and colleagues as we developed and evaluated the PREP approach and the Jewish and interfaith marriage programs. The list is now too long to include here, but we are greatly indebted to each of the people who have worked with us.

We've also had the good fortune to connect with many people who have aided our work in meaningful ways. Two people stand out for their encouragement and assistance in meeting the needs of couples: Bill Coffin and his colleagues in the U.S. Navy and Diane Sollee of the Coalition for Marriage, Family, and Couples Education.

We also want to express our great appreciation for the wonderful staff at PREP, Inc., who help so many couples through their hard work: Natalie Jenkins, Veronica Johnson, Phyllis Lemons, Janelle Miller, Glenda Roslund, Jonathan Wade, and Caroline Bagdasarian. As the co-director of the Center for Marital and Family Studies and the co-author of *Fighting for Your Marriage*, Scott Stanley's contribution has been invaluable.

The research studies underlying the content of this book have been supported by the American Jewish Committee, Jewish Family and Children's Services of San Francisco, the National Institute of Mental Health, the National Science Foundation, and the University of Denver. We are deeply grateful for this essential support, which has made our work possible.

Alan Rinzler, our editor at Jossey-Bass, has been determined to bring a book on Jewish identity and marriage to life for many years. He has made a major contribution to this book. We thank Alan and the entire staff at Jossey-Bass.

We want to express our deepest gratitude to the individuals, couples, and families who have shared their lives with us in our various research studies. They have opened their hearts and their relationships to our questionnaires, interviewers, and video cameras. The knowledge presented in this book comes from all they have taught us. We also thank our clients and seminar participants who have further shaped our ideas.

Finally, last but certainly not least, we thank our families. It is only in the crucible of family life that we learn the true lessons of love.

The support and assistance of everyone we have mentioned here, and of many more people we are not able to individually acknowledge, form the foundation of the book you are about to read. We share a common desire for you to use the knowledge we've gained through the years to deepen and enrich your relationship.

# Introduction

## Why Is This Book Different from All Other Books?

*Matchmaking may be a trivial thing in your eyes; but for the Holy One, it is as awesome an act as splitting the Red Sea.*

Genesis Rabbah 68:4

So why do we need a book called *Fighting for Your Jewish Marriage?* After all, aren't Jewish marriages like other marriages? What's so special about Jewish marriages?

In fact, in many ways Jewish marriages are becoming distressingly "normal." Whereas we used to pride ourselves on our low divorce rate, Jews under the age of forty are now divorcing nearly as often as everyone else. Between one-third and one-half of all new Jewish marriages will end in divorce. One-third of Jewish children under eighteen have had to deal with the pain and confusion of their family's coming apart. And of course, divorce statistics don't tell the full story. As many as half of all couples who don't divorce have less than satisfying relationships.

Jewish (and interfaith) relationships are under assault by the same forces that affect all marriages today. The breakdown of community, the lack of extended family support, economic pressures, frequent moves, difficulties balancing professional and home lives, and the material mania of our culture are hard on most marriages. *We believe that marriage is the most risky undertaking routinely taken on by the greatest number of people in our society.* What starts out as a relationship of great joy and promise can become the most frustrating and painful endeavor in a person's lifetime.

But for all the ways that Jewish marriages are similar to all others, they remain distinct in important ways. On the one hand, Jewish marriages still benefit in a variety of ways from Jewish heritage and tradition. Although Jews define themselves in many different ways, extended Jewish families, Judaism, synagogues, Jewish organizations, and a sense of belonging help support Jewish marriages. On the other hand, Jewish marriages suffer from special problems that are a result of our long, complex history and the ways it has affected our social, cultural, and psychological adjustment.

We need a book to help Jewish marriages because they are in trouble. For answers to our problems, we will turn both to ancient wisdom and to the findings of modern science. The best of Jewish tradition represents the accumulated wisdom of our ancestors. Its insights into the psychological, sexual, and spiritual foundations of human relationships remain relevant and meaningful to modern generations. And modern psychological research provides us with new ways to understand the pulse of human nature.

Our goal is not simply to understand but to refine and translate the insights of science and Jewish tradition into practical, useful, and learnable methods that support today's besieged marriages. In *I and Thou*, Martin Buber worked to show how the wisdom of Judaism and Jewish tradition could be used as part of a psychologically informed philosophy of human relationships. Our aim is similar: to integrate the insights of modern psychology with the wisdom of Jewish tradition to develop ways to support marriages and families.

Let's first look at some of the important issues that affect Jewish intimacy:

*Rapid assimilation.* The Jewish journey from shtetl to suburbia in one generation was dazzling and disorienting. Without time to digest the changes, Jews in America have paid a price for their rapid material success and assimilation. Many third- and fourth-generation Jews received mixed messages from their parents about the importance of being Jewish and about just what kind of Jew to be, leaving them ambivalent and confused about the meaning of being Jewish. Does it mean eating bagels and having a Seder once a year, or should it involve traditional observances like observing Shabbat, keeping kosher, or going to shul? Even in marriages between two Jews, partners may argue about what is "too Jewish" or "not Jewish enough."

*Intermarriage.* Half of Jews marrying today choose non-Jewish spouses, and intermarriage presents special challenges. Statistically, the marriages of interfaith couples are considerably more likely to end in divorce than marriages in which both spouses are Jewish. Sorting out and negotiating differences in cultural codes as well as religious and family loyalties can be a challenging task.

*Identity ambivalence.* Difficulties in establishing a positive Jewish identity can lead to problems between the sexes. This is especially true for Jews who have not found a positive meaning to their Jewishness. Internalized anti-Semitic stereotypes can lead to Jewish self-hatred and problems with self-esteem. "If only I didn't have such a big nose." "Why does she always talk about money?" Problems with Jewish identity can lead to the creation of negative stereotypes about Jews of the opposite sex, making romance and intimacy with other Jews problematic.

*Dealing with diversity.* Even when a Jew marries another Jew, they each may have very different cultural, religious, and behavioral expectations. Reform, Orthodox, Conservative, Renewal, Ashkenazi, Sephardic, East Coast, West Coast, Jews-by-choice, uninvolved, and "cultural" Jews, as well as immigrants from other countries, all call themselves Jewish. Nevertheless, they come to their relationships from very different backgrounds and with very different expectations about what being Jewish means and about gender roles, raising children, family obligations, and how to express emotions. When these differences are not clarified and negotiated, they can lead to misunderstanding and conflict.

*Shadow of the Holocaust*. Our legacy of suffering has left invisible wounds on the Jewish psyche, even among Jews brought up in secure and safe environments. Whereas the anxiety of older generations was based on the very real traumas they experienced, an unprocessed anxiety has been passed on to younger generations who have had little direct experience with anti-Semitism. This can create difficult-to-identify tension in individuals and their relationships. One recent national study, for example, found that Jewish men were twice as likely as men in the general public to suffer from depression;[1] depression can make creating and maintaining successful relationships very difficult. Even if we have never experienced the threat directly, the fact is that in recent memory, millions of individuals who were exactly like us—men, women and children—were horribly murdered just because they were Jews. This can make for some pretty understandable fear and loathing.

Let's look at some real-life examples that will help you understand the wide spectrum of issues that we explore in this book:

---

### I Like Being Jewish, But Jewish Women Are a Problem

Ed was thirty-seven and single; he felt under a lot of pressure, particularly from his mother, to marry and settle down. He came from a family with a strong Jewish background, and his parents made it clear that they expected him to marry a Jewish woman. But Ed never felt attracted to Jewish women. He said that he felt good about being Jewish, that almost all of his male friends were also Jewish, and that he was actively involved in Jewish organizations. "I would be glad to marry a Jewish woman if I could find one who didn't always want things her way," said Ed, "but I don't think they exist."

---

## When Jewish Practices Change

Sam was forty-four, and Katherine was forty; they had a four-year-old son, Andy. Sam was Jewish, and Katherine was raised as an Episcopalian, but their religious differences never seemed to be a big issue. Although Sam had always said he wanted to have a Jewish family, he never pushed Katherine.

Shortly after her mother died a few months ago, Katherine told Sam that she was tired of being a "nothing" and that she wanted something more spiritual in her life; she became increasingly interested in Judaism. She wanted Sam to go to synagogue with her and to begin observing Shabbat. He said he wasn't interested. One night Sam got really upset when he came home and found Katherine reading the Torah in bed. He told her, "I wanted you to be Jewish, but this is ridiculous." Because he had previously lived, as he would say, "as a typically uninvolved secular Jew," he found Katherine's new interest in Judaism to be actually threatening. "Suddenly," said Katherine, "it seemed to Sam that I had changed the deal, that I had become some sort of 'super-Jew.' All of a sudden I leapfrogged over him, and it has created a lot of tension in the relationship."

---

## Dealing with Jewish Diversity

Manny was twenty-nine. His parents were Sephardic and Moroccan and were born in Israel. Rebecca was also twenty-nine and was from a fifth-generation German American Jewish family. Because they were both Jewish, well educated, and from middle-class families, they didn't foresee any major differences in opinion—until the day their son was born. "I always assumed that we'd have a bris [ritual circumcision] at home and a big party for our family and friends," said Manny. Rebecca was horrified, and called it a "primitive ritual." Manny reluctantly agreed to a hospital circumcision, but the resentment about their different, unexpressed expectations began to build right then. "When we got married, I didn't realize the potential problems that might be created by the fact that I was attached to Jewish ritual while Rebecca couldn't care less. Neither of us considered ourselves that religious, so we hadn't anticipated the problems we now face," said Manny.

---

## Strangers in a Strange Land

Sylvia was twenty-six, Sacha twenty-eight. They were a young married couple who had emigrated from Russia three years ago. They had been fighting about whether to take advantage of social services offered by the Jewish community to Russian immigrants. In Russia, Sacha had been trained as an engineer at an elite school. Sylvia had finished dental school. Now, in the United States, Sacha was working as a mechanic's assistant in a garage, and Sylvia was working as a dental assistant. Under the Soviet regime of their youth, Sacha's family worked hard to disguise their identities as Jews, whereas Sylvia's family took the risk of being openly involved with the largely underground Jewish community. Sacha had trouble acknowledging that the idea of asking for help, especially from the Jewish community that his family had disavowed, made him feel anxious and humiliated. Sylvia, in contrast, insisted that the Jewish community was the natural place to turn for help.

---

## Is This Wedding Fun or Decadent?

Renee was twenty-six and had been raised in a suburb of Detroit; her family was involved in a Conservative synagogue. Her fiancé, Mike, was thirty-two; he had been raised by parents who had been actively engaged in radical politics and who prided themselves on the fact that they had never set foot in a synagogue.

Now that Renee and Mike were getting married, Renee's parents were insisting on spending $50,000 on a wedding that Mike's parents saw as totally decadent and materialistic. Renee and Mike found themselves fighting over how to deal with their respective sets of parents and about what was really important in life.

# THE PURPOSE OF THIS BOOK

Sam and Katharine, Manny and Rebecca, Renee and Mike. These couples and many more are struggling to deal with myriad issues in order to achieve harmony, a positive Jewish identity, and stronger, more satisfying marriages.

Good marriages take work. Contrary to popular belief, it is not how much you love each other that can best predict the future of your relationship but how you handle conflicts and disagreements. Unfortunately, conflict is inevitable—it can't be avoided. So if you want to have a good marriage, you had better learn to *fight right*.

Fortunately, these are exciting times in which to work with the most powerful yet fragile social institution we know—marriage. Advances in the "technology" of marital research have shed new light on why some marriages succeed while others fail. Until recently, most therapeutic advice for married couples was based solely on the experience and opinion of an individual "expert." Today, longitudinal research on thousands of married couples illustrates the key factors affecting marital success and failure.

The techniques and strategies in this book are based on the most up-to-date research in the field of marriage. We base our suggestions on solid research rather than on "pop-psych" speculation. This means that we don't just assume we know what may help couples— we use research and testing to see what really works. Although we discuss the problems and patterns that can destroy relationships, this book is less about what goes wrong and more about the specific things you can do to achieve and maintain a successful, satisfying relationship.

Our approach is based on the Prevention and Relationship Enhancement Program (PREP™) and twenty years of research at the University of Denver. Our research has been supported by

National Institute of Mental Health, National Institute of Health, and National Science Foundation grants and has resulted in over fifty scientific and professional publications. We developed our program to help couples beat the odds. In our workshops, we teach couples how to apply the skills and attitudes associated with good relationships.

Because of its roots in solid research and its straightforwardness, our approach has received a great deal of attention from couples across the country, professionals in the field of marital counseling, and the media. We have trained mental health professionals from around the world and leaders of such institutions as the U.S. Navy Family Service Centers. One of our primary goals is to give solid information to as many couples as possible about what they can do to prevent marital distress and divorce.

We have integrated the special issues that Jewish and interfaith couples face by incorporating the research of Dr. Joel Crohn. (This research, sponsored by the American Jewish Committee, led to Crohn's book on intermarriage, *Mixed Matches*.) *Fighting* for *Your Jewish Marriage* also includes the methods he developed in collaboration with Jewish Family and Children's Services of San Francisco. We will show how these findings can be adapted specifically to strengthen intimate relationships involving Jews. In each chapter, the examples, case histories, and exercises focus specifically on issues that are faced by Jewish and interfaith couples.

This book will teach you how to fight *for* your marriage. It is designed to provide you with the specific tools that twenty years of research have shown can make a real difference in your current and future happiness. At the same time, we will help you maintain and enhance intimacy, fun, commitment, friendship, and sensuality in your marriage.

*Fighting* for *Your Jewish Marriage* will give you exciting new ways to understand your personal, spiritual, and cultural differences. The innovative, thought-provoking exercises, first presented in *Fighting* for *Your Marriage*, have been successfully used by tens of thousands of couples across the United States and in countries around the world, and in this book have been adapted for the special needs of Jewish intimacy. We provide you with practical tools that will help you develop new insights, strengthen your communication skills, resolve conflicts, and deepen your pleasure in each other's company.

*Fighting* for *Your Jewish Marriage* also offers concrete, practical help for couples who are dealing with all the challenges of modern marriages, in addition to the special issues of Jewish intimacy. It shows how the traditional strengths of Jewish marriage and Jewish tradition can be reclaimed and built on, even by the most secular couples. And, using the findings of modern research as well as ancient wisdom, the book will help you develop specific skills and strategies to create more successful and satisfying relationships.

## WHO IS THIS BOOK FOR?

*Fighting* for *Your Jewish Marriage* is for

- Couples in which both partners are Jewish by birth

- Couples from different Jewish cultural and religious groups—Ashkenazic, Sephardic, Russian immigrant, and Israeli, as well as Reform, Reconstructionist, Conservative, Orthodox, and secular Jews

- Interfaith couples in which one partner is contemplating conversion *or* has opted to retain his or her original religious identity

- Couples including one or two Jews-by-choice

- Jewish partners whose lifestyles or religious and cultural commitment to Judaism differ sufficiently to create stress in the relationship

We want our Jewish marriages to be another sturdy link in the chain that has stretched for more than five thousand years, connecting families *l'dor v'dor*—from generation to generation. Wherever you are in your relationship, *Fighting* for *Your Jewish Marriage* has something to offer. It is for new couples who want to build the strongest possible foundation; for couples who have been together for years and are looking for ways to enrich, reinvigorate, and strengthen their bonds; and for singles who are looking for the communication skills that lead to lasting relationships. These are tools that *work:* research spanning twenty years has demonstrated that divorce rates can be reduced by as much as 50 percent in couples who learn and use the techniques and perspectives we teach in this book.

## MAKING YOUR MARRIAGE WORK

At the end of a Jewish marriage ceremony, the groom stomps on a wineglass wrapped in a napkin. To explain the ritual, most commentators note that the shattering of the glass brings a moment of solemnity to a joyous occasion, in memory of the destruction of the Second Temple. More practically, others add that happiness and trust are such delicate components in any marriage that great care must be taken not to damage them beyond repair.

The challenge of creating successful marriages lasts a lifetime. It is a joyful, sometimes painful, but ultimately deeply satisfying struggle in which the coauthors of this book, their respective spouses, and millions of Jewish families are engaged. We've been there. We are there. And we want to be there with you as well. L'chaim.

# Beyond the Chuppah

# Creating a Positive Jewish Identity
# That Supports Your Marriage

MAX: *I think "devouring" is the word that stands out in my mind when I think of Jewish women. Also "pushy, aggressive, neurotic, difficult, status-conscious, and self-destructive." I think a Jewish female's idea of sharing is that she deals with all of her problems, and then you deal with all of her problems. That's sharing?*

LIZZIE: *Being a Jew means really limiting my social life, because it's hard for me to stick to my commitment to marry another Jew when I meet Gentiles that I happen to like better. Being a Jewish woman means conflict for me, because I associate it with being passionate and intelligent, and that's not always so easy for Jewish men to handle.*

*Max and Lizzie, two participants in an ethnotherapy group for Jewish men and women*

In this chapter, we first explain the origins of our struggles with Jewish identity. We then describe methods—based on groundbreaking research on the connections between Jewish identity, self-esteem, and intimacy—to help you create a more positive sense of being Jewish. Sorting out your own conflicts and confusion about being Jewish can enhance your sense of self-worth, which is the foundation on which you build a successful intimate relationship. Going through this process is also a crucial step to take before trying to work out religious or cultural differences with your partner. By clarifying your own sense of identity, you will be much better prepared to use the communication and conflict resolution skills you will learn in later chapters.

Most of us are aware that our ability to create successful, loving relationships is built on our sense of self-worth. If we feel unworthy at some basic level, we will have difficulty giving or receiving love. In spite of their hunger to create enduring love, adults who were abused or neglected as children have great difficulty with intimacy. Children's ability to love and be loved is also damaged by parents who have unrealistic expectations of their children, who are never satisfied, or who treat their children simply as extensions of themselves. These pressured children are often mystified when, as adults, great success does not automatically erase self-doubt or make love easy.

Although it is less obvious to people living in our hyperindividualistic American society, our self-esteem is also rooted in our tribal history. At our core we are social animals. In order to feel whole, we need to have some sort of positive connection to something bigger than ourselves. Developing a positive sense of group belonging is especially important and often difficult for members of minority groups that have a history of persecution and discrimination. Self-esteem problems are common among Jews as well as among African Americans, Asian Americans, and Mexican Americans who are uncomfortable with or ashamed of their group identities. Just as a solid sense of self requires a person to come to terms with all of his or her personal history, a healthy tribal identity requires that the individual face the history of his or her group. For many minority group members, this means finding ways to integrate the collective pride *and* the pain of the past into an overall positive sense of group belonging. The extreme splits between the good and bad images of Jews—in the minds of both Jews and Gentiles—pose special challenges in creating a healthy Jewish identity.

Today, Jews face an additional challenge: choice. Identity as a Jew used to be a matter of destiny; now it is one of decision. We find ourselves at a smorgasbord of identity choices. How important to our lives shall we make Judaism, Israel, Jewish culture, ethnicity, or defense of Jewish interests? How much do we want to just blend in and be inconspicuous? How important is it to create a Jewish family? Some Jews are comfortable with the choices they have made, but many others are uncertain, ambivalent, and inconsistent about how they define being Jewish. They may act out this confusion in troubling ways in their intimate relationships, both with other Jews and with non-Jews.

## HOW HISTORY AFFECTS THE JEWISH PSYCHE

Our cultural and religious histories are woven into our psyches and souls. As surely as our ancestors' genes have passed from previous generations into us, our attitudes, beliefs, and emotional makeup are deeply influenced by the experiences of those who have come before us. Who we are, how we see the world, and how we relate to others are all colored by our collective pasts, often in ways we are unaware of. Whether you are married to another Jew or in an interfaith relationship, whether you are secular, Orthodox, or a Jew-by-choice, whether you are a sixth-generation American or a new immigrant, the triumphs and catastrophes of Jewish history influence how you think, feel, and, most important, how you love.

It is one thing to be hated, and quite another to be adored. But because Jews have been so despised and reviled, on the one hand, and literally worshiped, on the other, it is very difficult for the Jewish psyche to integrate these radical contradictions. The uneasy relationships between pride and pain are embedded deeply in the Jewish psyche and have a tremendous impact on the self-esteem of Jews and, as a result, on their intimate relationships. In *Portnoy's Complaint,* Philip Roth captured with painful perfection the Jewish abil-

ity to create children who experience themselves as "unique as uni-
corns . . . geniuses and brilliant like nobody has ever been brilliant
and beautiful before in the history of childhood—saviors and sheer
perfection on the one hand, and such bumbling, incompetent,
thoughtless, helpless, selfish . . . little *ingrates*, on the other."[1]

It's not just Portnoy. Rooted in our shared history are very mixed
feelings about success, power, money, and Judaism that we act out
in complex ways in our relationships.

## About Being Loved and Admired

No group of humans on earth has been as talented and influential,
relative to their numbers, as have the Jewish people. From Moses to
Jesus, from Freud to Marx and Einstein, the impact of Judaism and
Jews on world civilization has been nothing short of remarkable. It
is apparent that membership in this small tribe is like none other.

Although it can feel good to be somehow connected to greatness
through being Jewish, it can also be a burden. Given this legacy, it
is very easy to feel that one has somehow not measured up. Falling
short of greatness is, by definition, far more common than is attain-
ing it. Not all Jews are brilliant or rich or good. The focus on success
and achievement so prevalent in Jewish families no doubt helps create the drive that has supported the accomplishments of many Jews,
but the cost of these elevated expectations can be a nagging sense of
not ever quite measuring up to impossible standards.

> *Mr. and Mrs. Marvin Rosenbloom are pleased*
> *to announce the birth of their son, Dr. Jonathan*
> *Rosenbloom.*
>
> Rabbi Joseph Telushkin[2]

There is another dark side to the success of the Jews: the jealousy
and envy of others. Although many anti-Semitic stereotypes about
Jews are virulent lies, some are, at least in part, based on truth. Jews
have been very successful in America and in every nation where we

have been given the freedom to compete. Jews are the most educated and wealthy ethnic group in American society. But Jews are all too aware of the danger that the anti-Semite can (and will) twist the reality of Jewish success into lies: "Jews are cunning thieves; they take more than their share. Look at how they control the banks and the media." If Jews are admired for their success, it is also clear that they are hated for it. Thus our historical experience has created a troubling mix of pride and paranoia in our psyches.

## About Being Hated

> All Jewish holidays can be reduced to a simple for-
> mula: They tried to kill us all; they failed; let's eat.
> *Sacha, a twenty-eight-year-old Jewish man*

Jews historically have been among the most despised people on earth. From the destruction of the Second Temple, to the expulsion from England in 1290 and then from Spain in 1492, to centuries living under the threat of pogroms in Russia and Poland, and culminating in the recent horror of the Holocaust, Jews have wandered the earth for two thousand years, fleeing persecution. And although the birth of Israel finally created a Jewish homeland, the small state has existed in a state of war with many of its neighbors since it was founded in 1948.

Of course, the persecution of Jews has always been justified in the minds of their oppressors. Jews stole money, were parasites on society, cheated in business dealings, were oversexed (or undersexed), were effeminate, had horns, and were in alliance with the devil. They ritually killed Christian children to use their blood on Passover; they *did* kill Christ. Understanding that these beliefs and stereotypes were very real to their neighbors, Jews who lived in the fear of Easter pogroms were not paranoid; they understood that this was truly a dangerous time. Jews have repeatedly been used as "aliens in residence" by kings, czars, and dictators to focus and manipulate discontent. Hitler used the historical hatred of Jews to amass power by harnessing the fear, passion, and prejudice of a nation in chaos.

The shadow of the Holocaust has hung heavily over the generation of Jews born after the war. As the real fear of actual threats became part of the past, what got passed to the next generation was a kind of generalized and diffused anxiety and paranoia. For many baby-boomer Jews raised in the United States in the 1950s and 1960s, talking about the Holocaust was forbidden. Although some families couldn't stop reliving it, more buried it in silence.

Alex, born in 1952, described what it was like to be raised by his parents, survivors of the concentration camps: "Their suffering was on their faces. They would never trust a non-Jew, but they pushed us to succeed in the Gentile world. If we ever tried to talk to them about what they had been through, my father would get very angry, and my mother would get depressed. It was clear that we were not to bring it up. But it meant I could never talk to them about the ordinary growing up things I was struggling with. My problems always felt so petty compared to what they had been through."

In recent years there has been a shift in how Jews and non-Jews are dealing with the history of the war. As the aging survivors and killers from World War Two face their own deaths, we suddenly find ourselves barraged by images of and references to the Nazis and the Holocaust. Maybe we are now confident enough to face what happened, or maybe we sense that this is our last chance to learn from those who were there.

For the generation of Jews raised in silence, this recent focus on the past can be confusing and disturbing. Just when we thought that the Holocaust had become ancient history, images of it are constantly being resurrected. Such movies as *Schindler's List* met with unanticipated success. The Holocaust Museum in Washington, D.C., placed the memory of the Holocaust in the national consciousness. That which was hidden is now everywhere, and we are not always well equipped to deal with it. There is a part of the Jewish psyche that alternates between an adaptive numbness and a sense of being overwhelmed.

In some curious ways, understanding and dealing with the anxiety that Jews have passed on from generation to generation has become more difficult as we have become safer and more secure. The immigrant generations in the United States and refugees who had experienced persecution had little difficulty pinpointing the origins of their fear. There were plenty of painful memories to explain their anxiety. In succeeding generations, however, the dread that was passed on became less personal and therefore less understandable, even though its presence was still felt.

We also benefit from our identification with the suffering of our ancestors. Judaism and Jewish history have taught us to identify with the underdog. At the center of Judaism is a focus on *tikkun olam*—repairing the world. It is no accident that the story of Moses leading the Jews out of Egypt is crucially important not only to Jews but to African Americans and other oppressed groups. Jews have been disproportionately involved in social action, in the civil rights movement, and in the helping professions. Jews' voting patterns are much more similar to those of poor African Americans than to those of their middle-class neighbors. It seems that the impact of history on the Jewish psyche has been to create a curious mix of pain and pride, of fear and compassion that affects every aspect of our lives, including how we love.

## Conditional Acceptance and Self-Hatred

Prior to emancipation in late-eighteenth-century Western Europe, Jews did not suffer from a sense of self-hatred, in the modern sense of the word. Trying to "fit in" was not an option for most Jews, as they were physically, socially, and spiritually isolated from the mainstream community. Almost all Jews lived in ghettos, dressed differently, and lived a completely different way of life. We were the People of the Book. The pious Jew had the security of knowing how to do almost everything, because Jewish law prescribed it all. More important, suffering was offset by a sense of collective moral superiority. Suffering had its own rationale; we suffered because we were held to a higher standard. Those killed by anti-Semites were not victims; rather, they died for *kiddush hashem,* as holy martyrs to God. Whether Jews were celebrating the birth of a child or going to the gas chambers with the "Shema" on their lips, all pleasure and all pain had meaning and purpose.

As integration into the broader society seemed more in reach, the price of acceptance seemed to be that Jews had to abandon the distinct characteristics that separated Jew from non-Jew. Identifying with those in power meant trying to adopt Gentile standards of behavior and beauty, and minimizing the differences between Judaism and Christianity. The real paradox was that virulent stereotypes about Jews became truly destructive to the Jewish psyche only as Jews became free enough to mingle with those who held those stereotypes. In *The Jewish Mind,* Raphael Patai observed the psychological cost of the emancipation of the Jews. "The pathetic aspect of the situation was that the Jews themselves, once they became acquainted with as much as the rudiments of the Gentile cultural values, and, in particular, with the Gentile stereotype of the Jew, began to be influenced by them and to share them."[3]

## The Dilemmas of Assimilation

Rapid assimilation into American culture is the latest and, in some ways, most challenging phase of Jewish history. In societies in which we were barely tolerated or actively persecuted, there was never any question about our Jewish identity. Our lives, however difficult, were imbued with meaning *because* we were Jewish. However religious we were, whether we were rich or poor, our fates as individuals were intertwined with the fate of the Jewish community. For better and for worse, we were connected.

As integration into the larger society became more of an option, those traits that labeled us as "Jew" seemed to be increasingly troublesome. As a people who valued contact, engagement, debate, and emotion, we were too loud and intense to be accepted into the inner sanctums of Protestant life. We had to tone ourselves down, which was not always easy.

We also tried to tone down and Americanize our religious practices so as to avoid making our Christian neighbors uncomfortable with our alien ways. In recent years, the largest group of Jews has become the "unaffiliated." The successful and very rapid process of assimilation left many Jews without the burdens of anti-Semitism, but also without the benefits of community, meaning, and connection provided by traditional Jewish life. Under these conditions, identity as a Jew for some seemed increasingly a liability rather than an asset.

But hundreds of generations of connection are not so easily jettisoned. We mourned the losses caused by assimilation even as we passionately pursued the opportunities provided by an open and free society. Hence the modern and difficult phenomenon of Jewish ambivalence. *We want our cake*—to take advantage of American individualism and the freedom to do whatever we want, unbound by obligations of the past. *And we want to eat it too*—to experience the connection, sense of belonging, meaning, and identity that being Jewish can provide.

For many Jews, the process of assimilation resulted in a confusing jumble of tremendous pride and tremendous shame, of nostalgia and embarrassment, of wanting to merge with the tribe and also to escape its embrace. And as we shall see over and over again, the struggle to define our relationship with Jewish life gets played out in our intimate relationships. How could it not?

Ana's confusion is a good example of how this ambivalence can affect intimacy with other Jews. At thirty, she had been through four intense relationships, alternating between Jewish and non-Jewish men.

There are times when being Jewish is really important to me. I want to do Jewish things, to be around other Jews, to eat Jewish foods, to visit my parents. Even though I'm not very religious, there are even times when I am surprised that I actually feel a desire to go to synagogue, almost in spite of myself. It's during my "Jewish phases" that I feel like it's really important that I find a Jewish man to settle down with.

But there are other times when I wish I didn't have to think about being Jewish at all. I look in the mirror and wish I looked less Jewish, wish I were able to be less emotional and more quiet and demure. At those times, I feel uncomfortable around other Jews, like I am almost embarrassed by their behavior. Am I crazy?

## Be Jewish—But Not Too Jewish: Mixed Messages from Our Families and Society

Ana was not crazy, but she also wasn't totally aware of the conflicting messages about being Jewish with which she had grown up. It was inevitable that as the conflict between continuity and assimilation intensified, many Jewish families gave out mixed messages about the importance of Jewish continuity. The message usually took the form of "Be Jewish, but don't be too Jewish."

One of the authors of this book, Joel Crohn, realized that even his name is an interesting example of the ambivalence that molded the character of American Jews. As the story goes, in 1940 when his great-uncle, Nathan Cohn, a Chicago surgeon, the youngest and only educated and American-born of his siblings, changed his name to Crohn, the rest of the family *had* to follow suit.

"How would it look, me introducing my brother as 'Dr. Crohn,' while my name is Cohn?" complained Joel's grandfather. Joel's own father felt he had been denied the opportunity to apply for a job in the 1940s because his name revealed his Jewishness. With the change from Cohn to Crohn, his name was now generic enough for him to at last receive the job application.

What is particularly interesting about his family's decision was how *little* they changed their name. By adding just one letter, they simultaneously tried to annihilate *and* honor their Jewish distinctiveness. They didn't erase Cohn completely by choosing a generic, American-sounding name, as some Jews did.

His family wanted it both ways and attempted to walk an exquisitely fine line: to be invisible when they chose, but also to have access to the benefits of belonging to the group when they wanted and needed it. As for many other Jewish families, the ambivalence that led to name changes and nose jobs had an emotional cost. The price was confusion about what it meant to be a Jew.

## HOW HISTORY AFFECTS JEWISH RELATIONSHIPS

With our increasing success, acceptance, and assimilation in Western societies, our discomfort with our Jewishness—even self-hatred—grew in ways that had a particularly destructive impact on intimate relationships. Even as we were most comfortable with the sense of safety and familiarity that could be part of loving another Jew, we could also become uncomfortable with how he or she reminded us just how Jewish we were.

Psychologists use the word *projection* to describe how we protect ourselves against owning certain unpleasant aspects of our personalities and behavior by projecting them onto others. This psychological process of projection allows people to disown aspects of themselves they find unacceptable by seeing them in others.

The origins of the concept of projection lie in the Biblical ritual of imbuing a sacrificial goat—the scapegoat—with the sins of the community and then sending the animal into the desert to die. "The sacrificial goat unburdened the community of its collective guilt, freeing it . . . to begin anew."[4] Sigmund Freud developed the concept of projection when he lived in Vienna during the late nineteenth century, a time and place in which it was quite obvious how Austrian and German Gentiles could project unacceptable aspects of themselves onto Jews.

Unfortunately, as they attempted to integrate themselves into Western culture, many Jews began to absorb and internalize the anti-Semitic projections rather than resist them. The price of acceptance seemed to be the taking on of the perspective and prejudices of Gentiles. We looked in the mirror and searched for evidence of the stereotypes. "Am I too aggressive in my speech, are my shoulders too stooped, is money all I care about? I must be aware of these traits in order to eradicate them." This is the basis of Jewish self-hatred.

But it is hard to acknowledge these feelings in ourselves. One way Jewish men and women sometimes deal with this kind of self-hatred is to project these "negative" Jewish traits onto the opposite sex. In her pioneering research on Jewish identity and self-esteem, the late Dr. Judith Weinstein Klein found that this kind of self-hatred can lead to a thought process that justifies negative stereotypes about Jews—but only of the opposite sex. Klein's research showed how these kinds of unresolved personal conflicts about Jewish identity interfere with Jewish intimacy. When people project negative stereotypes about Jews onto Jews of the opposite sex, they unconsciously sacrifice themselves in a self-destructive bid for acceptance.[5]

As we discuss in Chapter Ten on intermarriage, marrying out of the group does not resolve the issues created by Jewish identity conflicts. Jewish self-hatred, ambivalence, and low self-esteem are destructive in all intimate relationships, be they between two Jews or a Jew and a non-Jew. These problems are not unique to Jews. Research on African Americans and Asian Americans, for example, has demonstrated very similar patterns that affect intimacy between members of those groups as well.

## CREATING A POSITIVE SENSE OF JEWISH IDENTITY

*am*biv*a*lence (noun): simultaneous and contradictory attitudes or feelings (as attraction and repulsion) toward an object, person, or action.*
*Merriam Webster's Collegiate Dictionary (10th ed.)*

Facing and acknowledging your own ambivalence and seeing how it has affected you is an important first step in clarifying your own sense of Jewish identity. Doing so helps you create a more consistent, cohesive, and clear sense of Jewish identity, which is so important in building strong intimate relationships.

## Healing the Wounds of Internalized Anti-Semitism

A first step in healing the psychological and spiritual wounds of internalized anti-Semitism is exposing to the light of day the painful stereotypes you have internalized. Psychologist Judith Weinstein Klein described how a process she called ethnotherapy involved a necessary but difficult opening of old wounds in order to let them heal. Listen in to the revealing and disturbing dialogue in an ethnotherapy group for young single Jewish men and women, most of whom had never directly experienced anti-Semitism in their own lives. It will give you a sense of the power and destructiveness of internalized negative stereotypes on Jewish relationships. As you read what the group members say, imagine what you would add to the discussion if you were there. Don't be surprised if your own responses sometimes seem contradictory.

> RINA:  They [Jewish men] are neurotic. Very out of touch with their sensuality. Nervous and uncomfortable with their bodies.
> BRAD:  There are two things I'm supposed to have along when I'm with a Jewish woman: my Dun & Bradstreet rating and the power of attorney that I'm supposed to turn over to them.
> SHELLEY:  Jewish men expect a lot of Jewish women, and they're very dependent. They're overachievers, egocentric, and selfish.
> GUY:  Jewish women have high material expectations—furs and jewelry.
> LOIS:  Jewish men expect to be waited on—psychologically as well as physically. They have to be the center of attention.
> SYLVIA:  When I think of Jewish men, I think of my father and my brother. I don't want to see them as sexual beings. I had always put that aside. Therefore, Jewish men have never been sexually attractive to me.

MAX:  You know, in a lot of ways, Christians have been my ideal. I've always wanted a muscular body, and I don't have one. Jewish men have flat feet, and they're soft and not very athletic. It's always bothered me. I'm not my father's son; in a way, I'm my mother's son.

The outpouring of negativity in the group eventually led to deeper sharing and a greater awareness of the mixed messages about being Jewish each of the participants had received from their own families and from society. Ultimately, revealing their own stories helped group members begin to take responsibility for working through their own conflicts about what it meant to be Jewish. When group members could begin to understand and admit their personal conflicts, they felt less need to project the negative onto the opposite sex.

Jane was a thirty-eight-year-old divorced woman with an eight-year-old daughter. She reflected on her experience growing up:

When I was twelve years old, I loved Barbara Streisand's singing and thought she was really beautiful and sexy. When we would watch her on TV, my parents would constantly talk about her nose: "How can she appear in public like that?" I didn't say anything, but as a young Jewish girl, I felt kind of proud of her and ashamed of my parents.

As an adult I always had trouble feeling good about the way I looked. When I was growing up, my father kept offering me a nose job. It really hurt. It was like my father was saying that I was ugly because I looked Jewish.

I was really pleasantly surprised when I found that Gentile men were so attracted to me in college. I had never felt comfortable with Jewish boys. When I was twenty-eight and on my own, I told my parents that I planned to marry Bob, a non-Jew. They became totally hysterical: "How could you do this to us? Marry a goy?" I couldn't believe it. They hadn't contributed a penny to the Jewish community or gone to synagogue in years. From talking in the group, I'm

starting to realize that not all Jewish men are like my father. What
a relief.

It is vitally important to be able to talk to each other, to uncover
our stories and our history. Only then can we begin to understand
and heal the ways our ambivalence, our doubts, and our fears about
being Jewish have undermined our intimate relationships. It is
painful to open old wounds, face the confusion, and try to deal with
the hurt, but the process can free up a tremendous amount of energy.
And it can help us build more successful and satisfying relationships.
The exercises at the end of this chapter will help you understand and
work through your own issues surrounding your Jewish identity.

## Ancestors' Shadows

Drs. Joel Crohn and Judith Klein developed a powerful process that
they use in groups to help people work through the mixed feelings
they have about their religious and cultural backgrounds. The process,
called Ancestors' Shadows, first described in *Mixed Matches*,[6] reveals
the chorus of your family members' voices and their mixed messages
that you carry within you.

In the groups, each participant describes in writing what he or
she imagines his or her grandparents, parents, and siblings would
say if they were really being honest in answering two crucial questions. The first question is "What does being Jewish mean to you?"
The second question is "How do you make your way in life?"

After all the group members have written down their responses,
a participant is asked to volunteer to be the central character. That
person stands in front of the group and chooses people from the
group to play the roles of his or her family members. The written
sentences become the script for a family drama.

In one group we conducted, Susan, a thirty-five-year-old woman
from New York, volunteered to be at the center of the psychodra-
matic exercise. She chose group members to play out the role of
each of her family members. After coaching them on how to speak

their lines, she faced her family and listened intently to the chorus of characters she had created.

MATERNAL GRANDMOTHER: I'm Jewish. That means living in fear and trying to forget what happened to my family in Europe. I make my way in life by devoting myself to my family and not expecting much.

MATERNAL GRANDFATHER: I am a Jew. For me, that means studying the Torah and observing the mitzvoth, and never forgetting what the Nazis did. I make my way in life by being a good Jew.

PATERNAL GRANDMOTHER: I am a Jew. That means focusing my life on the Jewish community. I make my way in life by helping others.

PATERNAL GRANDFATHER: I am a Jew, and to me that means fighting to protect other Jews. I make my way in life by being tough and smart.

MOTHER: To me, being a Jew means you don't advertise the fact that you are Jewish and that you do everything to help your children succeed. I make my way in life by pouring myself into my children and making sure that they get the best of everything that life has to offer.

FATHER: I'm Jewish and that means that you are proud of who you are, but your religion is a private matter. I make my way in life by working hard and providing for my family.

OLDER BROTHER: I identify with being an American and fitting in. Being Jewish doesn't mean anything except ridiculous expectations and rules that can never be fulfilled. I make my way in life by doing my own thing and by not making commitments that I can't keep.

YOUNGER SISTER: I am a Jew, and that means living in a Jewish community and going to shul and raising my children as Jews. I make my way in life by being part of something bigger than myself.

Then it was Susan's turn to talk about what being a Jew meant to her. Her eyes were full of tears as she addressed the family she had created.

SUSAN:  I am a Jew, and that means I am confused about who I am. I make my way in life by trying to please everybody.

As Susan looked at the people playing the roles of her family members, she began to cry. After a few minutes, she went on to describe her reactions to her experience with the group.

I'm really confused. My dad's father smuggled guns to Israel in 1948. Here I am, intermarried, uninvolved in the Jewish community, and living a safe middle-class life. So I can't tell you what kind of Jew I am. But I don't think you can equate being Jewish and Christian. And bringing a child into the world—that's a very heavy thing to do. So I don't know what I am going to want to tell and teach him. I feel so unprepared. I think that in a way, I've been trying to be like a lot of my family members—simultaneously—and it hasn't worked very well for me. I don't know how I want to be Jewish right now, but I don't think it's something that should be lost.

At the next week's meeting, it was clear that Susan had been thinking a lot about her Ancestors' Shadows experience.

I began to realize that my brother and sister and I, each in our own way, have been struggling to come to terms with the very mixed messages that we received from our family about the importance of being Jewish. I understand better why I have always felt so conflicted about my Jewishness. Sometimes I've been proud of being Jewish, but other times I just resented my family's attempts to control what that was supposed to mean. I guess it's my turn now to try to figure out what is important for me and then really try to talk to my husband about it.

## Healing Choices

Steve, a twenty-nine-year-old Jewish man, remembered a conversation he had with a friend: "When I was feeling really confused about my Jewish identity, I told an African American friend that sometimes I wish we had a distinct color like he did. If we were born green, we wouldn't always be burdened with having to choose whether or not to identify ourselves as Jews. He said, 'You have no idea what you are asking for. You better hope that your wish is never granted.'"

The vast majority of American Jews are Caucasian. Unlike members of racial minority groups whose identity is directly connected to their appearance, Jews are aware that today they have much more of a choice about how distinctive and important they make their Jewish identity.

Bob, forty-five, described the issue well:

> When I walked out on the streets of Chicago in my virtually all-Jewish ghetto in the 1950s, it didn't really matter if my parents were observant or not. Everything and everyone was Jewish, so I could absorb the feeling of being a Jew just by going out my front door. Now I live in a California suburb where less than 10 percent of my neighbors are Jewish. Out here that's considered a "Jewish neighborhood." If I want my kids to have any kind of positive identity as Jews, I am going to have to be a lot more conscious and active as well as a lot less ambivalent about being Jewish than my parents were.

Creating a clear sense of group identity in a rapidly changing world is very difficult—and very important. We are social creatures, and throughout human history identification with some combination of culture, faith, tradition, and shared group history has provided us with meaning and morality. People have always turned to their tribe for support and a sense of connection. To paraphrase John Donne, "No person is an island."

In *Mixed Matches*, Joel Crohn wrote of the dramatic shift in how group identity is created. He pointed out that throughout human history, "identity as a member of a group was a matter of destiny, not decision. . . . We now face the complicated task of *creating* our own sense of identity. Like painters standing before a palate of colors, we can choose the shades and shapes of our identities. This can be both an exhilarating and a confusing task."[7]

For you to create and maintain a successful and enduring intimate relationship, it is very important to resolve your confusion and work toward creating a clear and meaningful cultural and religious identity. Research on marital stability and satisfaction has demonstrated the importance of agreement on matters of identity and faith. In order to enter into a productive dialogue with your partner about the ways to connect your relationship and your family to a broader community, you need to be as clear as possible about what is important to you. Doing the work to clarify your own sense of identity will allow you to make wholehearted choices with your partner.

## Dimensions of Jewish Identity

There are many different ways that individuals identify with being Jewish. Some people identify as Jewish but have little or no interest in participating in any of the ways of being Jewish that we describe here. For these individuals, the challenge is to define why they choose to identify as Jews. For most Jews, however, one or several of the following dimensions define what is important about being Jewish.

- Judaism: practice and participation in synagogue life; observation of some or all of Shabbat, keeping kosher, the high holidays, Passover seders, or other rituals in the home; prayer, study of Hebrew, and related activities

- Ethnic, cultural, and communal connections: participation in Israeli dance; enjoyment of Jewish foods;

involvement in Jewish social, cultural, philanthropic,
or recreational activities

• Secular Zionism: interest in Israeli politics, culture,
and history; interest in traveling to Israel; participation
in groups or organizations that focus on Israel's welfare

• Jewish defense: involvement in organizations or activities that defend Jews against persecution and fight
anti-Semitism

• Study of culture and history: interest in books, film,
museums, and other ways of learning about Jewish history and Jewish life

• Children's education and activities, and meaningful
family time: working to create a positive sense of Jewish history, traditions, or religious practices for children
in a way that makes sense to them and has significance
in their lives; focusing on creating positive self-esteem,
a sense of belonging, and a social and moral consciousness connected to being Jewish, which may include
sending children to Hebrew school, teaching them
about traditions, supporting Jewish youth activities,
attending Jewish summer camps, or sending a child
on a summer trip to Israel

It is important to remember that these categories are not completely distinct; they often overlap. The study of Hebrew, for example, may relate more to an interest in Israel than in Judaism. A
person's passion for Judaism does not automatically mean that he
or she has the same interest in Israel or Jewish defense. Also, these
dimensions tend to take on different degrees of importance at different life stages. Marriage, the birth of children, aging, and the
death of loved ones are all emotionally and spiritually charged
events that catalyze changes in identity. Using these dimensions

creates a starting point and a kind of vocabulary with which to reflect on, talk about, and experiment with the meaning of that short but complex word *Jew*.

We hope that you will see the benefits of taking responsibility for shaping your own Jewish identity. Finding ways to connect yourself to the chain of generations that came before you can improve your sense of self-worth and self-acceptance, which are crucial to successful relationships. There is no one path that works for everyone; we urge you to find one that works for you. Take this opportunity to see identity formation as an ongoing and active process, not as an accident of fate.

# EXERCISES

The following exercises can help you to create a clear and healthy Jewish identity that can help you build a more supportive and resilient marriage. Remember, even though you may be very articulate about a wide range of topics, you may find exploring issues of identity to be both intellectually and emotionally difficult. Many Jews end their formal involvement with studying Judaism when they are thirteen years old or younger. It is a lot easier to work with these issues if you expect and accept that you are likely to feel all kinds of contradictory and seemingly mutually exclusive feelings. For many people, such confusion is the norm, and facing mixed feelings is an important step in clarifying your sense of identity. Save anything that you write for later discussions with your partner. Also, because these exercises can sometimes elicit strong emotions, don't push yourself to do more than you are comfortable with. What is important is that you learn more about yourself at a pace that works for you.

Finally, if you were not raised as a Jew, substitute "Christian" or whatever other identity was most meaningful to you for the words "Jewish" or "Judaism" whenever it is useful for you to do so. We will focus on intermarriage and conversion in Chapter Ten.

## Facing What You Internalized About Jewish Identity

This exercise involves exploring the negative as well as the positive stereotypes you have internalized about being Jewish. Such exploration helps clear the way for you to begin to more actively engage the process of shaping your own Jewish identity.

Take a pencil and write down the first ten words or phrases that come to mind when you think about the word *Jewish*. The difficult part of this exercise is that you will be very tempted to edit the list. The goal is simply to pay attention to the words and ideas that pop into your mind. It is useful to repeat this exercise at a later time to see how different your list may be from one day to the next.

## Clarifying Your Own Identity: Exploring Five Paths

As you look back over the course of several generations of your family, it probably becomes clear that cultural and religious identities are not static and unchanging. If you are truly happy and satisfied with your relationship to the ethnic, cultural, and religious aspects of your identity, that's fine. If, however, your sense of Jewish identity seems too vague, conflicted, or nebulous, you can work to shape your own identity in the future. The best way to make changes is to experiment, create new experiences, and then make choices.

First complete the following exercise by yourself. We will ask you to return to this exercise with your partner after you have worked through the next few chapters, which teach you important communication and conflict resolution skills. For now, it is important that you have begun the work to clarify and strengthen your sense of identity.

For each dimension of identity—Judaism; ethnic, cultural, and communal connections; Israel; Jewish defense; study of culture and history; and children's education and activities—make notes that answer the following questions:

1. At various times in your life—as a child, as an adolescent, and as a young adult—what was your connection to this

dimension of being Jewish? What is your connection today? Are there ways in which you would like to change or develop any aspect of your identity? What might some of your goals be? Think of ways you might want to explore each dimension in order to learn more.

2. Which individuals in your family were most important—in positive *or* negative ways—in shaping your attitudes toward each of the dimensions?

3. What would you hope you could pass on to children (even if you don't have any) about the dimensions of Jewish identity that are most important to you?

## Ancestors' Shadows: Exploring Your Past

It is very difficult to work out a clear sense of identity with your partner until you are able to acknowledge all the voices you carry within. Only then can you really come to terms with your own complex identity and make better choices. Look back at the Ancestors' Shadows group process we described earlier in the chapter.

This exercise can help you get a lot clearer about the contradictory messages you received and internalized from significant family members. Using this process can help you better understand why you feel one way about being Jewish today and a different way tomorrow.

Remember, all the significant people in your life, as well as those who were important in *their* lives, deeply affect you. Even if you never knew one of your grandparents, some version of that person (or reaction against him or her) lived on in your mother or father. Whereas it is easy for you to remember the voices that represent people you feel loved by and whom you respect, it is important to hear the voices you are less comfortable with as well; they can affect you just as much.

Begin by taking a piece of paper and drawing a circle (female) or square (male) representing each of the members of your family, including your grandparents, parents, siblings, and yourself. Leave enough room under each circle to write in two sentences. Underneath the symbol that represents each person, write down your fantasy of what each person would say (if he or she were being really honest) in response to each of the two statements that appear at the end of this exercise. After completing these sentences, imagine each of them speaking their lines to you as people did in the group exercise. Finally, after you have "heard" from each of your family members, write your own two lines and imagine saying them to your intergenerational family, gathered together as a group.

*I am a* [fill in whatever combination of religious or cultural identity that seems most important to the person], *and to me that means . . .*

*I make my way in life by . . .*

# 2

# Four Key Patterns That Can Harm a Relationship

*"Household peace" might be described more as a state of dynamic equilibrium than as unruffled serenity. A happy household is a swirl of people, all busy, all talking. There may be arguments and nagging, mutual recriminations. All this is part of being expressive, part of showing one's affection and interest, part of sharing in the experience of one's family. Life would be dull without constant discussion, and that is impossible without constant disagreement. Disagreement leads to excitement, and to heated argument. Nevertheless, until the boiling point is reached, sholem bayis [peace of the home] is not jeopardized.*

Mark Zborowski and Elizabeth Herzog[1]

Our greatest strengths and our worst weaknesses are often two sides of the same coin. Judaism and Jewish culture traditionally fostered an emotional environment in the home and in the synagogue where argument, debate, and struggling with ideas were the norm. To varying degrees, even among assimilated Jews in America, the pattern of emotional intensity and debate continues. In his classic study of Jewish psychology, Raphael Patai observed that Jewish Americans are more intense, sensitive, and impatient than their Gentile neighbors.[2] It should come as no surprise, then, that in Jewish marriages, *words* can be the most important tool—and a most destructive weapon—for dealing with differences.

Although generalizations about "Jewish psychology" can be useful, it is also important to remember how culturally complex Jewish marriages have become. Jewish marriages include people from many different cultural, national, and religious backgrounds. This can complicate how words are used to hurt or heal. Throughout the book, we pay attention to how the different frames of reference partners bring to their relationships affect the ways they deal with conflict and cooperation.

One of the most powerful things you can do to protect your marriage is to learn constructive ways to handle conflict, differences, and disagreements. As we emphasize throughout this book, all couples have disagreements; they are an inherent by-product of the blending together of two lives. Researchers from two major research labs in the United States, including that of coauthor Howard Markman and his colleagues Scott Stanley and Susan Blumberg, found that the likelihood of divorce can be predicted by studying how couples handle conflict. In their research, couples whose marriages were in distress consistently displayed four specific patterns of conflictual interactions:

1. Escalation
2. Invalidation
3. Withdrawal and avoidance
4. Negative interpretations

A series of questions (found in the exercises at the end of this chapter) can help couples identify how badly conflict has eroded their relationship. All couples will have a few danger signs at different times in their relationship. Some couples will have more consistent and higher levels of conflict, and some will be experiencing significant levels of distress. The material in this book is designed for all of these couples.

If you are currently happy together, you can use the approach we present in this book to prevent negative patterns from developing in the first place. If you are experiencing relationship problems, we want to motivate you to fight more constructively, so that you can actually resolve issues.

We will also begin to look at how the emotional and cultural patterns in your family of origin influence the ways you deal with anger. In later chapters, we focus in much greater depth on how you can protect your relationship from such negative patterns.

Let's start by looking at the four patterns that best predict distress in relationships.

## ESCALATION: WHAT GOES AROUND COMES AROUND

*Only God can give us credit for the angry words we did not speak.*

Rabbi Harold Kushner[3]

*Escalation* occurs when partners negatively respond back and forth to each other, continually upping the ante so that conditions get worse and worse. Negative comments often spiral into increasing anger and frustration. Couples who are happy now and likely to stay that way are less prone to escalation; if their arguments start to escalate, they are able to stop the negative process before it erupts into a full-blown, nasty fight.

You can clearly see the escalation process in the interactions of Alex and Miriam, who had been married for four years when we met them. Alex came from a highly assimilated Jewish family whose great-grandparents had come to America in the 1890s. Miriam was the first person in her family who had been born in the United States. Her parents had emigrated as a young couple from Hungary in 1952. Alex's family was as emotionally controlled as Miriam's was volatile. As with many couples, their fights started over small issues:

ALEX: *(sarcastically)* I can't believe that you forgot to bring the wine to the Stern's Shabbat dinner.

MIRIAM: *(equally sarcastically)* Oh, like you never forget to do anything.

ALEX: I don't forget to do the important things.

MIRIAM: Oh, I forgot just how compulsive you are. You're right, of course!

ALEX: Your hostility is too much. Why don't you go into therapy and work on it?

MIRIAM: *(hurt and angry)* Yeah, I'm defective, Dr. Perfect. Maybe marrying me was the only mistake you ever made. At least it's not too late to correct that one.

One of the most damaging things about arguments that are escalating out of control is that partners tend to say things that threaten the very lifeblood of their marriage. As frustration and hostility mount, partners often try to hurt each other by hurling verbal (and sometimes physical) weapons. You can see this pattern with Alex and Miriam; the stakes quickly rose to include an invitation to end the relationship. Once very negative, verbally abusive comments are made, they are hard to take back. The damage can be undone, but it takes a lot of work. Saying "I was just kidding when I said that stuff about divorce" may not help, because it doesn't address the hurt feelings.

Partners can say the nastiest things during escalating arguments, but such remarks often don't reflect what they actually feel about one another. You may believe that people reveal their "true feelings" in the midst of fierce fights, but we don't think that this is usually the case. Instead, partners mostly try to hurt the other person and to defend themselves. One of the biggest problems with this scenario is that the comments that hurt the other person the most tend to be related to confidences that were shared at earlier, intimate moments. Hence, in the heat of escalation, the weapons people choose are often based on intimate knowledge of the partner.

In Miriam and Alex's argument, for example, Miriam mentioned Alex's being compulsive because she really wanted to hit him below the belt. At a tender moment between them, he once shared his concerns about being so driven and emotionally controlled and said that he had learned this style to please his father when he was growing up. His father had prided himself on being successful in a WASP world, and expected Alex to do the same.

Alex also used his knowledge of Miriam's background to attack her in her most vulnerable places. He knew that Miriam's immigrant mother had never really adapted well to life in the United States and that her outbursts of anger and abuse had terrorized her children. Alex was the only man in whom Miriam had ever confided about her past. Now he was using it against her.

Although neither of them explicitly mentioned the other's family background during the argument, both felt that the other was using personal, intimate information to gain the upper hand. Such tactics are tantamount to marital terrorism and cause great pain and damage in the relationship. When escalation includes the use of intimate knowledge as a weapon, the threat to the future tenderness is great. Who is going to share deep feelings if the information may be used later when conflict is out of control in the relationship?

You may be thinking, "We don't fight like cats and dogs—how does this apply to us?" In fact, escalation can be very subtle. You needn't raise your voices to get into the cycle of returning negative for negative. Yet research shows that even subtle patterns of escalation can lead to divorce in the future.

The more arguments escalate, the more at risk couples are for future problems. It is very important for the future health of your relationship to learn to counteract whatever tendency you have for your arguments to escalate. If they don't escalate very much, great! Your goal is to learn to keep things that way. If they do escalate too much, your goal is to recognize this problem and learn how to stop it.

## Short-Circuiting Escalation

All couples have arguments that escalate from time to time, but some couples steer out of the pattern more quickly and much more positively. Compare Alex and Miriam's argument, earlier, with Phyllis and Bruce's. Phyllis, a forty-five-year-old realtor, and Bruce, a forty-nine-year-old attorney who works for the Department of Justice, have been married twenty years. Both of their parents had divorced when Phyllis and Bruce were teenagers. At that time, divorce was very unusual in the Jewish community, and both Phyllis and Bruce had been very upset by their parents' marital difficulties. They had talked a lot about their parents' divorces and resolved not to repeat their mistakes. They had used sharing the pain of the past to forge a deeper sense of connection and commitment.

Phyllis and Bruce were referred to one of our weekend communication workshops by a local marital therapist. Like Alex and Miriam, they also tended to argue about everyday events, as in this example:

> PHYLLIS:  *(annoyed)* You left the butter out again.
> BRUCE:  *(irritated)* Why are little things so important to you? Just put it back.
> PHYLLIS:  *(softening her tone)* Things like that are important to me. Is that so bad?
> BRUCE:  *(calmer)* I guess not. Sorry I was snotty.

Notice the difference. Like Miriam and Alex's argument, Bruce and Phyllis's argument showed escalation, but they quickly steered out of it. When escalation sequences are short-circuited, it is usually because one partner backs off and says something to de-escalate the argument, thus breaking the negative cycle. Doing so takes a touch of humility; humility is very powerful for breaking out of destructive communication cycles.

Phyllis and Bruce each did something constructive to end the escalation. For her part, Phyllis softened her tone rather than getting defensive. For his part, Bruce made the decision to back off and acknowledge Phyllis's point of view. Softening your tone and acknowledging your partner's point of view are powerful tools you can use to defuse tension and end escalation. As we go on, we will be teaching you specific and effective ways to do just this.

# INVALIDATION: PAINFUL PUT-DOWNS

*Invalidation* is a pattern in which one partner subtly or directly criticizes the thoughts, feelings, or character of the other. Whether they are made intentionally or unintentionally, such invalidating comments sometimes lower the self-esteem of the targeted person.

Invalidation can take many forms. Let's listen in on two other arguments between Alex and Miriam and between Phyllis and Bruce.

MIRIAM: (*very angrily*) You missed your doctor's appointment again! You're so irresponsible. I could see you dying and leaving me, just like your father.
ALEX: (*bruised*) Thanks a lot. You know I'm nothing like my father.
MIRIAM: He was a creep, and so are you.
ALEX: (*dripping with sarcasm*) I'm sorry. I forgot my good fortune to be married to such a paragon of responsibility. You can't even keep your purse organized.
MIRIAM: At least I am not so obsessive about stupid little things.
ALEX: You're so arrogant.

PHYLLIS: (*looking upset*) You know, I think Josh's Hebrew teacher is too hard on him. Josh works really hard and does his best, and I'm worried it's going to hurt his self-esteem.
BRUCE: I think you are being overprotective. He needs to learn to deal with a little criticism once in a while.
PHYLLIS: (*with a sigh and turning away*) You don't get it. It upset him, and it upsets me.
BRUCE: Yeah, I see that, but I still think you're overreacting.

Both of these examples show invalidation, but the first example is much more caustic than the second. With Miriam and Alex, you can feel their belligerence and contempt. The argument has shifted from confronting a behavior to each partner attacking the other's character. And although Bruce and Phyllis do not display the level of nastiness expressed by Alex and Miriam, Bruce is subtly putting down Phyllis for the way she is feeling. He may even think that he is being constructive or trying to cheer her up by saying, in effect, "It's not so bad." Nevertheless, this kind of communication is also invalidating. Phyllis feels more hurt now because Bruce has said, in effect, that her concerns about Josh are wrong.

You experience another subtle form of invalidation when you are expecting praise for some positive action that your partner ignores while he or she highlights some minor problem. For example, suppose that you worked hard all afternoon to reorganize and clean up the kitchen, and your spouse comes home and complains because you didn't get to the store. You are going to feel pretty invalidated. Going out of your way to do something positive and then being criticized for what you didn't do can be very painful and frustrating.

Invalidation hurts. It leads naturally to concealing how you feel and what you think, because it becomes just too risky to reveal yourself. People naturally cover up their innermost feelings when they believe that they will be "put down." Our research shows that invalidation is one of the very best predictors of future problems and divorce. It is interesting that the amount of validation, or positive support of the partner, in a relationship doesn't say as much about the health of the relationship as the amount of invalidation does. Invalidation is highly toxic to the well being of your relationship.

## Preventing Invalidation

In either of the arguments just described, both couples would have done better if each partner had shown respect for and acknowledged the other's viewpoint. Note the difference in how these conversations could have gone:

MIRIAM: (*very angry*) I'm very angry that you missed the doctor's appointment again.
ALEX: It really upset you, didn't it?
MIRIAM: You bet. I want to know that you're going to be there for me, and when you miss a doctor's appointment, I get really anxious about your health.
ALEX: I understand why it would make you worried when it seems like I'm not taking care of myself.

PHYLLIS: (*looking upset*) You know, I think Josh's Hebrew teacher is too hard on him. Josh works really hard and does his best, and I'm worried her criticism's going to hurt his self-esteem.
BRUCE: You're really worried about him?
PHYLLIS: Yeah, I am. And I also get worried about him losing his positive attitude about school.
BRUCE: I didn't know you were so concerned. What do you think is going on with him and the teacher?

These examples replay the issues but with very different outcomes for both couples. Now we see each explaining his or her own feelings, showing respect for each other's character, and putting an emphasis on validation. By *validation* we mean that the one raising the concern is respected and heard. You don't have to agree with your partner to validate his or her feelings. The issue we are dealing with here is *how* you and your partner talk to one another, not who is right. Validation is a powerful tool that you can use both to build intimacy and to reduce anger and resentment. But it takes discipline, especially when you are really frustrated or angry. We will teach you much more in later chapters about how to enhance your ability to use validation as the cornerstone of conflict resolution skills.

# WITHDRAWAL AND AVOIDANCE: HIDE AND SEEK

Withdrawal and avoidance are different manifestations of a pattern in which one partner shows an unwillingness to get into or stay with important discussions. Withdrawal can be as obvious as getting up and leaving the room or as subtle as "turning off" or "shutting down" during an argument. The withdrawer may tend to get quiet during an argument or may quickly agree to some suggestion just to end the conversation, with no real intention of following through.

Avoidance reflects the same reluctance to participate in certain discussions, with more emphasis on preventing the conversation from happening in the first place. A person prone to avoidance would prefer it if the difficult topic never came up, and if it did, he or she might manifest the signs of withdrawal.

Let's look at this pattern as it was played out in a discussion between Paula, a twenty-eight-year-old teacher, and Jeff, a thirty-two-year-old loan officer. Married for three years, they have a two-year-old baby girl, Lily, whom they both adore. They were concerned that the tension in their relationship was starting to affect their daughter:

PAULA:  When are we going to talk about how you're dealing with Lily's tantrums?

JEFF:  Can't this wait? I have to get these taxes done.

PAULA:  I've brought this up at least five times already. No, it can't wait!

JEFF:  (*tensing*) What's to talk about, anyway? It's none of your business.

PAULA:  (*frustrated and looking right at Jeff*) Lily is my business. I'm afraid that you may lose your temper and hurt her, and you won't do a darn thing to learn to deal better with your anger.

JEFF:  (*turning away and looking out the window*) I love Lily. There's no problem here. (*leaving the room as he talks*)

PAULA: (*very angry now, following Jeff into the next room*) You have to get some help. You can't just stick your head in the sand.

JEFF: I'm not going to discuss anything with you when you're like this.

PAULA: Like what? It doesn't matter if I'm calm or frustrated. You won't talk to me about anything important. Lily is having problems, and you have to face that.

JEFF: (*quiet, tense, fidgeting*)

PAULA: Well?

JEFF: (*going to the closet and grabbing sweater*) I'm going out to get some peace and quiet.

PAULA: (*voice raised, angry*) Talk to me, now. I'm tired of you leaving when we're talking about something important.

JEFF: (*looking away from Paula and walking toward the door*) I'm not talking, you are. Actually, you're yelling. See you later when you calm down.

Many couples do this kind of dance when it comes to dealing with difficult issues. One partner *pursues* dealing with issues (Paula) and one *avoids* or *withdraws* from dealing with issues (Jeff). This common scenario is very destructive to the relationship. As with the other patterns we have discussed, it doesn't have to be this dramatic to predict problems to come. It is one of the most powerful predictors of unhappiness and divorce.

The *pursuer* is the one in the relationship who most often brings issues up for discussion or calls attention to the need to make a decision about something. The *withdrawer* is the person who tends to avoid these discussions or pull away during them. Studies show that men tend to take the withdrawing role more frequently, whereas women tend to pursue. However, in many relationships this pattern is reversed. It is also common for partners to switch these roles, depending on the topic. For example, one of you may handle the budget and be more likely to pursue in discussions about money-related problems. Your partner may handle issues about the children's schooling more often and so may be more likely to pursue in talking about these concerns. Nevertheless, across a range of issues, males are more likely to take the withdrawing role.

## Avoiding Withdrawal

Research clearly shows that withdrawal and avoidance are good predictors of problems now and in the future. If you are seeing this pattern in your relationship, keep in mind that it will likely get worse if you allow it to continue. That is because as pursuers push more, withdrawers withdraw more, and as withdrawers pull back, pursuers push harder. Furthermore, when issues are important, it should be obvious that trying to avoid dealing with them will only lead to damaging consequences. You can't stick your head in the sand and pretend that important or bothersome problems are not really there.

In the case of withdrawal and avoidance, the first and best step you can take right now is to realize that the two of you are not independent of each other. Your actions cause reactions, and vice versa. For this reason, you will have much greater success if you work together to change or prevent the kinds of negative patterns discussed here. Withdrawers are not likely to reduce avoidance unless pursuers pursue less aggressively or more constructively. Pursuers will find it hard to cut back on pursuing unless withdrawers deal more directly with the issues at hand.

We get much more specific about ways to combat these pursuer-withdrawer patterns in the next few chapters. For now, try to agree that if you are having trouble with pursuit and withdrawal, you will work together to change the pattern.

## Physical Violence and Healthy Withdrawal

At times, withdrawal is better than the alternative, particularly if the conflict is likely to escalate to the point of physical aggression. Physical violence is a pervasive problem in our culture. Approximately 25 percent of all couples report incidents of pushing, shoving, or hitting within the previous year.[4] Both men and women in these relationships resort to physical tactics from time to time, although it is potentially more dangerous for the husband to become violent and control his wife through fear and threats. For many couples, physical aggression is the outgrowth of poor handling of escalation and withdrawal.

For some couples, there is a much more dangerous pattern, in which the husband batters the wife and intends to wear down, subjugate, and dominate his partner. If this sounds like your situation, please get help. In an emergency, you can call the police. Short of that, you can find help by calling organizations that help women find safety and obtain advice for dealing with domestic violence. Most communities have shelters or advocacy groups; you can obtain the phone numbers for such resources by calling your local police or mental health agency. This book is designed, in part, to help couples handle conflict, but conflict at this physically and emotionally dangerous level requires professional help and legal intervention.

Jewish women face an unusual problem in getting help with domestic violence. Although we often focus on the issue of negative stereotypes about Jews, positive stereotypes can create their own problems. One stereotype about Jewish men is that they aren't prone to violence. But recent studies have suggested that domestic violence is actually as common among Jews as among non-Jews. As many as 19 to 25 percent of Jewish women may experience abuse in their relationships.[5] An important difference between Jews and non-Jews, however, is that the myth of nonviolence results in Jewish women waiting up to twice as long as non-Jews before looking for help. Fearing the stigma, worrying that no one will believe them, or thinking that help is not available, Jewish women hesitate to reach out. In fact, numerous organizations have developed outreach and treatment programs for Jewish relationships in which abuse is an issue (see Resources).

If you are in a pattern that includes occasional physical aggression consisting of pushing, shoving, or slapping, the approach described in this book can teach you how to interrupt the cycle of escalation that leads up to such actions and how to use a constructive form of mutual, agreed-on withdrawal: Time Out. As we go on, we will teach you techniques for handling escalation and withdrawal in the most productive manner. Nevertheless, if you are worried about physical danger, please seek additional help.

## NEGATIVE INTERPRETATIONS: WHEN PERCEPTION IS WORSE THAN REALITY

> *What does a good guest say? "How much trouble*
> *has my host gone to for me. How much meat he set*
> *before me. How much wine he brought me. How*
> *many cakes he served me. And all this trouble he has*
> *gone to for my sake!" But what does a bad guest say?*
> *"What kind of effort did the host make for me? I have*
> *eaten only one slice of bread. I have eaten only one*
> *piece of meat, and I have drunk only one cup of*
> *wine! Whatever trouble the host went to was done*
> *only for the sake of his wife and children."*
> Babylonian Talmud, Berakhot 58a

*Negative interpretations* occur when one partner consistently believes that the motives of the other are more negative than is really the case. This can be a very destructive pattern in a relationship, and it will make any conflict or disagreement harder to deal with constructively.

You can see the effects of negative interpretations in the discussions of the next two couples, but to different degrees. Melissa and David have been married twelve years, and they are generally happy with their relationship. Yet their discussions have been plagued at times by a specific negative interpretation. Every year, they have had trouble deciding whether to travel to Melissa's parents' home for Passover. Melissa believes that David dislikes her parents, but in fact he is quite fond of them in his own way.

When they were first dating, Melissa's parents expressed concerns about David's work history. When David found out about what he felt was Melissa's parents' unwarranted criticism, he was hurt and angry. But he went on to have a satisfying career as a professor at a small college and had long since forgotten the event. Melissa held on to her belief that David still resented her parents, without ever having checked out this belief with him. Her negative interpretation of David's attitude affects them to this day. Here is how a typical discussion around their issue of holiday travel plans goes:

MELISSA: We should start looking into getting plane tickets to go visit my parents for Passover.

DAVID: (*thinking about their budget*) I was wondering if we can really afford it this year.

MELISSA: (*in anger*) My parents are very important to me, even if you don't like them. They're getting older, and I'm going to go no matter what.

DAVID: That's really not the issue. I'd like to go, really I would. I just don't see how we can afford a thousand dollars in plane tickets and pay the bill for Joey's orthodontist, too.

MELISSA: You can't be honest and admit you just don't want to go, can you? Just admit it. You don't like my parents.

DAVID: There's nothing to admit. I enjoy visiting your parents. I'm thinking about money here, not your parents.

MELISSA: That's a convenient excuse. (*storming out of the room*)

Even though David really does like to visit Melissa's parents, her negative interpretations are too powerful, and he cannot penetrate them. What can he say or do to make a difference as long as she believes so strongly that he dislikes his in-laws? If a negative interpretation is strong enough, nothing will change it. In this case, David wants to address the decision they must make from the standpoint of the budget, but Melissa's interpretation overpowers their ability to communicate effectively and come to a decision that makes both of them happy. Fortunately for them, this problem is relatively isolated and not a consistent pattern in their marriage.

When relationships become more distressed, the negative interpretations create a more pervasive environment of hopelessness and demoralization. Moshe and Eileen are a couple who met when Eileen traveled to Israel after graduating from college. They have been married thirteen years and have two children, but they have been very unhappy in their marriage for more than seven years, in part due to the corrosive effect of strong, negative interpretations. They seldom talk directly about the resentment left over from a number of important unresolved issues, including several years of arguing about whether or not to return to Israel. Moshe wanted to return to Israel, but Eileen did not. Although there are positive things in their marriage, almost nothing either of them does is recognized positively by the other, as seen in this recent conversation about parking their car:

MOSHE: You left the car out again.

EILEEN: Oh. I guess I forgot to put it in when I came back from Madge's.

MOSHE: (*with a bit of a sneer*) I guess you did. You know how much that irritates me.

EILEEN: (*exasperated*) Look, I forgot. Do you think I leave it out just to irritate you?

MOSHE: (*coldly*) Actually, that's exactly what I think. I've told you so many times that I want the car in the garage at night.

EILEEN: Yes, you have. But I don't leave it out just to tick you off. I just forget.

MOSHE: If you cared what I thought about things, you'd remember.

EILEEN: You know that I put the car in nine times out of ten.

MOSHE: More like half the time, and those are the times I leave the garage door up for you.

EILEEN: Have it your way. It doesn't matter what reality is. You'll see it your way.

This may sound like a minor argument, but it isn't. It represents a long-standing tendency for Moshe to interpret Eileen's behavior in the most negative light possible. For the sake of argument, assume that Eileen is absolutely correct when she says that she simply forgot to put the car in the garage and that this only happens about one in ten times. Moshe sees it differently, especially in his interpretation that she leaves the car out mostly to upset him.

If a marriage is at a point where one partner routinely and intentionally does things just to frustrate or anger the other person, it is generally in deep trouble. Much more frequently, however, one of the partners is interpreting the actions of the other negatively and unfairly. This also is a sign of a relationship heading for big trouble in the future. Negative interpretations are very destructive, in part because they are very hard to detect and counteract after they become woven into the fabric of a relationship. This intractability has its roots in the way we form and maintain beliefs about others.

Both experience and solid research tell us that people tend to see what they expect to see in others and in situations. In fact, we have a very strong tendency toward *confirmation bias*, which means that we look for evidence that confirms what we already think is true about a person or situation. We can be wrong in our assumptions, but we all have formed beliefs and expectations about why those we know well do what they do.

In the preceding example, Moshe has the expectation that "Eileen doesn't care one bit about anything that's important to me." This assumption colors the good things that do happen. In distressed relationships, partners have a tendency to discount the positive things they see, attributing them to causes such as chance rather than to any positive intentions of their partner. Because of Moshe's negative interpretations, he attributes the times Eileen does put the car in the garage to his own action of leaving the door open and not to her desire to please him. She can't win this argument, and because of his negative mind-set, she can't prove that she has positive intentions.

## Battling Negative Interpretations

We are not advocating some kind of unrealistic "positive thinking." You can't just wish away your partner's negative behaviors. However, you may even need to consider that your partner's motives are more positive than you are willing to acknowledge.

The bottom line with negative interpretations is that the person views positive behavior negatively and negative behavior as an extension of character flaws, even if the other person's actual intention was positive. We can show you how to work as a couple to overcome negative patterns such as escalation and invalidation, but negative interpretations are something you have to confront within yourself. Only *you* can control how you interpret your partner's behavior.

First, you have to ask yourself if you might be overly negative in your interpretation of your partner's actions. Second—and this is hard—you must push yourself to look for evidence that is contrary to the negative interpretation you usually make. For example, if you believe that your partner is uncaring and you generally see most of his actions in that light, you need to look for evidence to the contrary. Does your partner do things for you that you like? Could this be because she is trying to keep the relationship strong? It's up to you to consider your interpretation of behavior. In fact, sometimes the best way out of this cycle is to ask your partner why he did something, in order to understand what he was really thinking.

Of course, negative interpretations can be accurate. But suppose you begin to suspect that you are being hard on your partner. A third constructive step you can take is to ask yourself if you might have any personal reasons for maintaining a pattern of negative interpretation with your spouse. If you are being unfair, there must be some reason. Perhaps growing up you learned a certain style of thinking. As we saw in Chapter One, your family history as well as your family's Jewish history can affect your tendency to interpret events negatively.

Perhaps you have some deeper need to see yourself as the partner who truly cares about the relationship. Perhaps you want to feel sorry for yourself and think of yourself as a kind of martyr. Suffering was not only the objective experience for many generations of Jews but also a common Jewish style of controlling others in family relationships. *I suffer, therefore you should change!* Reflecting on how you may be repeating patterns learned in your family of origin can be difficult but may be very productive if doing so can help you discover whether you have a tendency to persist in seeing things negatively.

In Moshe's case, he grew up in a home with judgmental, perfectionist parents, both of whom were Holocaust survivors. Negative interpretations come as easily to him as they did to his parents. It was not at all unusual for him to hear his father say, "If you cared at all about what's important to me, you'd have worked harder in school." Even though his father never said it directly, the message was clear: "After all I've been through, you owe me obedience and respect."

Like his father, Moshe developed a pattern of interpreting the motivations of others negatively unless they performed to meet his perfectionist standards. And as we saw in Chapter One, problems with self-esteem can lead a person to project unacknowledged negative feelings about himself onto his partner.

Ultimately, it doesn't matter how Moshe came to think this way; only he can really confront his internal bias against Eileen. The way he thinks is his responsibility—not hers. If he doesn't deal with this pattern—and Eileen doesn't deal with areas where she has similar problems—their marriage is certain to fail. Even if Eileen were an angel (and no one is), Moshe's incessant accusations would eventually result in her getting angry and withdrawn, which Moshe would use as evidence to confirm his own worse expectations. Psychologists call this a self-fulfilling prophecy, meaning that if we believe something strongly enough, we tend to behave in ways that might make it come true.

As you work through this book and are considering positive changes in your relationship, make sure to give your partner the benefit of the doubt about wanting to make things better. Confront your negative bias. Don't allow inaccurate interpretations to sabotage the work you are trying to accomplish.

## HOW POSITIVE FEELINGS ERODE IN MARRIAGE: THE LONG-TERM EFFECT OF NEGATIVE PATTERNS

Contrary to popular belief, positives in marriage do not slowly fade away for no reason in particular. We believe that the chief reason that marriages fail at alarmingly high rates is that the partners handle conflict poorly, as demonstrated by patterns such as those described in this chapter. Over time, these patterns steadily erode all the good things in a relationship.

For example, when couples routinely resort to escalation when problems arise, they may come to the conclusion that it is just as easy not to talk at all. After all, talking leads to fighting, doesn't it? When partners become more concerned with getting their own way, invalidation becomes a weapon easily taken in hand. Over time, no issue seems safe.

Not only do many couples deal with issues poorly; they also may not set aside time to discuss them or come to any agreement about how they will handle them. Even in what starts out as the best of marriages, these factors can lead to growing distance and a lack of confidence in the relationship. Remember Jeff and Paula, earlier in this chapter? Even though they are a genuinely caring couple, their inability to discuss tough issues—in this case, his anger—has caused a rift that will widen and perhaps destroy the marriage if nothing is done.

When negative patterns in a relationship are not changed, real intimacy and a sense of connection die, and couples settle for frustrated loneliness and isolation. If you want to keep your relationship strong or renew one that is troubled, you must learn to counteract destructive patterns such as those we have described. Fortunately, you can do this. You can prevent the erosion of happiness in your relationship in the years to come.

———————

In this chapter we have described four patterns in handling conflict that predict future marital discord and divorce. We have made the point that certain ways of dealing with conflict are particularly destructive in a relationship. Keep in mind that most couples show some of these patterns to some degree. It isn't important whether you currently engage in some of these patterns as long as you decide to do something about them.

How can couples manage their tendencies toward destructive patterns and limit the damage they cause? In the following chapters, we will suggest specific agreed-on rules and strategies for handling conflict and difficult issues in your relationship. As a first step, use the following exercises to shed light on how your relationship is affected by negative patterns. We hope that this will encourage you to work to replace such patterns with the positive behaviors and attitudes we demonstrate later in the book.

# EXERCISES

Sometimes the process of considering questions like the ones in the following exercises and reflecting on where your relationship stands at this point causes anxiety or sadness. Although it may not be pleasant to think about negative patterns, we believe that honestly confronting your relationship patterns will help you as you move ahead in this book and learn constructive ways to keep your marriage strong.

## How Do You Handle Conflict?

Take a pad of paper and write down your answers to these questions independently from your partner. When you have finished, we suggest that you share your perceptions. However, if doing so creates conflict, put off further discussion of your answers until the two of you have worked through the next few chapters and learned more about how to talk safely about the tough topics.

Before getting into specific questions about the four negative patterns, consider the following question about your overall impression of how you handle conflict together: When you have a disagreement or argument, what typically happens? In answering this question, think about the four key patterns described earlier.

### Escalation

Escalation occurs when you say or do something negative, your partner responds with something negative, and off you go into a real battle. In this snowball effect, you become increasingly angry and hostile as the argument continues.

1. How often do you think you escalate arguments as a couple?
2. Do you get hostile with each other during escalation?
3. What or who usually brings an end to the fight?
4. When angry, does one or the other of you sometimes threaten to end the relationship?
5. How do you feel when you are in an escalating argument with your partner? Do you feel tense, anxious, scared, angry, or something else?

### Invalidation

Invalidation occurs when you subtly or directly put down the thoughts, feelings, actions, or worth of your partner. This is different from simply disagreeing with your partner or not liking something he or she has done. Invalidation includes belittling or disregarding what is important to your partner, out of either insensitivity or outright contempt.

1. Do you often feel invalidated in your relationship? When and how does this happen?

2. What is the effect on you?

3. Do you often invalidate your partner? When and how does this happen?

4. What do you think the effect is on him or her? On the relationship? What are you trying to accomplish when you do this? Do you accomplish that goal?

### Withdrawal and Avoidance

Men and women often deal quite differently with conflict in relationships. Most often, women are more prone to pursue and men are more prone to withdraw from discussion of issues in the relationship.

1. Is one of you more likely to be in the pursuer's role? Is one of you more likely to be in the withdrawer's role?

2. How does the withdrawer usually withdraw? How does the pursuer usually pursue? What happens then?

3. When are you most likely to fall into this pattern as a couple? Are there particular issues or situations that bring out this pattern?

4. How are you affected by this pattern?

5. When are you or your partner likely to be the pursuer in an argument? The withdrawer in an argument? Why do you think this happens?

### Negative Interpretations

Negative interpretations occur when you interpret the behavior of your spouse much more negatively than he or she intended. It is critical that you open yourself to the possibility that your view of your partner could be unfair in some areas. These questions will help you reflect on this.

1. Can you think of some areas where you consistently see your partner's behavior as negative? What are the advantages to you in making these interpretations?

2. Do you really think that your negative view of your partner's behavior is totally justified? Or just in certain situations?

3. Are there some areas in which you have a negative interpretation but are open to considering that you may be ignoring evidence to the contrary?

4. List two issues for which you are willing to push yourself to look for the possibility that your partner has more positive motivations than you have been thinking he or she has. Next, look for any evidence that is contrary to your interpretation.

5. Look for an opportunity to take a deep breath and let go of anger or irritation with your partner at least once each day. Then find two things your partner does each day to compliment or praise. This doesn't mean you have to be positive all the time; it simply means that you take on the difficult work of challenging yourself to be less negative and more positive.

## Thinking Personally and Culturally

We usually find it far easier to interpret and judge others' behavior than we do our own. And we usually feel that our anger is justified by our partner's "bad" behavior. But it is important to recognize how your life experiences prior to meeting your partner affect the ways you deal with differences and anger. The emotional "climate" of your family of origin as well as the norms of the cultural and religious milieu in which you were raised have a deep impact on what you consider normal and expectable behavior in intimate relationships. Your relationship with Judaism and the Jewish community helped shape important values about family, conflict, privacy, and emotional sharing. If you were not raised Jewish, the norms of your cultural, religious, and class background shaped your values in different ways. The following questions will help you learn to focus more on your own behavior and motivations and less on those of your partner.

1. How did your mother and father deal with differences in their relationship? Did you see them fight? How did they fight? Did either or both of them use silence, suffering, yelling, or violence as weapons?

2. In what ways would you want to emulate your parents' marriage? Are there aspects of their relationship that you would not want to have as part of your own?

3. How did your parents deal with anger toward you and your siblings? How did they set limits? Were the rules clear? Did you feel that you or any of your siblings got preferential treatment or unfair treatment?

4. Which of those patterns do you wish to avoid, change, or emulate when dealing with anger? How does the way you handle your anger resemble, if at all, the way anger was handled in your family of origin?

5. What was the cultural and religious composition of the neighborhood(s) in which you were raised? How similar or different did your family seem from most of the Jewish families you knew? How was your family similar to or different from the non-Jewish families you knew?

## Relationship Dynamics Scale: Where Are You in Your Marriage?

Please answer each of the following questions in terms of your relationship with your partner. We recommend that you answer these questions by yourself (not with your partner). Use the following 3-point scale to rate how often you and your partner experience the situations described: 1 = almost never, 2 = occasionally, 3 = frequently.

1. Little arguments escalate into ugly fights with accusations, criticisms, name calling, or bringing up past hurts.

2. My partner criticizes or belittles my opinions, feelings, or desires.

3. My partner seems to view my words or actions more negatively than I mean them to be.

4. When we have a problem to solve, it is like we are on opposite teams.

5. I hold back from telling my partner what I really think and feel.

6. I think seriously about what it would be like to date or marry someone else.

7. I feel lonely in this relationship.

8. When we argue, one of us withdraws—that is, doesn't want to talk about it anymore or leaves the scene.

We devised these questions based on fifteen years of research at the University of Denver on the kinds of communication and conflict management patterns that predict if a relationship is headed for trouble.

This measure in and of itself should not be taken as a predictor of who is going to fail in their marriages. It is designed to help motivate high-scoring people to take a serious look at where their relationships are heading—and take steps to turn negative patterns around for the better.

### 8 to 12 "Green Light"

If you scored in the 8–12 range, your relationship is probably in good or even great shape *at this time*, but we emphasize "at this time" because relationships don't stand still. In the next twelve months, you may have a stronger, happier relationship, or you could be heading the other direction. Continue to look for ways to strengthen and deepen your relationship.

### 13 to 17: "Yellow Light"

If you scored in the 13–17 range, you are coming to a yellow light. You need to be cautious. Although you may be happy in your relationship now, your score reveals warning signs of patterns you don't want to let get worse. You should be taking action to protect and improve what you have. Spending time to strengthen your relationship now could be the best thing you could do for your future together.

### 18 to 24 "Red Light"

If you scored in the 18–24 range, you are approaching a red light. Stop and think about where the two of you are headed. Your score indicates the presence of patterns that could put your relationship at significant risk. You may be heading for trouble—or already be there. But there is *good news*. You can stop and learn ways to improve your relationship now!

# 3

# Changing Roles, Changing Rules
## Men and Women in Conflict

*An Israeli mayor in a small town is walking past a construction site with his wife. One of the construction workers calls out to the woman: "How you doing, Ofra?"*

*"Good to see you, Itzik," the woman answers. She introduces the construction worker to her husband, and chats pleasantly with him for a few minutes.*

*After they walk away, the mayor says to his wife: "How do you know that man?"*

*"We were sweethearts in high school. He even proposed to me once."*

*The husband laughs. "You should be very grateful to me then. If I hadn't come along, today you'd be the wife of a construction worker."*

*"Not at all," the wife answers. "If I had married him, he'd now be the mayor."*

*Rabbi Joseph Telushkin[1]*

The Torah states that after God created Adam and saw that Adam was lonely, God created Eve as an *Ezer K'negdo*, which can be translated as "help against" or as "opposed/counterpart," an idea embodying both opposition and harmony. These two fateful words shape a paradox that has defined the relationships between the sexes ever since creation. They suggest that both help and confrontation are crucial to dynamic relationships.

From a Jewish perspective, conflict is a crucial ingredient in relationships that are generative and creative. Jacob was given the Hebrew name *Israel* to symbolize his role as the father of our people only after wrestling with God. Struggle was the catalyst for his transformation. Like Jacob, our intimate relationships reach their potential to help transform and complete us only through the ways that we engage in and deal with conflict.

Jewish tradition recognizes that dynamic tension is inevitable in all important relationships. Although one of the highest values of Jewish tradition is *shalom bayit,* "peace in the home," peace doesn't necessarily mean unruffled civility. There is nothing wrong with occasional silence, but the peace defined by shalom bayit in the traditional Jewish household more often meant active engagement in the form of teasing, yelling, or kvelling (praising). Everything was acceptable, except for those two actions that most threatened family cohesion: violence and withdrawal. Both violence and the failure to engage were seen as destructive.

Nowhere is the balance between support and confrontation more important than in marriage. Our spouse is the one person who can soothe our pain and self-doubt at life's most important moments. But when we look into the mirror of our partner's eyes and see anger and pain rather than love and compassion, our most important ally can be transformed into our worst critic. Who else knows better our strengths and weaknesses? Who else has the same power to nurture and challenge, to build up and tear down? Conflict is the fire of love: handled wisely it warms, carelessly it burns.

In this chapter, we look at a number of factors that affect how men and women approach conflict and intimacy. By exploring how history, culture, and even biology affect the different ways that men and women fight and love, we will be better able to build relationships that remain alive and vital.

# FROM TRADITIONAL TO MODERN ROLES

In *Fiddler on the Roof*, when Tevya asked Golda, "Do you love me?" she seemed incredulous and annoyed. What was this talk of love? In the shtetl life of arranged marriages, poverty, and persecution, love was a luxury that few could afford. Marriage was more the merging of two families than the union of two individuals. But *Fiddler* portrayed a tradition-shattering historical moment. Tevya's questions about love were catalyzed by his struggles with his daughters. They had broken with tradition by choosing to marry for love. The mass migration of the Jews to America required a further wrenching break with the past that opened the floodgates to new possibilities. All that had been taken for granted became open to question.

Before the great migrations of Jews that began in the 1880s, the shtetl society of Eastern Europe was a patriarchy. Men were responsible for the most important task, that of religious study. The book *Life Is with People* describes the ideal shtetl man as dignified, poised, and reflective. The ideal woman was competent, earthy, and practical.[2] Women took care of much of what was seen as the "less important" aspects of family life: dealing with officials and peasants, earning and budgeting money, making decisions about the functioning of the family, and participating in community work. In contrast to the contemplative Jewish man, the shtetl woman, as anthropologist Barbara Meyerhoff observed, needed to be purposive, robust, intrepid, and efficient. "No doubt some of these women were domineering, shrill, and implacable. But this was forgiven, since it was felt that woman's nature inclined her to great vigor and volatility."[3]

But Jewish communities throughout the Diaspora shared a terrible difference from most other cultures described as patriarchies. In patriarchal cultures around the world, men's status and power were related to their ability to protect and provide for their wives and children, something Jewish men often were unable to do. In *Jewish Women/Jewish Men*, Aviva Cantor documented the rabbinical prohibitions that restrained Jewish men from retaliating against

Gentiles for their crimes against Jews. The rapes of Jewish women and the pillage of Jewish communities largely went unavenged. From the time of the Zealots' resistance to the Romans up until the Holocaust, Jews suffered brutal collective punishment following their infrequent and doomed attempts to resist the violence of others. Spiritual resistance and nonviolence became survival strategies in a world where Jewish male aggression threatened group survival.[4]

## The New American Roles

The German Jewish and Sephardic communities were already established in the United States well before the great wave of Eastern European Jewish immigrants who arrived between 1880 and 1924. For the new Jewish arrivals, the first task was survival. For the most part, these immigrants who washed up at Ellis Island came with no English, little money, and few marketable skills. The sweatshops and streets of New York, Chicago, and Philadelphia were filled with thousands of Jewish men and women, struggling to establish a foothold in the United States.

As they had in Eastern Europe, the immigrant Jewish women continued to earn money and organize the household. For the men, the mind continued to be valued over the body—but with an important difference. Increasingly, it became work and money rather than piety and Talmudic study that came to define success.

## The Transition Generation

By the 1940s, many American-born Jewish women left the workforce and returned to the home as soon as their families were able to make do with one income. The prodigious energy of Jewish women, which had been so crucial to the functioning of shtetl life and the establishing of a base in their new land, was now transferred to the home front.

The daughters of the immigrants were an in-between generation with neither the responsibilities of their mothers and grandmothers nor the freedom of their daughters. Although there was much

to celebrate in the success of the involved Jewish mother in pro-
ducing accomplished children, the strategy sometimes backfired,
and children rebelled against what they experienced as impossible
demands. Clearly, the stereotype of the overly controlling, overly
involved Jewish mother is based in part on the experience of this
middle generation.[5]

Jewish men of this transition generation were very successful
professionally and financially. But financial security and safety in
America didn't seem to erase self-doubt. If, as Freud suggested,
depression is caused by stifled aggression turned inward, the legacy
of the past seemed to endure in the high rates of depression in
American Jewish men. Research recently conducted at Harvard
University found that Jewish men were nearly twice as likely as
non-Jews to suffer from clinical depression.[6]

## The Next Generation: The Boomers Come of Age

The boomer generation of Jews has been the most financially successful ethnic group in American society. Success, however, has had
a price.[7] In the late 1950s and into the 1960s, greater acceptance in
the larger culture led to ever-increasing contact with non-Jews, adop-
tion of American cultural norms, assimilation, and intermarriage.
Judith Klein's research on the relationship between positive Jewish
identity and self-esteem found that Jewish men and women began
to view each other through newly adopted American standards.[8]

Comparing the Jewish man to the idealized American man, who
is supposed to be tough, independent, and stoic, Jewish women
began to perceive Jewish men as too sensitive, dependent, and
weak. When comparing Jewish women to the WASP ideal, Jewish
men increasingly perceived Jewish women, who had been bred for
generations to take charge, as too aggressive and emotional. Even
while criticizing the opposite sex, Jewish men secretly wondered
whether they were tough enough to be "real men," and Jewish
women wondered whether they were gentle and submissive enough
to be "real women."

The Jewish woman's brief banishment to the kitchen ended as quickly as it had begun. As the generations of Jewish women who were born after World War Two came of age, history was once again turned on its head. The mythical Jewish mama, self-sacrificing and child centered, was transformed into the consummate career woman, who also had full responsibility for her home and kitchen. Today, Jewish women are among the most educated, most accomplished, and most affluent group of women in society.[9]

Ironically, the cultural revolution of the 1960s and, most important, the women's movement and feminism beginning in the 1970s led to changes that began to transform sex roles in the broader culture to be more like traditional Jewish gender roles. It should come as no surprise that Jewish women, who had long practiced balancing multiple roles, would be at the forefront of the battle for the economic and social empowerment of women. At the same time, men in the broader culture were urged to be more gentle, thoughtful, and in touch with their feelings, traits that Diaspora Jewish culture had cultivated in its men.

All of these changes seem to have left Jewish men and women confused. Studies of American Jews, described in *The Jewish Family and Jewish Continuity*, reveal unsettling facts. Of all ethnic groups, Jews now marry later and have fewer children. Whereas Jews used to pride themselves on their low divorce rates, now they are quickly catching up to national norms of 50 percent. Half of all Jews marrying today will intermarry. Of those marriages, more will end in divorce than marriages between Jews. Even more disturbing, increasing numbers of Jews are not marrying at all.[10]

---

Jewish family used to connote connection, closeness, interdependence, and tradition. Today, it seems that there are more questions than answers about the Jewish family. But one thing should be clear: the future success of Jewish marriage and Jewish families depends on developing and learning new ways of managing conflict in relationships where the roles and the rules are rapidly changing and are often unclear. The goal of this book is to give you the tools you need to help navigate these uncharted waters.

For all that is unique about Jewish history, the fact remains that Jewish men and women share much in common with non-Jews. This is especially true for the majority of American Jews who are highly assimilated into the mainstream culture. We believe, therefore, that it will be useful to examine some of the more universal differences between men and women.

## WHAT DO WOMEN AND MEN WANT?

Sometimes you can tell what people want by looking at what they complain about. The themes of men's and women's complaints tend to be consistent across cultures. Women more often voice concerns about withdrawn, avoidant husbands who won't open up or talk about their views or feelings. When men avoid too much, women can feel shut out and can feel that their husbands don't care about the relationship. In fact, this is the primary complaint we hear from women who come in for marital counseling. For many women, a lack of talking equals a lack of caring. It is very important to women for their husbands to communicate often and openly.

Men often complain that their wives get upset too much, griping about this or that and picking fights. Men may feel hassled; they want peace, often at any price. In one way or another, peace is what we most commonly hear men asking for when they come in for marital counseling. It seems very important to them to have harmony and calm in their relationships with their wives.

That's the way it was for Mel and Ruthie. They both worked and had done well at the same company, but Ruthie had been the more successful. In four years, she had been promoted to an important and well-paid position as director of marketing. Mel was respected as a technical writer, but he felt frustrated by what he saw as his failure to rise higher in the company, especially when he compared himself with Ruthie.

Ruthie had wanted to talk with Mel about some difficulties she was having at work, but he never seemed interested in hearing what was on her mind. Her frustration grew daily. She felt that he was avoiding talking with her about anything more important than the weather. The following conversation was typical, taking place one Saturday morning as their two kids were out playing:

RUTHIE: *(sitting down by Mel and looking at him)* I really would like to talk with you about this problem I've been having at work. You know all the people, and maybe you could help me get some perspective.

MEL: *(not looking up from his paper)* Uh huh, sure.

RUTHIE: *(She thinks, He doesn't want to hear me. I wish he'd put down that paper.)* I don't like some of the stuff Steve has been doing at work. His tone with me is really sarcastic, and he stole some of my ideas for promoting the new product and acted like they were his own. I'm really angry.

MEL: *(not looking up from the paper)* I'm sure it will all work out.

RUTHIE: *(starting to get agitated)* I'm telling you, he took credit for my ideas and then told me that I was being paranoid and abusive when I confronted him. I felt like he was telling me that I was a pushy Jew and an overly aggressive woman. I really think the guy is a sexist, anti-Semitic pig. I wish you would help me with this.

MEL: *(He tenses while thinking, What does she have to complain about? She's doing great at work. She's always looking for problems. If I tell her what I really think, we'll just end up fighting.)* I'm sure that it's not that big a deal. Why don't you use the weekend to think about other things? Remember, this is supposed to be our Sabbath.

RUTHIE: *(getting angrier)* Oh great, now you're going to use Judaism to shut me up. I can tell that you really don't want to talk about it. It really bothers me that you can't talk with me about this. You always either change the subject or get real quiet.

MEL: (*He takes a deep breath and lets out a loud sigh. He wants to say something to stop the escalation, but no good idea comes to mind. He says nothing. He feels tense.*)

RUTHIE: That's exactly what I mean. You just close me out, again and again, and I'm tired of it!

MEL: (*He thinks, I knew it. We always fight when we talk about work.*) Why do you do this? I'm just sitting here relaxing. It's the only time I have to sit still, and you pick a fight. I hate this! (*He throws the paper down, gets up from the table, and walks into the living room.*)

If we summed up their concerns bluntly, Ruthie wants Mel to open up, and he wants her to back off. Even more disturbing, she feels that he is not at her side in a battle where she feels she is being taken advantage of. At face value, it sounds as though they have very different goals for their relationship. Such patterns are commonly explained by saying that she wants intimacy and he doesn't. However, if you look underneath this pattern, you usually see something very different.

Many partners and therapists have concluded that men are less interested in intimacy and seek to avoid it. Our research and clinical experience suggest otherwise. Moreover, we don't believe that women desire conflict or take delight in stirring up turmoil. We believe that men and women want most of the same things in a relationship: respect, connection, intimacy, friendship, peace, and harmony. Our beliefs are not fueled by armchair speculation but are based on many studies of men and women in marriage and on our experience with couples.

## WHAT IS INTIMATE TO YOU?

Often the problems between men and women are less about their differences in values or needs, and more about how those values or needs are expressed. Research shows that although both men and women desire intimacy, women tend to define intimacy in terms of verbal communication, whereas men are more likely to define it in terms of shared activities. This is a critical point to keep in mind. When a wife asks her husband to spend some time talking about feelings, she may be showing her preference for intimacy, but so is a husband who asks his wife to take a walk or make love. These preferences parallel men's and women's upbringing: little girls spend much more energy mastering verbal intimacy, and little boys become intimate through activities, especially through play that has rules, such as sports.

Even in their goals for therapy, men and women are not as different as it may appear. Whereas a man's number one goal may be to reduce conflict and a woman's is to improve communication, we often find that her second most important goal is to reduce conflict and his is to communicate better. So even in the typical goals for marital counseling, what men and women want is similar: both want improved communication and reduced conflict, but they differ in the priority attached to each goal. Thus, the key difference between males and females regarding intimacy is one of preference, not one of interest or even capacity. In fact, one important study, conducted by Judy Schwartz and her colleagues, found that when conditions are right, men are nearly as capable of verbal intimacy as women.[11]

Couples in relationships that are working well have learned to use their understanding of their similarities and differences to work as a team rather than as enemies. They have usually developed the capacity to connect on several dimensions of intimacy, including verbal communication, shared activity, and sensual partnership, to name a few. They are also more accepting of their differences and recognize that they can't be soul mates on every dimension of life. We'll help you with all of these issues as we go on.

## CONFLICT: THE REAL DIFFERENCE

If men and women both want intimacy and are only different in the ways they prefer to attain it, why do so many couples have trouble preserving, protecting, and nurturing intimacy? Conflict! The important difference between men and women lies not in their desire for intimacy but in how they handle conflict. More specifically, we believe that when men go into a conflict management mode, they become overly focused on preventing conflict from erupting. They tend to avoid or withdraw from it at all costs. Women tend to interpret these more typically male responses to conflict or potential conflict as motivated by a lack of caring.

## Are Men Really Less Emotional?

No! Reconsider the case of Mel and Ruthie. When they have arguments, Mel appears fairly calm, and Ruthie appears very emotional. In fact, Mel usually looks totally shut down, which really hurts and annoys Ruthie. She wants him to respond, and he looks almost dead to her. But to say that Mel isn't emotional during these conflicts is to rely on a limited definition of what emotional means.

Suppose we hooked Ruthie and Mel up to equipment designed to measure physiological reactions to stress, such as variations in blood pressure, heart rate, or galvanic skin response. These are ways of gauging a person's inner emotional state, independent of how outwardly expressive he or she seems to be. Studies using such equipment have found that men may be responding more intensely than women on the physiological level even though they outwardly display little emotion. So although it may not be obvious on the outside, a man's emotional experience on the inside is very intense. This is why Mel can seem very calm one minute, then blow up the next, when he has reached his limit.

We can conclude from this type of research that many men can be very emotional, whether they show it or not. One study showed that the degree of physiological arousal men feel just contemplating talking to their wives at the end of the day strongly predicts divorce.[12] In other words, the more anxious and aroused you are just imagining a conversation with your partner, the greater the risk of divorce in the future.

Hence, even though there does seem to be a difference in the way men and women express emotion, it's not accurate to think that men do not respond emotionally, especially to conflict. Could this high degree of physiological arousal help explain the common occurrence of men shutting down in conversations with their partners? We believe so, and we'll explain why.

It seems that instead of being the stronger sex, males are physiologically weaker along a number of dimensions. Sure, men tend to be physically stronger, but they are not more durable. Considering that research shows they often experience higher levels of physiological stress during conflict with their partners, we can see a clear reason for them to be motivated to avoid or withdraw from conflict. Women tend to be more expressive and more physiologically resilient; they therefore have less reason to avoid discussing the issue in question, at least in a physically safe relationship. They simply don't feel the same aversion to conflict that men do.

We have talked with many men who report a very unpleasant sense of tension and anxiety during conflict with their wives. They bottle up unpleasant feelings, without finding any appropriate outlet to express themselves. In Mel and Ruthie's case, Mel only expressed his frustration when he could no longer hold it in. Even when he did this, he was still trying to shut the conversation down.

Biology isn't the only relevant factor in explaining these gender differences in handling conflict. Upbringing plays an important role as well. There is ample reason to believe that women are more comfortable with verbal relationships than men are. As we mentioned earlier, this may partially explain why women prefer verbal intimacy more than men do. Women typically have practiced verbal skills with their family and friends since childhood. It's not that men haven't done this, but little girls are socialized to do so much more. Girls tend to play in small groups or in pairs. From the start, their play focuses on relationships: playing house, role-playing with dolls, and even physical activities, such as jump rope games or taking turns on slides or swings. Dealing with issues verbally as they grow up gives girls greater confidence in handling conflicts through communication when they become adults. Boys are much more likely to play games that require a leader telling other boys what to do and how to do it. Boys' games have winners and losers, and rules take paramount importance. Overall, men appear to be socialized to be more action oriented, geared to problem solving and reaching specific goals. When rules don't exist or don't cover the situation at hand, men seem more uncomfortable, more at a loss to know what to do than women.

The common reaction for anyone dealing with a situation that causes anxiety and in which one feels inadequate is avoidance or withdrawal. Hence, when men and women get into conflict, men are more prone to choosing the wrong approach to dealing with it: withdrawal.

## Different Attitudes Toward Rules

Men may hate personal conflict, but they love rules. And who has more rules than Jews? Starting with the Ten Commandments, Judaism prescribes 613 *mitzvot*, which translates as "commandments": 248 positive and 365 negative.

So where are the rules that govern marriage and intimacy? In Chapter Fourteen, where we focus on sexuality, we will see that there are many traditional Jewish guidelines about relationships between the sexes. But in modern society, it seems that men experience more distress than women do about not knowing the rules of the game of love. Research indicates that when conflict arises in a game, girls are more likely to break off the activity, whereas boys are more likely to try to work through the conflict to keep the game going. Boys do this by resorting to rules or by creating new rules to resolve conflicts. This does not suggest that the girls are avoiding the conflict, but rather that the relationship is more important than the game for them, whereas for the boys the game *is* the relationship; it results in activity-oriented intimacy.

Culturally, we tend to think of men as more oriented toward conflict, not toward avoiding it, as so often seems to be the case in marriage. We might think that the experiences men have as boys would offer some guidance they could use as adults in handling marital conflicts. But whereas the presence of rules in games allows boys to cope with conflict, the absence of clear rules for dealing with emotional conflict in marriage sets the stage for men to withdraw. Women, who are not socialized to look as much to rules and who are freer to engage in the verbal process, usually don't have the same problems with conflict in marriage.

## THE IMPORTANCE OF RULES

It is evident that there are few rules or widely accepted methods designed to help men and women deal with emotional conflict in marriage. We aren't saying that none exist, but it is difficult for many couples to understand them. We suggest that many men, and women too, can handle conflict and differences better when the rules are clearly spelled out.

Rules are agreed-on techniques and strategies for dealing with conflict in marriage. For example, in the next chapter, we teach you the rules for a very powerful communication technique. The rules do not remove the conflict or solve the problem, but they set the stage for the discussion. They provide agreed-on guidelines for what is inbounds and what is out, who can speak when and in what way, and how both partners will take turns listening to each other. As you will see, the kinds of rules we emphasize don't take the emotion out of the issues being discussed, but they are of great help in making the emotion manageable.

When you have agreed on such rules and strategies ahead of time and have mastered them through practice, you will find that you can increase your ability to deal with issues without avoidance, withdrawal, escalation, or invalidation. In one sense, the next few chapters present what we think of as a set of marital mitzvot. Although some couples need them more than others, they can be helpful to all couples in handling their conflicts skillfully and respectfully.

---

All couples will experience disagreements and conflicts. This means that all of them will experience unpleasant emotions, such as anger, hostility, mistrust, fear, and sadness. A major task for partners in a close relationship, therefore, is to be able to handle these negative feelings constructively, without destructive levels of conflict or the loneliness of avoidance.

In light of the gender differences we have discussed, research from our colleague John Gottman and his associates has highlighted some important gender-linked dynamics of marital success that add a nice contrast to the kinds of frustrating patterns we have been discussing here. Gottman and his associates note that a major predictor of the future success of marriages is whether wives can constructively bring up issues, including negative feelings, and whether husbands can respond by listening and talking, rather than by avoiding and shutting down.[13] In other words, instead of falling into a pattern in which the woman feels compelled to raise the roof to get problems addressed and in which the man withdraws, the most successful couples demonstrate patterns through which issues get raised and dealt with gently and respectfully. And when issues are raised by the women in these more successful couples, even if they use a slightly irritated tone, the men tend *not* to escalate or withdraw but to respond more calmly in return. We have observed that it can have a very powerful and positive effect if partners who tend to withdraw learn to raise issues on their own, and not discuss a matter solely because their partners have brought it to light.

We can help you learn to respond to one another in ways more associated with great marriages. We advocate agreed-on rules for handling conflict that can greatly facilitate your ability as a couple to handle conflict in a manner that protects intimacy and promotes growth in your relationship. You may be thinking that this sounds like a rigid approach, but as you will see, it isn't. The kinds of rules we suggest are very effective in helping couples keep poorly handled conflict from destroying the great things in the relationship.

In Chapter Four, we begin by presenting the rules for the Speaker-Listener Technique; Chapter Five describes an effective method for solving problems. When couples regularly use such rules and techniques for dealing with the issues in their relationships, they develop increased confidence and satisfaction.

## EXERCISE

The exercise we suggest here calls for reflection. Mostly we want you just to think about the questions here, perhaps jotting your thoughts down on a separate pad of paper. Plan some time to talk together about your own perceptions of how these patterns work for you. Most of the exercises in this book will have you focus together on your relationship. Here, we ask that you first look at your individual styles.

1. If you tend to avoid or withdraw, why do you do this? How does your physiology or upbringing fit in with your pattern? That is, does thinking about conflict make you feel anxious or emotionally uncomfortable?

2. If you tend to pursue, why? What are you seeking when you pursue? You may consider many factors, such as the model presented to you by the way your parents and other significant people in your life managed conflict, as well as your temperament.

After reflecting on your own understanding of what you do in your relationship, plan some time together to discuss your perceptions. You should focus on this being an open, nonconflictual talk. Share with each other your perceptions of why *you* do what you do, not why you think your partner does what he or she does. If this type of discussion leads to conflict, you may want to wait to have this talk until you have learned the techniques presented in the next chapter.

# 4

# Communicating Clearly and Safely
## *The Speaker-Listener Technique*

*Learning begins with listening.*

　　　　　　　　　　　　*Noah Ben Shea[1]*

*It's so simple to be wise. Just think of something
stupid to say and say the opposite.*

　　　　　　　　　　　　*Sam Levenson[2]*

Why does the most important Jewish prayer begin with the word "Hear"? *Sh'ma Yisra'el, Adonai Eloheinu, Adonai Ekhad*: "Hear, O Israel, the Lord Is Our God, the Lord Is One" (Deuteronomy 6:4) commands our attention before God gives us the message of monotheism. Perhaps it is because we have so much difficulty attending to the truly important words in life. Clearly, many partners in intimate relationships have great difficulty listening to, as well as speaking clearly about, what matters most.

Do you really want to communicate well? Most couples do, but many have never learned to communicate when it counts most—in conflict. As you learned in Chapters Two and Three, handling conflict well is critical to the future of your marriage. And communicating well is critical to handling conflict. There are two keys to good communication: making it clear and making it safe.

In this chapter, you will learn the Speaker-Listener Technique. When you use this technique, you protect your communication from destructive patterns, allowing you and your partner to share clear and safe communication that can bring you closer together.

# MAKING IT CLEAR: THE PROBLEM OF FILTERS

Have you ever noticed that what you are trying to say to your partner can be very different from what he or she hears? You may say something you think is harmless, and suddenly your spouse is mad at you. Or you may ask a question such as, "What do you want for dinner?" and your partner starts complaining that you are not doing your share of the work.

We have all experienced the frustration of being misunderstood. We think we are being clear, but our partner just doesn't seem to "get it." Or we "know" what our partner said yesterday, but today he or she says something that seems completely different.

Many of our biggest arguments begin with a failure to understand what our partner is saying. Too often, our misunderstanding leads to anger. What gets in the way? *Filters*.

Filters change what goes through them. A furnace filter takes dust and dirt out of the air. A filter on a camera lens alters the properties of the light passing through it. A coffee filter lets the flavor through and leaves the grounds behind. As with any other filter, what goes into our "communication filters" is different from what comes out.

We all have many kinds of filters packed into our heads, and they affect what we hear, what we say, and how we interpret things. They are created by how we are feeling, what we think, what we have experienced in our life, and our family and cultural backgrounds, among other factors. Sometimes these filters can distort communication in ways that lead to problems. In this chapter, we emphasize six types of filters that can interfere with clear communication:

1. Inattention

2. Emotional states

3. Beliefs and expectations

4. Differences in style

5. Cultural differences

6. Self-protection

## Inattention

A very basic kind of filter is operating if you don't have the attention of the person with whom you are trying to speak. Both external and internal factors can affect a person's attention. Some examples of external factors are noisy children, a hearing problem, a bad phone line, or the background noise at a party. You are not likely to have a good conversation about an important matter if there is a crying child or a blaring television in the room. For important talks, when you really need to communicate well, find a quiet place if you can, and don't answer the phone. Make it easier to pay attention to one another by getting rid of filters created by external distractions.

Internal factors affecting attention include feeling tired, thinking about something else, mentally forming a rebuttal, and being bored. These internal factors distract a person from the conversation. It's common for one partner to think—correctly—that the other isn't paying attention. There are many times in relationships when you say something only to find that your partner didn't hear it. When one partner believes that this happens consistently, he or she will feel increasingly frustrated and invalidated.

Sometimes the listener who doesn't hear is rude or really doesn't care what the speaker has to say. In most cases, however, this is probably not the best explanation. Choosing to believe that your partner doesn't care can be a destructive interpretation if you are wrong. More often, the listener is tired or preoccupied, distracted by an internal filter. Psychological studies reveal that people differ in their ability to attend to several things at once. Multitasking is not for everyone.

Often the unhearing listener is focused on something else and truly doesn't hear what the other is saying. People also differ in their ability to break off their focus from one stimulus and turn their attention to another. And for everyone, the ability to switch focus or maintain attention suffers greatly with fatigue.

So be sure you have your partner's attention when you are trying to get your point across. It is just as rude to begin a point when your partner is focused on something else as it is for your partner not to respond.

We recommend that you accept lapses in attention as part of life. Sometimes they will affect your communication in frustrating ways. Try not to make too much of them. The key is to make sure you have your partner's attention and give your attention when it counts the most.

## Emotional States

Emotional states or moods become filters that affect communication. For example, a number of studies demonstrate that we tend to give people the benefit of the doubt more frequently when we are in a good mood and less frequently when we are in a bad mood. If you are in a bad mood, you are more likely to perceive whatever your partner says or does negatively, no matter how positive he or she is trying to be. Have you noticed that sometimes, when your spouse is in a bad mood, he or she jumps on you no matter how nicely you say something?

The best way to keep this kind of filter from damaging your relationship is to acknowledge when you are aware that one is operating. Here's an example. It's dinnertime. The kids are hungry and complaining. Adam just got home, and Barbara is working on dinner in the kitchen:

ADAM: Hi, did you get Izzy signed up for soccer today?
BARBARA: *(snapping with anger)* No, I didn't have time. Can't you see I have my hands full? Do something helpful.

ADAM:  I'm sorry. I should have seen you were busy. Rough day?
BARBARA:  Yes. I'm just really upset. I don't know if you remembered, but tomorrow is my father's yahrzeit. I can't believe he died seven years ago. I'm sorry I snapped at you. Sometimes when I feel depressed, I just get angry really quickly.
ADAM:  Maybe we can talk about it some after dinner.
BARBARA:  Thanks.

Without using the term *filter*, Adam and Barbara were acknowledging that one was there. Barbara was struggling with her sorrow about her father's death. It would have been easy to let this conversation escalate into an argument, but Adam had the good sense to see he had raised the issue at the wrong time, and Barbara was self-aware enough to understand why she felt on edge.

Barbara responded by essentially telling Adam that she had a filter going: her sad and angry mood. Furthermore, because she was in the middle of getting dinner ready, it was a bad time for Adam to get her attention. Once Adam became aware of her mood, he could interpret her behavior in light of it and understand that her negative mood was not his fault. His knowing this reduced the likelihood that he would become defensive in reaction to her mood.

Many kinds of emotional filters can exist in any one person. If you are angry, worried, sad, or upset about anything, it can color both your interpretation of what your partner says and your response to it.

## Beliefs and Expectations

Many very important filters arise from how you think about your relationship and what you expect from it. As we mentioned in Chapter Two, research and experience tell us that people tend to see what they expect to see in others. This kind of expectation becomes a filter that distorts communication.

Studies show that expectations not only affect our perceptions but also actually can influence the behavior of others. For example, if you believe that someone is an extrovert, that person is more likely to sound like an extrovert when talking with you, even if she or he is in fact introverted. In one infamous study, teachers were given false information about their new students' test scores. By the end of the year, the teachers' incorrect beliefs about their students significantly influenced the students' performance—for better and for worse. We "pull" behavior from others that is consistent with what we expect.

The next example shows how difficult it can be to get around such filters. Andy and Heidi are a Jewish couple we met in one of our workshops. They were having problems deciding what to do for fun when they had free time. With three children in elementary school, free time without the kids was very valuable. But they often disagreed about what to do, and both felt very frustrated.

Andy had grown up in a large extended Jewish family. Most of the family belonged to the same synagogue, and they always spent the holidays together. Heidi, in contrast, was an only child whose parents divorced when she was seven. Her father moved to another city, and she lived with her mother, who had no relatives who lived nearby. Her mother was not actively involved in the Jewish community, and taking care of Heidi, working, and friends filled her life.

In many ways, each partner's beliefs and expectations about one another were based in reality. Heidi was correct in her understanding that Andy's idea of fun was to be with lots of people. When the two of them would go out, he usually liked to be with at least one or two other couples. He also liked attending synagogue at least once a month, and Heidi didn't like to go. Andy was correct in his belief that Heidi, like her mother, had always seen individual friends as most important and liked being with one person at a time. When Heidi started dating in high school, she was intensely romantic and would always focus all of her attention on her boyfriend to the exclusion of almost anything else.

Heidi had often complained that Andy wasn't interested in spending time alone with her. Andy often felt annoyed that Heidi never wanted to do anything that he thought was fun and felt that if she cared more about him she would do things he liked. Both of them had been feeling rejected. Recently, though, Andy had been thinking a lot about Heidi's dissatisfaction and wanted to try something new. He decided to surprise her by suggesting that they do something alone, but filters based on their expectations got in the way. Note that they both act as if they can read each other's mind:

ANDY: (*He is excited about trying to please Heidi by suggesting that they spend time alone.*) We have some free time tonight. I wonder if we should try to do something.

HEIDI: (*She assumes that he wants to do be together with other couples and starts feeling hopeless.*) Oh, I don't know. What do you think?

ANDY: (*He hears the tone of resignation in her voice and feels disappointed, thinking that she really doesn't want to spend time alone with him. He hedges on his "romantic" agenda.*) Well, we could go to dinner, or we could call and see what Sal and Mimi are doing.

HEIDI: (*She thinks, "I was really stupid to think for a moment that he wanted to be with just me.*) Fine, let's call them. I think they're free tonight.

ANDY: (*He is disappointed and thinks, "I knew it. She really just likes complaining and doesn't want to make things better.*) Yeah, OK.

In this conversation, there was no apparent escalation, invalidation, or withdrawal. Nevertheless, Andy and Heidi didn't communicate well because of their filters. Heidi's belief that Andy didn't want to be alone with her colored her perception of his invitation. She assumed that he didn't want the two of them to be alone. It didn't help that Andy wasn't very clear in expressing what he wanted, and he was quick to assume that Heidi wasn't really receptive to his changing. In fact, negative interpretations acted as filters to distort and interfere with effective communication.

Although this couple's assumptions were not unreasonable considering their history together, neither of them took the chance to be curious about what the other really meant. Instead, they used "mind reading" to interpret what was going on. Heidi "knew" that Andy wasn't really interested in being alone with her. Andy "knew" that Heidi had given up on him. You are mind reading when you assume that you know what your partner is thinking or feeling. It is a common form of filtering based on your predetermined beliefs and expectations.

## Differences in Style

Everyone has a different style of communicating, and different styles can create filters that distort communication. Perhaps one of you is much more expressive, the other more reserved. You may have some trouble understanding each other because you use such different styles. Styles are influenced by many factors, including culture, gender, and upbringing. Sometimes, differences in style that are rooted in family backgrounds can cause serious misunderstandings, becoming powerful filters that disrupt communication.

Even though they are both Jewish, Sue and Samy come from very different families with very different emotional styles. Samy is forty-seven years old and is a Sephardic Jew who was born in Cairo, Egypt. His family first moved to France and then to the United States by the time he was ten years old. His family has always been very expressive, showing great intensity when they are emotional. Shouting and crying could quickly shift to laughing and kissing; all feelings were part of being close and connected.

Sue was raised in Southern California in a predominantly Christian neighborhood. Her parents did not like to call attention to themselves, and she remembered being "shushed" whenever she and her brother played too boisterously. She remembers "The neighbors will hear" as her mother's refrain. When anyone did get angry in her family, it usually led to a tense silence that could last hours and sometimes even days. By temperament and experience, Sue has always been more reserved.

As a result of their different upbringing, Sue and Samy interpret a slight rise in the loudness of someone's voice very differently: in Sue's family such a rise could be very anxiety provoking, whereas in Samy's it would hardly be noticed. In many conversations, therefore, Sue overestimates the intensity of Samy's feelings, and Samy underestimates Sue's feelings, as in this example:

SAMY:  How much was the doctor's bill?

SUE:  Four hundred and twenty-eight dollars.

SAMY:  (intense, quickly getting red) What? How could he possibly charge that much? That's outrageous.

SUE:  (lashing out) I wish you could stop yelling at me! I've told you over and over that I cannot listen to you when you are yelling!

SAMY:  I'm not yelling at you. I just can't believe that it could cost that much.

SUE:  Why can't we have a quiet conversation like other people? My sister and brother-in-law never yell at each other.

SAMY:  Yeah, and they're a couple of cold fish. Look, four hundred and twenty-eight dollars is too much to pay. That's all I'm reacting to.

SUE:  Why don't you deal with the doctor's office next time? I'm tired of being yelled at for things like this.

SAMY:  Honey, look. I'm not upset at you. I'm upset at them. You know I can get pretty hot, but I'm not trying to say you did anything wrong.

SUE:  (calming down) It seems that way sometimes.

SAMY:  Well, I'm not upset at you. Let me call them. Where's the number?

Samy and Sue are caught up in a misunderstanding based on differences in style. But in the conversation here, they do a great job of not allowing things to escalate. As in preceding examples in which a conversation got back on track, one partner figures out that a filter is distorting the intended message, and takes corrective action. Here, Samy skillfully clarifies that he is not mad at Sue.

Becoming more aware of the effects of your differing communication styles can go a long way toward preventing misunderstandings. Give some thought to these differences between you and your partner.

## Cultural Differences

Cultural differences in a marriage can create misunderstandings that are difficult to identify. What each of us thinks of as "normal" is built upon the invisible cultural rules that were part of our growing up. You can see from the example of Samy and Sue that sharing a common identity as Jews does not automatically mean sharing cultural values.

In interfaith marriages, even when one partner converts, culturally based misunderstandings can play a major role in conflict. Religious conversion does not erase ethnic experiences and expectations. Although it is important not to overgeneralize about the effect of cultural differences, it is also crucial to be able to recognize them when they create problems. Although some couples blame too much of their conflict on the differences in their backgrounds, far more never find a way to acknowledge the power of the past.

Almost all differences become more obvious in the process of raising children. Ron and Sharon were in their early forties and had an eight-year-old daughter and a twelve-year-old son. When they married, Ron chose to convert to Judaism from Catholicism. Even though Sharon never made conversion an issue, Ron felt strongly about the importance of a unified family faith.

They had both always lived in Chicago and came from large, cohesive families. Ron and Sharon shared a love of cooking, eating, and talking with their hands.

But for all their similarities, they discovered that their culturally based expectations about how they defined "appropriate" behavior for children were quite different. Ron's father was a foreman in a small factory. In the blue-collar Italian neighborhood he grew up in and in the church he attended, there was a high value placed on unquestioning obedience to parents, especially the father.

Even though Sharon had grown up in a Jewish suburb only a few miles away from Ron, the cultural rules in her world were quite different. Her father was an attorney who encouraged his two daughters' inclination toward debate. The rabbi at their temple was frequently in conflict with several groups of congregants who had very different ideas about how he was supposed to adapt Jewish ritual. Challenging authority sometimes seemed to be a communal sport in Sharon's family and community.

Sharon and Ron's differences about children and authority came out in a recent interaction.

SHARON: I can't believe how angry you got with Jonathan for expressing his feelings about going to the movies.

RON: (indignant) You call talking back to me after I said no three times "expressing his feelings"?

SHARON: He is doing really well in school and deserves a little down time. You shouldn't get so upset by what he said. I really respect his ability to argue his point. I don't want you to squash that out of him.

RON: (sarcastic) Great, so now you're going to make him into a lawyer too.

SHARON: (taking a deep breath and pausing for a few seconds) Look, I don't want to get into a big fight. It's true that in my family, discussion was really valued. My dad would be proud of me when I would argue with him.

RON: (calming down a little) Yeah, and in my family, talking back to my father was the best way to feel the back of his hand. I always think of myself as so much more liberal than he was.

SHARON: (teasing) Your dad was the infallible pope and mine was just a poor rabbi who everyone argued with. I guess some things never change.

Ron and Sharon had a very lively relationship. Their frequent arguments would usually subside as quickly as they began. Their style of managing their conflicts kept them feeling very connected. They were aware of the culturally based filters they each brought to their marriage, and they had learned to use that awareness in ways that helped them de-escalate conflict. Neither of them was frightened by the other's emotional intensity, and they both appreciated each other's wit and humor, even when it was somewhat caustic.

When couples learn to discuss their different cultural perspectives, they often can deal more effectively with differences. Much of what we aim to do in this book is help you understand your partner's perspective, *especially* when it differs from your own. Jennifer and Len had worked together a great deal to understand how their different backgrounds affected the ways they defined withdrawal and escalation. Jennifer had been raised as a Methodist in a small midwestern town; Len was a Jewish man from New York City. They learned that understanding their differences doesn't always make unpleasant feelings disappear, but it certainly could make the feelings easier to deal with.

JENNIFER: One of the things that is very different between us on the cultural level is that my family used silence a lot. If somebody disapproved of something, they wouldn't say anything at all. And growing up with that you get real sensitive to silence.
LEN: My family fought and bickered a lot, and I always heard more than I wanted to hear when my parents were unhappy about something. For me, silence was a rare reward.
JENNIFER: For me it was a punishment. Even though I understand the differences intellectually, to this day, when Len is quiet I get a little uneasy because I worry that he is angry about something.
LEN: When Jennifer is quiet, I always take it as a good sign.

## Self-Protection

This kind of filter has its origins in the fear of rejection, with which we all struggle in some ways. Because of this fear, we sometimes avoid saying what we really want or feel. Even saying something as simple as "Wouldn't you like to go see that new movie with me?" is a way of hedging our bets—of being a little indirect in the service of self-protection. Instead of stating our desires directly ("I'd like to see that new movie with you; want to go?"), we often partially conceal them because expressing them more directly reveals more of who we are—raising the risk of rejection. This may not matter a lot when the topic is movies, but when it comes to the important issues of marriage—feelings, desires, and expectations—the tendency to self-protect can lead to a lot of miscommunication.

Another way people protect themselves is by not directly dealing with issues that make them uncomfortable. Mitzi and Al had been married for forty years. He was sixty-two years old, and she was fifty-nine. Their two children were grown and had families of their own. Both Mitzi and Al worked in a small family business they had inherited from Al's parents.

They were both a little anxious about dealing with retirement, because they had not put away enough money to be able to retire in five years, which had been their goal. Without consulting Mitzi, Al had taken $50,000 out of their savings and invested it in an Internet stock that his friend told him was about to skyrocket. Al was excited about the idea of surprising Mitzi with the windfall he expected to collect.

It didn't work out as he had hoped—the stock crashed, and Al lost almost all the money he had invested. He hadn't yet told Mitzi about what had happened—instead, he became increasingly controlling and irritable about anything having to do with money.

The damage created by Al's attempts at self-protection became obvious when Mitzi brought up the idea of a vacation.

MITZI: *(excited)* You know, we've been pretty careful about spending this year. What do you think about the idea of us taking a vacation in Mexico this winter? We haven't been in years, and I think we've earned it.

AL: *(getting a little tense)* I think that we should just drive down south and visit the kids. They have an extra room, and it would be great to see them.

MITZI: *(a little disappointed)* But I really wanted to be alone with you. It's been a long time.

AL: *(angrily)* Is all you can ever think about is ways to spend money? What do you think, it grows on trees? I'm going to see the kids. If you want to come with, it's up to you.

MITZI: *(really hurt but trying to hide it)* Sure, whatever you want. That would be nice to see the kids.

It's clear that Al's efforts to protect himself from his embarrassment about losing their money motivated his aggressive rejection of Mitzi's ideas. In the past, Al had loved going away with Mitzi and would have really wanted to go this year—if he hadn't lost the money. Instead of being open, he is using anger to protect himself from feeling the shame he will experience when he tells Mitzi the truth.

For her part, Mitzi is also protecting herself a little when she backs down and says, "Sure, whatever you want." She doesn't want Al to see how hurt she is; in trying to appease him, she is putting off dealing with her discomfort. Later, when Al finally told Mitzi what had happened to the money, he broke into tears. That was the first step that began a process of forgiveness between them—and of dealing more directly with financial issues.

## FILTERS AND MEMORY: THAT'S NOT WHAT I HEARD!

*A man meets his friend, the story goes, and complains, "Whenever I have a fight with my wife, she becomes historical." The friend thinks he didn't hear right and says, "You don't mean historical, you mean hysterical." "No," says the first one, "I mean historical. The minute we have an argument, she remem-*

*bers everything wrong I ever did from the minute I*
*met her!"*

Rabbi Benjamin Blech[3]

Some of the biggest arguments couples have are about what they actually said in the past. How often have you wished that you had a tape recording of an earlier conversation? This happens to all of us. These differences in memory occur in great measure because of the variety of filters that operate in all relationships. Any of the filters we have discussed here can lead to differences—and arguments—about what someone actually said or did in the past.

We recommend two things that can save your relationship from such fruitless arguments about the past. First, don't assume that your memory is perfect. Accept that it isn't. Countless studies in the field of psychology show how fragile human memory is and how susceptible it is to the distorting influence of our motivation and beliefs. This is a tremendous problem in our legal system, and it's just as great a problem in relationships. Accept that you both have filters and that plenty of room exists for something to be said or heard differently from what was intended.

Second, when you disagree, don't persist in arguments about what one of you said in the past; you will get nowhere. Memory matching is a game with no winner. Instead, accept that you each remember the conversation differently and that filters were in operation on both sides. Then move forward by focusing on what you think or feel about the issue right now. Don't get stuck in the past, even if it was five minutes ago. Deal with what you think and feel in the present.

We all have filters. Either we react to them with little awareness, which can cause damage to the relationship, or we learn to look for them when conversations go awry. Try to get in the habit of announcing your filter when you are aware that you might have one, for example, "I know I'm sensitive about sex, so I may not be real clear in what I'm trying to tell you right now." We all have different moods, levels of attention, and beliefs. We also have differences in experience and upbringing that can result in filters that prevent successful communication. After discussing the importance of safety in your relationship, we will show you a very effective communication technique for reducing the effect of filters on your important discussions.

# MAKING IT SAFE: THE VALUE OF STRUCTURE

To have a great marriage, both of you must be able to express your beliefs, concerns, and preferences clearly, without damaging the relationship in the process. The four negative patterns we discussed in Chapter Two can make it unsafe to express your views about what is most important to you. Filters compound the problem, making it a wonder that couples can communicate about anything truly important.

Unless you feel emotionally safe, you are not likely to share important thoughts or feelings with your partner. For many couples, the relationship ends up feeling more like a minefield than a safe haven. Unless they feel safe enough, people generally don't share openly with anyone, including their spouse. Are marriages necessarily safe? No. Most married people want the safe haven of a friendly relationship, but many of them simply don't know how to achieve or sustain that safe, supportive friendship.

To play it safe, people often decide not to share important parts of their life. Marriages can feel like miserable cages when spouses lock away their personal dreams, sexual desires, and tender feelings. In a way, the belief that a relationship isn't safe becomes yet another kind of filter, as you learn to hide what you think, feel, and want. If your relationship does feel safe for sharing your heart and soul, learn to keep it that way. If it isn't safe, learn to make it that way. We'll help you get started.

By "safe" we do not mean risk-free. If you are going to share what you are concerned with, hurt by, or hoping for, you are going to take risks. There is a direct relationship between risk and reward in much of life. You can't be accepted deeply without offering something personal and important for your partner to understand. Conversely, you can take the risk, share deeply, and be rejected. This hurts a lot, because you have chosen to risk a deeper part of yourself in the relationship. But if it goes well, you find a deep, soul-satisfying acceptance of who you are, warts and all. And, happily, when occasional or unintended hurts do occur, safe communication can help you repair these wounds.

When you disagree, or think you do, more is at stake and more can go wrong. For your relationship to grow through conflict, instead of being damaged by it, it is necessary to use agreed-on strategies and techniques for keeping conversations safe and under control. This doesn't mean that every conversation will be pleasant. But it does mean that you work to keep escalation, invalidation, withdrawal, and negative interpretations from overwhelming your efforts to hear and be heard.

Using agreed-on strategies and techniques adds structure to your interaction. This is exactly what is done in work and political settings. Consider for a moment what the U.S. Congress would look like if there were no rules for how and when opinions could be expressed. With adequate structure, you can manage conflict with less chance of damage to your relationship.

## THE SPEAKER-LISTENER TECHNIQUE

The Speaker-Listener Technique offers couples an alternative mode of communication when issues are too hot or sensitive, or likely to get that way. Any conversation in which you want to enhance clarity and safety can benefit from this technique. We don't expect couples to use the technique during normal conversations, however. Many (though not all) couples can decide whether to go out for Chinese food without it, but when it comes to handling sensitive issues concerning money, sex, or in-laws, for example, having the safety net that such a technique provides can be a real comfort. In order to use these skills to talk through difficult issues, though, you will need to learn how to use them when things are going well.

We have found particular success with the Speaker-Listener Technique because it is so simple and very effective. Most couples seem to really appreciate this technique. In our research, couples taking the PREP program overwhelmingly report that learning this technique was very helpful for them. The key is this: you need some way in your marriage of communicating well when you really need to do a good job of it. This technique also is a great way to practice better communication habits that can affect how you interact even when you are not trying to use the technique as taught here.

What follow are the rules for the Speaker-Listener Technique. After you learn and practice these rules, you may find ways you want to modify them to work best in your relationship.

## Rules for Both of You

1. *The Speaker has the floor.* Use a real object to designate the "floor." In seminars, we hand out pieces of linoleum or carpet for couples to use as the floor. You can use anything, though: the TV remote control, a piece of paper, a paperback book. If you don't have the floor, you are the Listener. Speaker and Listener follow the rules for their roles.

2. *Share the floor.* Share the floor over the course of a conversation. One person has it to start and may say a number of things. At some point switch roles and continue as the floor changes hands. An equitable flow, with give and take, is the goal.

3. *Don't attempt to solve problems.* When you use this technique, focus on having good discussions, not on trying to come to solutions. You need to understand one another before you can resolve differences.

## Rules for the Speaker

1. *Speak for yourself. Don't try to be a mind reader.* Talk about your thoughts, feelings, and concerns, not your perceptions of the

Listener's point of view or motives. Try to use "I" statements, and talk about your own point of view. "I think you're a jerk" is not an "I" statement; "I was upset when you forgot our date" is.

2. *Don't go on and on.* You will have plenty of opportunity to say all you need to say. To help the Listener listen actively, it is very important to confine what you say to brief statements. If you are in the habit of delivering long monologues, remember that having the floor protects you from interruptions, so you can afford to pause and be sure that your partner understands you.

3. *Stop and let the Listener paraphrase.* After you have talked a short while, stop and allow the Listener to paraphrase what you just said. If the paraphrase wasn't quite accurate, you should politely restate what was not heard the way you intended it to be heard. Your goal is to help the Listener hear and understand your point of view. This is not a test—help make sure that the Listener really hears you.

## Rules for the Listener

1. *Paraphrase what you hear.* You must paraphrase what the Speaker is saying. Briefly repeat back what you heard the Speaker say, using your own words if you like, and make sure that you understand what was said. The key is to show your partner that you are listening by restating what you heard. If your paraphrase is not quite right (which happens often), the Speaker will gently clarify the point being made. If you truly don't understand some phrase or example, you may ask the Speaker to clarify, but do not ask questions on any other aspect of the issue unless you have the floor.

2. *Focus on the Speaker's message. Don't rebut.* In the Listener's role, do not offer your opinion or thoughts. This is the hardest part of being a good Listener. If you are upset by what your partner says, you need to edit out any response you may want to make and pay attention to what your partner is saying. Wait until you get the floor to respond. As the Listener, you may speak only in the service of understanding your partner. Any words or actions that would reveal your opinion are not allowed, including making faces!

Before showing how this technique works in a conversation, we want to give you some ideas about what good paraphrases can sound like. Suppose that your spouse says to you, "I really had a tough day. Mom got on my case about how I handled the arrangements for Ari's bar mitzvah. Ugh!" Any of the following would be an excellent paraphrase:

"Sounds as though you had a really tough day."

"So, your mom was critical of how you handled the party, and really got on you about it."

"Bad day, huh?"

Any one of these responses conveys that you have listened and displays what you understood. A good paraphrase can be short or long, detailed or general. If you are uncertain how to get a paraphrase started, it can help to begin with "What I hear you saying is. . . ." Then fill in what you just heard your partner say. Another way to begin a paraphrase is with the words "Sounds like. . . ."

When using the Speaker-Listener Technique, the Speaker is always the one who determines if the Listener's paraphrase was on target. Only the Speaker knows what the intended message was. If the paraphrase was not quite on target, it is very important that the Speaker gently clarify or restate the point rather than responding angrily or critically.

One more key point: when you are in the Listener's role, be sincere in your effort to show that you are listening carefully and respectfully. Even when you disagree with the point being made by your partner, your goal is to show respect for—and validation of—his or her perspective. To validate your partner means that you understand how it makes sense for your partner to feel that way, even if you disagree. Show respect and listen well. Remember, you will have your chance to share your point of view when it is your turn to have the floor.

## Using the Speaker-Listener Technique

The most frequent concern that we hear from couples about the Speaker-Listener Technique is that "it's not natural." Yes, that is very true. But you do many things in life that prove beneficial that didn't seem natural when you first learned them. Besides, as we have observed, what many couples "naturally" do is fight. When they disagree or when they talk about something sensitive, their natural style looks more like the danger signs we described than great communication. So try something unnatural for a change. You just might like it. Also, if you practice, you truly will find that the unnaturalness of the technique diminishes with time.

Here is an example of how this technique can change a conversation that is going nowhere into a real opportunity for communication. Paul and Jessica are both forty years old and have two children, ages four and eight. For years they have had a problem dealing with difficult issues. Paul consistently avoids discussing problems, and if Jessica corners him, he withdraws by pulling into himself. They know they need to communicate more clearly and effectively about tough topics and have agreed that the structure of the Speaker-Listener Technique might help.

In this case, Jessica and Paul have been locked in the pursuer-withdrawer cycle over the issue of Jeremy's preschool. Jessica felt that it was really important for him to attend a nursery school connected to a synagogue. Paul once said he wanted to consider a nearby Montessori school, but had avoided talking about the issue. They had recently been practicing using the Speaker-Listener Technique and were feeling more confident about tackling more difficult issues. Let's see what happens:

JESSICA: I'm really getting tired of leaving Jeremy's preschool up in the air. We've got to deal with this, now.
PAUL: (not looking up from the newspaper) Oh?

JESSICA: *(walking over and grabbing his newspaper)* Paul, we can't just leave this decision hanging in the air. I'm getting really ticked about your putting it off.

PAUL: *(recognizing this would be a wise time to act constructively and not withdraw)* Time out. I can tell we need to talk, but I've been avoiding it because it seems that talking just leads to fighting. Let's try that Speaker-Listener Technique we've been practicing.

As we said, using the Speaker-Listener Technique isn't a "normal" way to communicate, but it is a relatively safe way to communicate about a difficult issue. Each person will get to talk, each will be heard, and both will show their commitment to discussing the problems constructively. When the person who usually withdraws moves toward the pursuer (like Paul does), the effect on the relationship is often very positive. The action attacks the foundation of the pursuer's belief that the withdrawer does not care about the relationship.

The conversation proceeds with Paul picking up a piece of carpet they use for the floor.

PAUL (SPEAKER):   I've also been pretty concerned about where we send Jeremy to preschool, and I'm not totally sure about where I want him to go. I've been leaning toward the Montessori school because I really like their philosophy.

JESSICA (LISTENER):   You've been concerned, too, and you've been thinking you would like to consider the Montessori school because you think their teaching methods would work well for Jeremy.

PAUL (SPEAKER):   Yeah, that's it. Also, I worry that a Jewish school would be too limiting for him. I want him to get to feel comfortable with all kinds of kids.

Note how Paul acknowledges that Jessica's summary is on the mark before moving on to another point.

JESSICA (LISTENER):  You want him to be exposed to a diverse group of kids, and you're concerned that the Jewish nursery school would be too limiting socially, right?

Jessica is not quite sure she has understood Paul's point, so she makes her paraphrase tentative.

PAUL (SPEAKER):  Well, that's partly it, but I also don't want to be limited either. I never went to a Jewish school, and it makes me a little uncomfortable.

Note how Paul reveals more about himself to help Jessica understand his feelings. He is moving forward in the conversation, rather than backward. In general, whenever you, as the Speaker, feel that it would be helpful for your partner to reach a deeper understanding of your perspective, use your next statement to restate or expand on what you are trying to get across.

JESSICA (LISTENER):  So, you never went to a Jewish school, and you're worried about your own comfort as well.
PAUL (SPEAKER):  That's right. Here, you take the floor. (He hands Jessica the floor.)
JESSICA (SPEAKER):  Well, I appreciate what you're saying. Actually, I hadn't realized you'd thought this much about it. I was worried that you were just negative about anything Jewish and didn't want to talk about it.

As the Speaker, Jessica validates Paul in the comments he's made.

PAUL (LISTENER):  Sounds as though you're glad to hear that I'm concerned and that I'm willing to really think about why I feel the way I do.
JESSICA (SPEAKER):  Yes. I agree that this isn't an easy decision. The Jewish nursery school is farther from home and costs more

money. And I like to meet all kinds of people too. But I feel that helping him get a firm foundation in feeling Jewish is really important and worth the effort.

PAUL (LISTENER): You feel that there are reasons to consider sending him to another school. But you feel that it's even more important that we give him real exposure to a Jewish setting while he's young.

JESSICA (SPEAKER): Exactly. That's just how I feel. I got the sense that you never really had a good Jewish experience and that you're leery of things that seem "too Jewish." But for me feeling comfortable as a Jew only happened after I got involved in a Jewish school.

Jessica feels good with Paul listening so carefully, and she lets him know it. She also gives Paul room to disagree by being tentative ("I got the sense") when she talks about how she understands Paul's feelings.

PAUL (LISTENER): You realize that I'm kind of uncomfortable in Jewish settings, but for you, being involved in a Jewish school was really important to feeling good about yourself as a Jew.

JESSICA (SPEAKER): Yes to all of the above. I'm glad that we can talk about this more openly. I'm not sure how we will resolve this issue, but it feels really good to talk so openly about it.

PAUL (LISTENER): You're happy we are finally talking about the preschool issue, even though you're not sure what our final decision will be.

JESSICA (SPEAKER): Right. Here, you take the floor again. (*They pass the floor again.*)

As you can tell, Paul and Jessica have been practicing quite a bit. They are both doing an excellent job following the rules and showing concern and respect for each other's viewpoints. Couples can have discussions like this on difficult topics, even when they disagree. The key is making it safe and showing respect for your partner's thoughts, feelings, and opinions.

## The Advantages of Using the Speaker-Listener Technique

The Speaker-Listener Technique has many advantages over unstructured conversation in discussing difficult issues. Most important, it counteracts the destructive styles of communication described in this chapter and in Chapter Two—escalation, invalidation, pursuit and withdrawal, and filters:

1. *Escalation.* It's nearly impossible to escalate if you both follow the rules and work at showing respect. You can't scream at one another if you have to stop every few sentences and ask for a paraphrase! The momentum of escalation is interrupted.

2. *Invalidation.* The simple process of paraphrasing intervenes effectively with invalidation because the Speaker gets immediate feedback. You can enhance the validation by saying "I understand" or "I see what you mean" at the end of a paraphrase or when you get the floor. This doesn't mean that you agree, just that you can see the situation from the other person's perspective. Save agreement or disagreement for your turn as Speaker. *You don't have to agree with your partner to be a good listener!*

3. *Pursuit and withdrawal.* For the spouse who is usually in the role of pursuer, structure in conversations ensures that you will be heard and issues will be addressed. For the spouse who tends to withdraw from potentially conflictual conversations, the structure of this technique makes it much safer to remain in the conversation. When you have a clear sense that both of you are committed to keeping things from getting out of hand, there is less to be anxious about, because conflict is less likely to occur in an unmanageable way. As you feel safer and more willing to address issues, withdrawing becomes less useful or necessary. This moves you both closer to a win-win situation and away from hopeless win-lose cycles.

4. *Filters.* The Speaker-Listener Technique makes it much easier to identify filters as soon as they come up. They will be evident in the paraphrases. The Speaker will then have a nonthreatening opportunity to say, "That's not quite what I meant. I said. . . . Could you paraphrase again, please?" All kinds of filters can be reduced using this technique, especially negative interpretations.

---

Practicing this technique regularly for some time can improve all of your communication in your marriage, not just when you are using all the rules of the technique. Our research strongly suggests that practicing such skills for a period of time can result in long-term, positive changes in how you communicate. We also think such practice makes couples more aware of ways to inhibit the negative patterns we discussed in Chapter Two. So even if you don't think you want to communicate this way very often, practicing these kinds of skills can produce big benefits.

When you choose to use the skills and ground rules we present for handling conflict, you are choosing to use more structure. One of the most important things you can do as a couple is learn to identify when you need more structure and when you need less. If you practice, you will learn as a couple how and when to increase structure to handle the tough times. Practice is the key. If you want to strengthen your marriage and reduce your chances of divorce, learn to move toward each other and deal constructively with those issues that have the potential to drive you apart. We cover many other important principles in this book, but none is more critical. Remember that the prayer, Sh'ma Yisra'el, begins with the command *Hear.* By hearing your partner in the fullest sense of the word, you take an important step toward enriching and preserving your relationship.

In the next chapter, we teach you a structured model for solving problems. If you work at it, you will find that using it together with the Speaker-Listener Technique can make a tremendous difference in your ability to deal with whatever issues you must face as a couple.

# EXERCISE

The Speaker-Listener Technique does not work miracles, but it is a powerful tool. If it is going to be useful, though, you have to practice. Like any new skill, you are likely to be a bit unsure at the start. You need to learn this technique so well together that applying the rules becomes automatic when you have something really difficult to discuss.

If you were learning to play tennis, you would not try to perfect your backhand at center court at Wimbledon. Instead you would hit backhands against the back wall for hours to get it just right. Trying to learn a new skill while in a high-stress situation is not advisable. Hence we recommend that you follow the suggestions here to learn the Speaker-Listener Technique.

Practice this technique several times a week for fifteen minutes or so each time. If you don't set aside the time to practice, it will never feel natural, and you will never find this technique very helpful.

For the first week, try the technique only with nonconflictual topics. Talk about anything of interest to either of you: your favorite vacation ever, news, sports, your dreams for the future, concerns you have at work, and so on. Your goal here is not to resolve some problem but to practice new skills.

After you have had three successful practice sessions on nonconflictual topics, choose areas of minor conflict to discuss. Sometimes couples are poor at judging what will and will not trigger a fight. If the discussion gets heated on a topic you choose, drop it and agree to come back to it later, after you have had more time to practice together.

Practice several discussions in which you both exchange some thoughts and feelings on these minor issues. Don't try to solve problems; just have good discussions. Your goal is to understand each other's point of view as clearly and completely as possible. In the process, you may solve some problems, simply because all that was needed was to understand what the other person was thinking. That's OK, but don't set out—or intentionally try—to find solutions. You are focusing on good discussions with clear understanding right now. You will learn and practice problem solving in the next chapter.

When you are doing well on the last assignment, move up to tougher and tougher issues. As you do, remember to work at sticking to the rules. The technique works if you work at it.

# 5

# Problem Solving

*The wise man hears one word—and understands two.*
*Not to answer is an answer.*

Yiddish folk sayings

I n Chapter Four we focused on the need for clear and safe communication when it counts most. If you are progressing in your
ability to talk about things effectively, you are better prepared for
what we will now say about solving problems.

All couples want to solve problems that affect their relationships. This is natural. But we have waited to discuss this subject
until now because most couples try to solve problems prematurely,
before they have developed a thorough, mutual understanding of
the issues at hand. Understanding, before trying to solve problems,
is crucial for maintaining respect and connection in your relationship. In this chapter, we present a straightforward approach to problem solving that can help you through those times when you really
need practical, workable solutions.

## THREE KEY ASSUMPTIONS

Before presenting the specific steps that can help you solve problems effectively in your relationship, we would like to describe three
assumptions, all of which have been confirmed by research:

1. All couples have problems.

2. The couples who are best at working through their problems work together as a team, not against each other as adversaries.

3. Most couples rush to find quick solutions; because these quick solutions don't take into account the real concerns of each partner, they do not last.

Let's explore these three points.

## All Couples Have Problems

Have you ever wondered why some couples seem to sail through marital life? It's not that they don't have problems. Although the nature of the problems changes for couples over time, all couples encounter problems.

During their engagement, couples report that their key problem areas are jealousy and in-laws. These issues reflect the core task they have early in their relationship: that of establishing boundaries with others. By the first year of marriage, they report other problems as being more important, such as communication and sex. These are issues central to how the partners interact with each other. Looking even at this simple data, it is clear that communication becomes a greater concern for couples over time. And whether they are in a new or long-standing relationship, most couples report money as a top problem, no matter how much they have.

So although the nature of the conflicts may change over time, all couples report problems that reflect a set of core issues they have to resolve. Granted, some couples are dealt a more difficult hand in life than others are. However, our observations of couples in PREP and in our research dovetail to indicate that those who handle problems well tend to display a common set of problem-solving skills— skills that can be learned.

## You Need to Work Together as a Team

Some couples combine their mutual respect and skill to produce a powerful sense that they are a team working together to find solutions that will enhance their life. You have a choice when dealing with a problem. Either you will nurture a sense that you are working together against the problem or you will operate as if you are working against each other. This principle holds true for all problems, great or small.

All too often, people approach problems as if their partner is the enemy to be conquered. For such couples, issues are approached as if there will be a winner and a loser—and who wants to lose? That kind of attitude is guaranteed to produce tension and conflict. People don't get married to have an enemy to struggle with for years; nevertheless, sadly, many couples end up in this type of brutal situation. Marriage is about cooperation, not competition. You can be sure that if one partner is forced to do something against his or her will, it will foster resentment, and the relationship will suffer.

The good news here is that you don't have to remain locked into the cycle of one partner trying to win at the expense of the other. *You can learn to work as a team.* But even when couples work well as teams, many fail to take the necessary time to move toward solid, lasting solutions to problems.

## Don't Rush to Find Solutions

Is rushing a particularly Jewish affliction? We live in a very hurried society, and certainly Jews do not have a monopoly on trying to do more than is humanly possible. But as Rabbi Harold Schulweis quipped, "Remember that Jews are just like everyone else, only more so."[1] The "more so" certainly seems to apply to the modern Jewish attitude toward time.

Jews have a reputation for rushing that predates the computer. As we mentioned earlier, a number of social observers and researchers have described the Jewish tendency toward intensity and impatience.[2] More recently, Letty Cottin Pogrebin, in *Getting Over Getting Older,* captured this essential Jewish attitude toward time: "Time is life. Use it or lose it. Seize it as if you have every right to it, like air; take it in, hold it, expand it, shape it to your dreams or it will gallop out of control and disappear."[3]

As we all know, too much of a good thing can become a bad thing. The same traits that define our greatest assets also point toward our worst vulnerabilities. The incredible productiveness of Jews in America has not resulted from our being a relaxed people. If we pride ourselves on our accomplishments, we also need to be aware of the cost. For many, the price has been *time*.

Many well-intentioned attempts at problem solving fail because couples don't take time to understand the problem together; this prevents them from working out a solution that both partners can support. If you are deciding which movie to see, not much is at stake in rushing to a solution—except maybe the prospect of sitting through a boring film. But if you are deciding something more important, such as how to parent or to divide up the household responsibilities, it is critical to take the time to develop a mutually satisfying solution.

Two major factors propel couples to rush to solutions: time pressure and conflict avoidance.

### Time Pressure

Most of us are not all that patient. We want it now. This tendency reflects the hurried pace of our lives. We usually don't take the time to plan what we are doing in our family relationships.

We have had many colleagues visit us from Europe over the years, and they often comment about how crazy we are in America. They see Americans as rushed and always busy, with little attention left for the really important things. When this time pressure is combined with our desire to be in control of our lives, we experience an overwhelming desire to solve problems quickly and move on to the next challenge.

But when it comes to dealing with important issues in families, hasty decisions are often poor decisions. We must be committed to spending the time to work things out if we are going to make good decisions together. One colleague recently remarked that "time is today's currency." Failing to spend enough of this currency on marital and family relationships becomes a major problem for many people.

### Conflict Avoidance

The following example is fairly typical in describing how, because of a desire to avoid further conflict, a couple can rush to a solution that is destined to fail. Francine and Ari have been married twenty-four years, with one child through college and one a senior in high school.

The family legend was that Ari's grandfather came to America with pennies in his pocket and ended up a millionaire. Ari's parents had also done well financially, at least in the early years of their marriage. Then they lost much of their inheritance on some risky investments when Ari was a teenager. They kept their money problems a secret from everyone, including their children. Members of a prosperous Jewish community in Cleveland, they continued to live for several years as if nothing had changed. When he graduated from high school, Ari was shocked and hurt when his parents confessed that they would not be able to help him with paying for college.

Francine was raised in a middle-class family in the suburbs of Philadelphia, and her family had never had nor lost a lot of money. Her grandparents had worked in the garment industry after immigrating to the United States, and were modestly successful. Her father had a career in sales, and her mother was a housewife who had saved enough for a comfortable retirement.

Now, thirty years later, Ari and Francine are dealing with the financial burden of educating their children. Ari is an insurance broker, and Francine works nearly full-time as a volunteer for a Jewish day school. They have always had enough money, but things have gotten much tighter with college bills piling up. An issue for Ari is that Francine devotes so much time to work that doesn't pay. The following conversation is typical of their attempts to solve the problem:

ARI: *(testily)* I noticed that the Visa bill was over three thousand dollars again. I just don't know what we're going to do to keep up. It worries me. I'm doing all I can, but . . .

FRANCINE: *(gives no indication that she's paying attention to Ari)*

ARI: *(frustrated)* Did you hear me?

FRANCINE: Yes. I didn't think we spent that much this time.

ARI: *(really annoyed now)* How many clothes did Janet need, anyway?

FRANCINE: *(annoyed, but calm)* Well, we agreed she needed one really nice outfit for applying for jobs. I guess we got more extras than I thought, but it was all things she can use. It's very important to her to look good on interviews. And you know, the sooner she gets a job, the better off our budget will be.

ARI: *(settling down a bit)* I understand, but this kind of thing adds to my worry. *(long pause)* We aren't saving anything at all for retirement, and we aren't getting any younger. If you had some income coming in for all your work, it would help a lot.

FRANCINE: Why don't we just get rid of that credit card? Then you wouldn't have to worry about it anymore.

ARI: We could do that, and also plan to put aside an extra hundred-and-fifty dollars a month in my retirement plan. That would help a lot to get us going in the right direction. What about a part-time job?

FRANCINE: I can think about it. What I'm doing seems a lot more important. For now, let's try to get rid of the credit card and save more. That sounds good. Let's try it out.

ARI: OK, let's see what happens.

End of discussion. The one good thing about this discussion is that they had it. However, what are the chances that they came to a satisfactory resolution of their money problem? Two months later, nothing was changed, no more was saved, the credit card was still being used, interest was accruing, and they were no closer to working together on the budget. In addition, they didn't really address Ari's central concern about Francine's volunteer job.

One of the main difficulties is that there are no specifics about how their agreement will be implemented. Ari and Francine are not generally into quick fixes, but they do rush to solutions at times because they hate conflict. For them, this conversation was a relatively big fight. Both were eager to get back to being nice to each other after a disagreement.

Finding a solution can be a relief when you and your spouse are talking about an issue that causes some anxiety. However, when you settle on a solution prematurely, you are likely to pay for the lack of thorough planning with more conflict later. The good news is that once you agree on a solution to a nagging issue, it will be under rule control and will stop being a cause of ongoing conflict. *Rule control* means that you have agreed together on a principle or rule to guide you whenever this issue comes up in the future.

## HOW TO SOLVE YOUR PROBLEMS

*The flip side of expressing disproportionate anger is not expressing it at all. Always address your grievances to their source.*

*Rabbi Joseph Telushkin*[4]

The approach we take here to solving problems—consistent with the approach we have taken throughout the book—is structured. In other words, we recommend a specific set of steps that successful problem solvers follow. The steps we present, based on the original PREP book, *Fighting for Your Marriage* (1994), also contain some ideas that can be found in other works, such as *We Can Work It Out: Making Sense of Marital Conflict* (Notarius and Markman, 1993) and *A Couple's Guide to Communication* (Gottman, Notarius,

Gonso, and Markman, 1976). Although these steps are very straightforward, don't be misled by the simplicity of the approach. You must be creative and flexible, willing to work together, and able to experiment with change. Under these conditions, you will be able to discover solutions to most of the problems you have to grapple with together.

Following are the steps to handling problems well:

I. Problem Discussion

II. Problem Solution

    A.  Agenda setting
    B.  Brainstorming
    C.  Agreement and compromise
    D.  Follow-up

## Problem Discussion

Problem Discussion is critical to handling problems well. In this step, you are laying the foundation for the next step: Problem Solution. Although you may not agree about how to solve the problem, a good discussion can lead to a clear sense that you are working together and respecting each other.

Whether the problem is large or small, you shouldn't move on to Problem Solution until you both understand and feel understood by your partner. This means that you have each expressed your significant feelings and concerns on the topic and believe that the other person has clearly understood your point of view. We recommend you use the Speaker-Listener Technique for this step. Placing a premium on validation in this phase results in an atmosphere of mutual respect, which allows Problem Solution to proceed much more smoothly.

Couples experience greater pain and distance when they fail to take the time to discuss the issues before coming to an agreement. We have repeatedly seen that when it is preceded by good discussion, problem solving can often go quickly and smoothly, even for difficult issues. With all the relevant facts and feelings on the table, the foundation is laid for working as a team.

During Problem Discussion, it is likely that one or both of you may have a specific gripe that needs to be expressed. When this is the case, it is very important for each of you to present your feelings and concerns constructively. One way to do this is to use what Gottman, Notarius, Gonso, and Markman call an XYZ statement. Using an XYZ statement, you put your gripe or complaint into this format:

**"When you do X in situation Y, I feel Z."**

When you use an XYZ statement, you are giving your partner usable information: the specific behavior, the context in which it occurs, and how you feel when it happens. This is much preferred to what is often offered: a vague description of the problem and some character assassination instead of an "I" statement. Often we just express an overall sense of anger or frustration, without giving any concrete information about what we are angry about. Remember our earlier discussion of mind reading; all too often, we expect our partner to know what we are upset about, and it increases our anger when he or she plainly does not know—certainly a very unfair situation all around.

For example, suppose that you have a concern about your partner making a mess at the end of the day. Which of the following statements do you think gives you a better shot at being heard?

"You are such a slob."

"When you drop your pack and jacket on the floor [X] as you come in the door at the end of the day [Y], I feel angry [Z]."

Or suppose you are angry about a comment your spouse made at a party last Saturday night.

"You are so inconsiderate."

"When you said that what I did for work wasn't really that hard [X] to John and Susan at the party last Saturday [Y], I felt very embarrassed [Z]."

Unless you are careful, it is all too easy to fall into a nonspecific attack on your partner's character. Such statements are guaranteed to cause defensiveness and escalation or withdrawal. These types of statements are accusations or judgments about the person, rather than comments about the behavior. XYZ statements are far more constructive: you are identifying a specific behavior in a specific context. It is difficult to change one's character, but it is possible to change a behavior. The "I feel Z" part requires you to take responsibility for your own feelings. Your partner doesn't "make" you feel anything in particular—you are in charge of how you feel.

Keep in mind that no one really likes to hear a gripe or criticism, no matter how constructively it is expressed. But unless you are a hermit, there are times when you need to voice a concern, and you should do it without fostering unneeded conflict. The XYZ format will help you do just that.

Before we turn to Problem Solution, we want to remind you that in Problem Discussion, you are really laying the foundation for productive problem solving as a team. So we repeat: *do not move from discussion to solution unless you both agree that the issue or problem in question has been fully discussed.* In many instances, however, you will find that after an excellent discussion, there is really no problem solving to be done. Just having a good discussion is enough. In fact, in our PREP seminars we often shock couples by announcing that our experience indicates that approximately 70 percent of the issues couples deal with don't really need to be solved, just discussed well. "How can that be?" they ask.

It's hard to appreciate this point without experiencing the power of a Problem Discussion that leaves you with what therapists call an "ah-ha!" experience. After such a discussion, there's often nothing left to resolve. That's because we often want something much more fundamental in our relationships than solutions to problems. When partners are upset, most of the time what they want most is not agreement or even change, but just to feel heard and understood.

Nevertheless, there are many times when your discussion of problems or issues will naturally lead to the next step: working together to find specific solutions. When you need to come up with a specific solution, the steps of the Problem Solution phase can help you get there.

## Problem Solution

We have found the following steps to work very well for couples, provided that the work of Problem Discussion has been done.

### Agenda Setting

The first step in Problem Solution is to set the agenda for your work together. The key here is to make very clear what you are trying to solve at this time. Often your discussion will have taken you through many facets of an issue. Now you need to decide what to focus on. The more specific the problem you are tackling now, the better your chances of finding a workable and satisfying solution. Many problems in marriage seem insurmountable, but they can be cut down to size if you follow these procedures.

For example, you may have had a Problem Discussion about money that covered a range of issues, such as credit card problems, checkbooks, budgets, and savings. As you can see, the general problem area of money can contain several more specific problem areas to consider, so it is necessary to take apart a large problem such as this and focus on the more manageable pieces, one at a time. It is also wise to work on an easier piece of a problem first. For example, you might initially decide who should balance the checkbook each month, then deal with budget plans later. Be sure to set a specific time to talk about those other issues.

At times, your Problem Discussion will have focused from start to finish on a specific problem. In this case, you will have already defined the agenda for problem solving. You might be working on the problem of where to go for the holidays—your parents' home or that of your spouse's parents. There is no way to divide this problem into smaller parts, so you will set the agenda to work on all of it.

### Brainstorming

As far as we know, the process referred to as brainstorming has been around at least since the 1940s. However, it seems to have been refined and promoted by NASA during the early days of the U.S. space program. NASA needed a way to bring together the many different engineers and scientists who were looking for solutions to the varied problems of space travel. The method worked for NASA and came to be used frequently in business settings. We have found that it works very well for couples, too. There are several rules regarding brainstorming:

- Any idea can be suggested. One of you should write down the ideas.

- Be creative. Suggest whatever comes to mind.

- Don't evaluate the ideas either verbally or nonverbally. (This includes making faces!)

- Have fun with it if you can. This is a time for a sense of humor; all other feelings should be dealt with in Problem Discussion.

The best thing about this process is that it encourages creativity. If you can stifle your tendency to comment critically on the ideas the two of you generate, you will encourage each other to come up with some great stuff. Wonderful solutions can emerge from considering the points you made during brainstorming. Following the rules helps you resist the tendency to settle prematurely on a solution that isn't the best you can find.

### Agreement and Compromise

In this step, the goal is to come up with a specific solution or combination of solutions that you both agree to try. We emphasize the word *agree* because the solution is not likely to help unless you both agree to try it. We emphasize *specific* because the more specific you are about the solution, the more likely it is that you will follow through. This is the time to discuss the ideas you came up with during the brainstorming step. Usually it is not necessary to use the Speaker-Listener Technique for this discussion, as potentially upsetting feelings and concerns have already been fully explored in your more structured Problem Discussion. Explore combinations of ideas that you each think might work well. This isn't the time for heavy discussions but rather for working toward a specific solution.

Although it is easy to see the value of agreement, some people have trouble with the idea of compromise. To some, it sounds more like lose-lose than win-win. We recommend that compromises be directed at fulfilling both of the partners' underlying needs, as well as they can be expressed to each other. In Chapters Seven and Eight, we will discuss more fully how to accomplish this.

Marriage is about teamwork. Two separate individuals may see things differently and might make different decisions. But often the best solution will be a compromise in which neither of you gets everything you wanted, except the satisfaction of knowing you successfully solved a problem. You probably don't have a great marriage if you get your way all the time. Our goal is to help you win as a team, with solutions that show mutual respect and bring you closer as a couple. Sure, at times you may give up some of getting your own way. But what you can gain as a couple by creating effective compromises can be worth far more than being totally in control.

### Follow-Up

Many couples can make an agreement to try a particular solution to a problem. It is just as important to follow up to see how the agreement is working out. Following up has two key advantages. First, solutions often need to be "tweaked" a bit after trying them out and seeing how well they work. Second, following up builds accountability. Often we don't get serious about making a change unless we know there is some point of accountability in the near future.

Sometimes a lot of follow-up is needed in the Problem Solution phase; at other times, it's not really necessary. You reach an agreement and it works out, and nothing more needs to be done. Keep in mind, though, that many agreements will by nature require periodic updates—for example, as children grow or as the current situation changes. As your relationship develops, you need a fluid process of updating solutions.

Some couples choose to be less formal about follow-up, but we think they are taking a risk. Most people are so busy that they don't plan the next step, and nothing happens. There's an old but true saying: "If you fail to plan, you plan to fail." Set a specific time (in a week or a month) to sit down and talk about how well your solution is working or to discuss any changes needed to help it work better.

Writing down what you have agreed on can help you in following up. Doing so can clear up any differences in memory later on, as well as serve as a reminder to talk about how the solution is working out. However, we caution you not to go so far as to think of these agreements as contracts. The legal metaphor may not enhance your sense of working together as a team. If you do like the term *contract*, make your solutions "good faith" agreements, in which you each try your best to keep up your end no matter what your partner does.

# A DETAILED EXAMPLE: ARI AND FRANCINE

Let's return to Ari and Francine's discussion about money. It did not take them very long to realize that their problem-solving attempts concerning the credit card, her volunteer work, and their retirement savings were not working. They decided to try the steps we have described here.

First, they set aside the time to work through the steps. Depending on the problem, these steps may not be very time-consuming, but specifically setting aside time is nevertheless very wise.

## Problem Discussion

Let's follow Ari and Francine through the steps:

> FRANCINE (SPEAKER):  I can see that we really do have to try something different. We aren't getting anywhere on our retirement savings.
>
> ARI (LISTENER):  You can see we aren't getting anywhere, and you're concerned, too.
>
> FRANCINE (SPEAKER):  *(letting Ari know he had accurately heard her)* Yes. We need to come up with some plan for saving more and for doing something about the credit cards.
>
> ARI (LISTENER):  You agree we need to save more, and can see that how we use the credit cards may be part of the problem.
>
> FRANCINE (SPEAKER):  I can also see why you're concerned about my volunteer work—when I could be spending some of that time bringing in some income. But my volunteer work is really important to me. I feel like I'm doing something good in the world.
>
> ARI (LISTENER):  Sounds like you can appreciate my concern, but you also want me to hear that it's really important to you— it adds a lot of meaning to your life. *(Here he validates her by listening carefully.)*
>
> FRANCINE (SPEAKER):  Yeah. That's exactly what I'm feeling. Here, you take the floor. I want to know what you're thinking. *(She hands Ari the floor.)*
>
> ARI (SPEAKER):  I've been anxious about this for a long time. If we don't save more, we're not going to be able to maintain our lifestyle in retirement. It's not all that far away.
>
> FRANCINE (LISTENER):  You're really worried, aren't you?
>
> ARI (SPEAKER):  Yes, I am. You know how things were for Mom and Dad. I don't want to end up living in a two-room apartment.
>
> FRANCINE (LISTENER):  You're worried we could end up living that way, too.
>
> ARI (SPEAKER):  I'd feel a lot better with about three times as much saved.

FRANCINE (LISTENER): Too late now. (*She catches herself inter-jecting her own opinion.*) Oh, I should paraphrase. You wish we were much further along in our savings than we are.

ARI (SPEAKER): (*This time, he feels he's really getting her attention.*) I sure do. I feel a lot of pressure about it. I really want to work together so we can both be comfortable. (*This lets her know he wants to work as a team.*)

FRANCINE (LISTENER): You want us to work together, reduce the pressure, and plan for our future.

ARI (SPEAKER): Yes. (*suggesting some alternatives*) We'd need to spend less to save more. We'd need to use the credit cards more wisely. I think it would make the biggest difference if you could bring in some income.

FRANCINE (LISTENER): You feel that to save more we'd need to spend less with the credit cards. More important, you think it's pretty important for me to bring in some money.

ARI (SPEAKER): Yes. I think the income is a bigger problem than the outgo.

FRANCINE (LISTENER): Even though we could spend less, you think we may need more income if we want to live at the same level in retirement. Can I have the floor?

ARI (SPEAKER): Exactly! Here's the floor. (*He hands Francine the floor.*)

FRANCINE (SPEAKER): (*responding to Ari's clarification*) Sometimes I think that you think I'm the only one who overspends.

ARI (LISTENER): You think that I think you are mostly at fault for spending too much. Can I have the floor again? (*Francine hands the floor back to Ari.*)

ARI (SPEAKER): Actually, I don't think that, but I can see how I could come across that way. (*validating Francine's experience*) I think I overspend as much as you do; I just do it in bigger chunks.

FRANCINE (LISTENER): Nice to hear that. (*validating his comment and feeling good about hearing him taking responsibility*) You can see that we both spend too much, just differently. You buy a few big things we may not need, and I buy numerous smaller things.

ARI (SPEAKER): Exactly. We're both to blame, and we can both do better.

FRANCINE (LISTENER): We both need to work together. *(They switch the floor again.)*

FRANCINE (SPEAKER): I agree that we need to deal with our retirement savings more aggressively. My biggest fear is losing the work I love so much. It's been the most meaningful thing I've done since the kids got older.

ARI (LISTENER): It's hard to imagine not having that—it's so important to you.

FRANCINE (SPEAKER): Exactly. Maybe there's some way to deal with this so I wouldn't lose all of what I'm doing, but where I could help us save what we need for retirement at the same time.

ARI (LISTENER): You're wondering if there could be a solution that would meet your needs and our needs at the same time.

FRANCINE (SPEAKER): Yes. I'm willing to think about solutions with you.

At this point they discontinue the Speaker-Listener Technique.

ARI: OK.

FRANCINE: So, are we both feeling understood enough to move on to the Problem Solution step?

ARI: I am, how about you?

FRANCINE: *(She nods her head, yes.)*

Here they are agreeing together that they have had a good discussion and are ready to try some problem solving. They are consciously turning this corner together to move into problem solving.

## Problem Solution

Ari and Francine now go through the four steps of Problem Solution.

## Agenda Setting

Here the important thing is for them to choose a specific piece of the whole issue that was discussed. This increases their chances of finding a solution that will really work.

> FRANCINE:  We should agree on the agenda. We could talk about how to put more into the retirement accounts, but that may not be the place to start. I also think we need a discussion to deal with the issue of how we spend money and the credit cards.
>
> ARI:  You're right. We're going to need several different stabs at this entire issue. It seems we could break it all down into the need to bring in more and the need to spend less. I don't want to push, but I'd like to focus on the "bring in more" part first, if you don't mind.
>
> FRANCINE:  I can handle that. Let's problem-solve on that first, then we can talk later this week about the spending side.
>
> ARI:  So, we're going to brainstorm about how to boost the income.

## Brainstorming

The key here is to generate ideas freely.

> FRANCINE:  Why don't you write the ideas down? You have a pen handy.
>
> ARI:  OK. You could get a part-time job.
>
> FRANCINE:  I could ask the board of directors about making some of my work into a paid position. I'm practically a full-time staff member anyway.
>
> ARI:  We could meet with a financial planner so we could get a better idea of what we really need to bring in. I could also get a second job.
>
> FRANCINE:  I could look into part-time jobs that are similar to what I'm already doing, like those programs for kids with only one parent.

ARI: You know, Jack and Maria are doing something like that. We could talk to them about what it's about.

FRANCINE: I feel this list is pretty good. Let's talk about what we'll try doing.

### Agreement and Compromise

Now they sift through the ideas that they generated during brainstorming. The key is to find an agreement that they both can get behind.

ARI: I like your idea of talking to the board. What could it hurt?

FRANCINE: I like that, too. I also think your idea of seeing a financial planner is good. Otherwise, how do we really know what the target is if I'm going to try to bring in something extra? But I don't think it's realistic for you to work more.

ARI: Yeah, I think you're right. What about talking to Maria and Jack?

FRANCINE: I'd like to hold off on that. That could lead them to try and get me involved, and I'm not sure I'm interested.

ARI: OK. What about seeing if there are any kinds of part-time jobs where you could do something that has meaning for you and make some bucks, too?

FRANCINE: I'd like to think about that. It'd be a good way to go if they don't have room in the budget where I am now. I sure wouldn't want to do more than half-time, though. I'd hate to give up all of what I'm doing now.

ARI: And I wouldn't want you to. If you could make a part-time income, I'll bet we could cut back enough to make it all work.

FRANCINE: So how about I talk to the board, you ask Frank about that financial planner they use, and I'll also start looking around for part-time jobs.

ARI: Great. Let's schedule some time next week to talk about how we're moving along toward the solutions we need.

FRANCINE: Agreed. (*They set a time to meet and follow up.*)

*Follow-Up*

At the end of the week, Francine and Ari meet to discuss what they have found out and what to do next. To Francine's surprise, the board member she talked with seemed eager to try to work something out. She had also started looking into various part-time jobs that would meet her needs. Meanwhile, Ari had scheduled a meeting for them with a financial planner for the following week.

In this case, the solution involved a process made up of a series of small steps and agreements. Things were now moving on an issue that had been a problem between them for a long time. They felt good working together and realized that they were no longer avoiding a tough issue.

Later they went through the steps again and came to a specific agreement about spending less. They decided how much less to spend and agreed to record all the credit card purchases in a checkbook register so they would know how they were doing compared to their target. In contrast to their problem solving about income, which was a process that lasted for several weeks, they implemented their solution on spending right away.

## WHEN IT'S NOT THAT EASY

We wish we could tell you that this model always works as well as it did for Ari and Francine, but there are times when it doesn't. What do you do then? In our experience with couples, there are a few difficulties that commonly come up in dealing with problems:

Discussions sometimes can heat up quickly. If you or your partner become so tense that you resort to negative behavior, it is time for a Time Out. We will have more on that in Chapter Six. If you can get back on track by staying with the structure (for example, by using the Speaker-Listener Technique), great. If not, you need a break until you can be constructive again.

Sometimes negative feelings can arise during the Problem Solution phase. They need to be talked out. To do this, it is usually best to cycle back to Problem Discussion. Simply pick up the floor again and resume your discussion. Acknowledge that you have shifted back to the Problem Discussion stage and keep going through the process as many times as needed. It is better to slow things down than to continue to press for a solution that may not work.

The best solution you can reach during a session may not always be the best solution for the whole problem. At times, you should set the agenda just to agree on the next steps toward the best solution. For example, you might brainstorm about the kind of information you need to make your decision.

Your agreement phase could focus on who will gather specific sources of information and when you will meet again to work on a decision based on what you find out. This is what Ari and Francine did in our example. They broke down a very complex problem into much smaller pieces.

Remember this tactic when the problem seems too big or when you don't know what to do next. If you use it consistently, you will increase your chances of regular, effective problem solving.

## WHEN THERE'S NO SOLUTION

Although some problems don't have mutually satisfying solutions, there are far fewer unresolvable problems than couples sometimes think. If you have worked together for some time using the structure we suggest and no solution is forthcoming, either you can let this lack of a solution damage your marriage or you can plan how to live with the disagreement. Sometimes couples allow an otherwise good marriage to be damaged by insisting on a resolution to a specific unresolved conflict.

If you have an area that seems unresolvable, you can use the agenda in the Problem Solution step to protect your marriage from the fallout from that one problem area. You literally "agree to disagree" constructively. This kind of solution comes about through both teamwork and tolerance. You can't always have your spouse be just the way you want him or her to be, but you can work as a team to deal with your differences.

––––––––––

We have given you a very specific model that will work well to help you preserve and enhance your teamwork in solving the problems that come your way in life. We don't expect couples to use such a structured approach for minor problems, but we do expect that most couples could benefit from this model when they are dealing with more important matters, especially those that can lead to unproductive conflict. This is one more way to add structure when you need it most to preserve the best in your relationship.

In the next chapter, we build further on the techniques presented so far to help you prosper in your relationship together. The ground rules we present help you take control of the conflict in your relationship rather than allowing it to take control of you.

## EXERCISES

There are three separate assignments for this chapter. First, we want you to practice making XYZ statements. Second, we invite you each to rate some common problem areas in your relationship. Third, we ask you to practice the problem-solving model presented in this chapter. Remember, these techniques won't help unless you practice them until they feel natural. Be patient—it will pay off.

### XYZ Statements: Constructive Griping

Spend some time thinking about things that your partner does that bother you in some way. On a separate piece of paper, list your concerns as you normally might state them. Then practice putting your concerns into the XYZ format: "When you do X in situation Y, I feel Z."

Next, repeat the exercise, but this time list the things your partner does that please you. You will find that the XYZ format also works well for giving specific positive feedback—for example, "When you came home the other night with my favorite ice cream, I felt loved." Try sharing some positive thoughts and feelings with your spouse.

## Assessment of Problem Areas

The following inventory is a simple measure of common problem areas in relationships. It was originally developed by Knox in 1971, and we have used it for years in our research as a simple but very relevant measure of the problem areas in couples' relationships. As we will explain, doing this exercise will help you practice the problem-solving skills we have presented. You should each fill out your own list independently.

Consider the following list of issues that all relationships must face. Please rate how much of a problem each area currently is in your relationship by writing down a number from 0 (not at all a problem) to 100 (a severe problem). For example, if children are a slight problem in your relationship, you might write 25 next to Children. If children are not a problem, you might put down a 0, and if children are a severe problem, you might write 100. Feel free to add other areas that aren't included in our list. Rate each area on a scale of 1 to 100 and be sure to rate all areas.

_____ Money                    _____ In-laws

_____ Recreation              _____ Sex

_____ Communication       _____ Children (or potential children)

_____ Alcohol and drugs   _____ Friends

_____ Jealousy                  _____ Religion

_____ Careers                   _____ Other (relatives, housework,
                                            and so on)

## Practice Problem Solving

To practice this model, it is critical that you follow these instructions carefully. When you are dealing with real problems in your relationship, the chances of conflict are significant, and we want you to practice in a way that enhances your chances of solidifying these skills.

Set aside uninterrupted time to practice. Thirty minutes or so should be sufficient to begin using the sequence on some of the problems you want to solve.

Look over your problem inventories together. Make a list of those areas in which you both rated the problem as being less serious. These are the problem areas we want you to use first to practice the model. Practice with very specific problems and look for very specific solutions. This will boost your skills and help you gain confidence in the model.

We recommend that you set aside time to practice the Problem Discussion and Problem Solution sequence several times a week for two or three weeks. If you put in this time, you will gain skill and confidence in handling problem areas together. Keep this chapter open while you are practicing, and refer back to the specific steps of the model.

# 6

# Ground Rules for Handling Conflict

*If you are not going to be any better tomorrow than you*
*were today, then what need have you for tomorrow?*
*Rebbe Nachman of Bratslav (1772–1811)*[1]

The concept of *teshuva,* or repentance, is a reminder that it is always possible to strive to be your best self and to heal relationships that need repair. The methods we present throughout this book will help you repair your relationships when damage has been done. Even better, as we show you in this chapter, there are effective ways you can protect your relationship in the future.

Remember, conflict is not the enemy; vital relationships are never without friction. Conflict is not only part of the human condition but also essential to learning, creativity, and love. Jewish tradition teaches us the importance of talmudic debate, of challenging injustice, of questioning the status quo. It is *poorly managed* marital conflict that can lead to emotional pain, violence, and divorce. Conflict is like fire: used well, it provides the warmth and energy we are so dependent on as humans; handled carelessly, it can destroy us.

As we have discussed in previous chapters, upbringing, gender and cultural differences, and the personal choices partners make during arguments can put couples at risk if they don't learn to manage the inevitable conflicts and differences that arise in marriage. If you do not have the skills to minimize negative patterns, the resulting anger, contempt, and hostility can seriously damage the love and commitment in your relationship. Now that you understand some powerful techniques for communicating and solving problems, we turn to our six ground rules for protecting your relationship from mishandled conflict.

We call these principles *ground rules* to highlight their importance for your marriage. Used properly, these rules can help you control the difficult issues in your relationship—these issues need never control you. Ground rules sum up many of the key points we have made so far. These rules give you the opportunity to create more structure and safety in how you communicate and handle conflict.

In sports, ground rules specify what is allowed and not allowed, what is inbounds and out. To be sure, marriage is not a sport. Further, we don't mean to invoke the image of competition by using the term *ground rules*. However, when things go downhill for couples, competition is a fact—competition over who will get his or her way. In our experience, these ground rules are powerful in helping couples stay on track and work as a team. Think of these ground rules as marital mitzvot.

GROUND RULE 1: TAKE A TIME OUT. *When conflict is escalating, we will call a Time Out or a Stop Action and either (1) try talking again, using the Speaker-Listener Technique, or (2) agree to talk about the issue later, at a specified time, using the Speaker-Listener Technique.*

If we could get the attention of every couple and have them all agree to only one change in their relationship, we would recommend following this ground rule. It's that important. This simple ground rule can protect and enhance relationships by counteracting the negative escalation that is so destructive to close relationships.

We suggest not only that you agree to this ground rule but also that you refer to it with a specific term such as Stop Action or Time Out—whichever term you like best. Doing so will help you interpret it positively when your partner invokes the ground rule. Otherwise, it becomes too easy to interpret a Time Out as avoidance. In fact, calling a Stop Action is one of the most positive things either of you can do for your relationship. You are recognizing old, negative behaviors and deciding to do something constructive instead.

We want you to approach this as something you are doing *together* for the good of your relationship. Sure, one of you may call Time Outs more often than the other, but if you both agree to the rule, you are really doing the Time Outs together. A Time Out is a gesture that should be met with appreciation and respect when used in this way.

It is important to know that you can call Stop Action if you realize that you, your partner, or both of you are getting out of control. Stop Action is called on the process of communication, not on a person or relationship. Don't simply say "Stop action" and leave the room—unilateral actions are usually counterproductive. Instead, say something like "This is getting too hot for me. Let's stop the action and talk later, OK?" By including your partner in the decision, you are making the process mutual and thus de-escalating conflict.

Another key aspect of this ground rule is that you are agreeing to continue talking—but productively—either right now or in the near future, after a cooling-off period. If you are a pursuing partner, this part of the ground rule addresses your concern that Time Outs could be used by an avoider to stop discussions about important issues. *This ground rule is designed to stop unproductive arguments, not to stop all dialogue on an issue.* You do need to discuss important issues—just do it in a productive manner. In agreeing to use the Speaker-Listener Technique when you come back to talking about an issue, you are agreeing to deal more effectively with the issue that got out of hand.

The Stop Action itself can give the partner prone to withdrawal confidence that the conflict won't get out of hand. Some withdrawing partners are even able to tolerate conflict better, because they know that they *could* stop it at any time. The Speaker-Listener Technique makes it still safer to deal with an issue by providing that all-important structure. This technique may work without using the Speaker-Listener Technique, but we're convinced that using both when necessary is more effective.

If you do decide to talk later, set a designated time immediately, if possible. Perhaps an hour later would be a good time to talk, or maybe the next day. If one of you was really angry when the Time Out was called, you may find that you still can't talk when you come back to the discussion. That's OK. You can set a time after both of you have calmed down. Here is an example of this ground rule being used correctly by a couple who came to our workshop.

Les and Teresa had been married for only one year, but they had already developed a pattern of frequent, intense arguments that ended with shouting and threats about the future of the relationship. Although Les was raised Jewish and Teresa Catholic, both came from homes where open, intense conflict was relatively common, so changing their pattern was not easy for them. As you will see, their arguments still escalate rather easily, but now they know how to stop when the argument gets going:

> TERESA: (annoyed and showing it) I really hate these holiday services. I think the rabbi is really being judgmental about people who didn't convert.
>
> LES: (also annoyed, looking up from the paper) I think you're really being overly sensitive. He was just saying that having one faith in the family made things easier for everybody.
>
> TERESA: Yeah, right. I can just imagine that next time we see him, he'll say that we'll damage our children if I don't convert.
>
> LES: (irritated) Look, when we got married, we agreed that we weren't going to make religion a big issue. If you can't deal with listening to what the rabbi has to say, then don't go.
>
> TERESA: (very angry now, voice raised) Oh great, leave your shiksa wife at home while you go off and shmooze with your friends at synagogue. Forget it. Why did you even marry me if you're more comfortable without me there?

LES: Look, this is something we have really avoided talking about, but I don't think this is the best time to do it. We're both tired, and I really don't feel prepared to talk about it right now. How about we call a Time Out and talk about it tomorrow morning—this isn't getting us anywhere right now.

TERESA: OK. But I really need to talk about this. Do you promise we can talk in the morning?

LES: Yeah. I agree we need to talk about it. Let's do it in the morning over breakfast. We have the day off, we'll be less tired, and maybe we can do a better job. It seems like right now we're just too tense to deal with it.

There's nothing magic here. It's really very simple, but the effect is potentially powerful for your relationship. This couple used a Time Out very effectively to stop an argument that they could see wasn't going to be productive. Later, using the Speaker-Listener Technique, they sat down and talked about Teresa's concern that Les didn't really accept her not being Jewish. They used the Speaker-Listener Technique to begin a dialogue about an issue that they had both avoided for a long time.

GROUND RULE 2: USE THE SPEAKER-LISTENER TECHNIQUE. *When we are having trouble communicating, we will use the Speaker-Listener Technique.*

We hope you don't need much convincing about the wisdom of this ground rule. The key is to have a way to communicate safely and clearly when you really need to do it well. With this ground rule, you are agreeing to use more structure *when you need it.* You don't always need to call a Stop Action, but you may need to make the transition to a more structured mode of communication.

For example, suppose that you wanted to talk about a problem such as how your family is spending money. You know from your history that these talks usually get difficult. You would be wise to follow this ground rule, raising the issue in this way: "Honey, I'm really concerned about money right now. How about if we sit down and use the Speaker-Listener Technique to talk about it?" Such a statement tells your partner that you are raising an important issue and that you want to talk it out using added structure. It is a lot easier to prevent destructive escalation about a hot topic when you agree to use the safety of structure.

GROUND RULE 3: SEPARATE PROBLEM DISCUSSION FROM PROBLEM SOLUTION. *When we are using the Speaker-Listener Technique, we will completely separate Problem Discussion from Problem Solution.*

As we stated in Chapter Five, it is critical to be clear at any given time about whether you are discussing or solving the problem. Too often, couples quickly agree to some solution in order to avoid the anxiety involved in a deeper discussion of the issues. When one or both partners do not feel well enough understood, solutions are more likely to fail. A lot of added problems and hassles come from rushing to agreements without laying the proper foundation by communicating fully with each other.

Discussion and solution are different processes, and each works better when you recognize this fact and act on it.

GROUND RULE 4: PAY ATTENTION TO THE TIMING OF YOUR CONFLICT DISCUSSIONS. *We can bring up issues at any time, but the Listener can say, "This is not a good time." If the Listener doesn't want to talk at that time, he or she takes responsibility for setting up a time to talk in the near future.*

This ground rule accomplishes one very important thing: it ensures that you won't have an important or difficult talk about an issue unless you both agree that the time is right. How often do you begin talking about a key issue in your relationship when your partner is just not ready for it? There's no point in having a discussion about anything important unless you are both ready to talk about it.

We emphasize this ground rule in appreciation of a fact of life: most couples talk about their most important issues at the worst times—over dinner, at bedtime, when they are getting the kids off for school, as soon as a partner walks in the door after work, or when one partner is preoccupied with an important project or task. Sound familiar? These are times when your spouse may be a captive audience, but you certainly don't have his or her attention. In fact, these are the most stressful times in the life of the average family.

This ground rule assumes two things: (1) that you each are responsible for knowing when you are capable of discussing something with appropriate attention to what your partner has to say and (2) that you can each respect the other when he or she says, "I can't deal with that right now." There simply is no point in trying to have a discussion if you are not both up for it. Important issues should be treated as important and given the time and focus they deserve.

You may ask, "Isn't this just a prescription for avoidance?" That's where the second part of the ground rule comes in. The person who isn't ready for a discussion takes responsibility for making it happen in the *near* future. This is critical. Your partner will have a much easier time putting off the conversation if he or she is confident that you really will follow through. We recommend that when you use this ground rule, you agree to set up a better time within twenty-four to forty-eight hours. This may not always be practical, but it is a good guideline to use.

For one variation of this ground rule, you may want to come to an agreement that certain times are never good for bringing up important things. For example, we have worked with many couples who have agreed that neither will bring up anything significant within thirty minutes of bedtime. These couples decided that they were just too tired at bedtime and that it was more important to relax, wind down, and get some good sleep.

GROUND RULE 5: RITUALIZE MEETINGS. *We will make "couple meetings" a weekly ritual in our life.*

All of Jewish tradition teaches us about the importance of ritual, specifically the role rituals play in separating regular day-to-day life from sacred and special moments. There are daily, weekly, and yearly rituals around which Jews have traditionally organized their lives. Today, however, for many people of all faiths, overly busy lives strip away the rituals that support spirit, mind, and body. You need time to talk to the person with whom you share your life. Too often people treat their marriage as if it is the one important relationship that can be put on hold until everything else is done—which it never is. Creating a ritualized time to talk about important issues can help you sustain a love that will last a lifetime.

Most couples do not set aside a regular time for dealing with key issues and problems. The importance of doing so has been suggested by so many marriage experts over the years that it is almost a cliché. Nevertheless, we want to give you our view on this sage advice.

The advantages of having a weekly meeting time far outweigh any negatives. First, this is a tangible way to place a high priority on your marriage by carving out time for its upkeep. We know you're busy. We're all busy. But if you decide that having a good relationship is important, you will find the way to give it the time it needs.

Second, following this ground rule ensures that even if there is no other good time to deal with issues and problems in your marriage, you at least have this weekly meeting. You might be surprised at how much you can get done in thirty minutes or so of concentrated attention to an issue. During this meeting, you can talk about the relationship, discuss specific problems, or practice communication skills. That includes using all the skills and techniques we have recommended in previous chapters.

A third advantage of this ground rule is that having a weekly meeting time takes much of the day-to-day pressure off your relationship. This is especially true if you have gotten tangled up in the pursuer-withdrawer pattern. If something happens that brings up a gripe for you, it's much easier to delay bringing it up until another time if you know there *will* be another time. If you are the pursuing partner, you can relax; you will have your chance to raise your issue. If you are the withdrawing partner, you will feel encouraged to bring up your concerns, because you have a meeting set aside for just this purpose. Devotion to this process can really cut down on sniping, criticism, and complaining during the rest of the week.

You may be thinking that this is a pretty good idea. But to put this good idea into action, *you must be consistent in taking the time to make the meetings happen*. We have repeatedly heard from couples that when they are getting along well, they are tempted to skip the meetings. Don't succumb to this temptation.

Consider Elliot and Diane. They had set aside Wednesday nights at nine as a time for their meeting, but if they had been getting along well during the week, when Wednesday night rolled around, each of them would begin to think, "We don't need to meet tonight. No use stirring things up when we're getting along so well." Then one or the other would say, "Hey, dear, we're doing fine—let's just skip the meeting tonight."

What Elliot and Diane came to realize is that they were having fewer conflicts partly because they were regularly having their meetings. After they canceled a few meetings, they noticed that more conflicts would come up during the week. They had given up their time to deal with issues and had begun reverting to the uncertainty of dealing with problems if and when they could. They finally decided that "if and when" was not placing the proper importance on their marriage, and they resumed their meetings.

If you actually do have little to deal with, fine. Have a short meeting, but *have a meeting*. Use these meetings to air gripes, discuss important issues, plan for key events coming up, or just take stock of how the relationship is going. When you are focusing on a specific problem, work through the steps for Problem Discussion and Problem Solution presented in Chapter Five. When there is nothing more pressing, practice some of the other skills described in this book. Take the time and use it to keep your relationship strong.

Take care of your marriage at least as well as you take care of your car—preventive maintenance tends to work a lot better than waiting for the car to explode while you're on the road.

Ground Rule 6: Ritualize Time for Fun. *We will ritualize time for the great things: fun, friendship, and sensuality. We will agree to protect these times from conflict and the need to deal with issues.*

Just as it is important to set aside time to deal with issues in your relationship, it is also critical to protect key times from conflicts. You can't focus on issues all the time and have a truly great marriage. You need some time for relaxing together—having fun, talking as friends, making love—when conflict and problems are off-limits. This is a key point that we will discuss in the chapters on friendship, fun, and sensuality later in the book.

For now, we emphasize two points. First, make time for these great things. Second, when you are spending time together in one of these ways, don't bring up issues that you have to work on. And if an issue does come up, table it until later—for example, until your couple meeting.

———

One essential benefit for your relationship is embedded in all these ground rules. When you use them properly, *you are agreeing to control the difficult issues in your marriage rather than allowing them to control you.* Instead of having arguments whenever issues come up, you are agreeing to deal with the issues when you are both able to do it well.

One of the most destructive things that can happen to your marriage is to have the growing sense that you are walking on eggshells. You know the feeling. You begin to wonder when the eggs will break, and you are too anxious to pay attention to where you are going. You no longer feel free to just "be" with your partner. It doesn't have to be this way. These ground rules do a lot toward getting you back on safe ground. They work. You can do it.

In the next five chapters, we turn our attention to deeper issues and more complex processes in relationships. Please continue to practice all the skills we have presented thus far as we move ahead into discussion of hidden issues, expectations, commitment, core beliefs, and forgiveness.

# EXERCISE

Your exercise for this chapter is very straightforward: discuss the ground rules and begin to try them out. You may want to modify one or more of them in some specific manner to make them work better for you. In fact, you may already be using some of these concepts in an unspoken way to set limits around conflict in your relationship. That's fine. The key is to review the rules and give them a chance to work in your relationship and, after you have given them a try, to talk about them again and agree on which ones you will use regularly.

We have listed the rules again here. We want you to actually set times to talk about them and how they are working for you. You might want to write them down, taking note of any changes you make to them.

### *Suggested Ground Rules for Handling Issues*

1. When conflict is escalating, we will call a Time Out or a Stop Action and either (1) try talking again, using the Speaker-Listener Technique, or (2) agree to talk about the issue later, at a specified time, using the Speaker-Listener Technique.

2. When we are having trouble communicating, we will use the Speaker-Listener Technique.

3. When we are using the Speaker-Listener Technique, we will completely separate Problem Discussion from Problem Solution.

4. We can bring up issues at any time, but the Listener can say, "This is not a good time." If the Listener doesn't want to talk

at that time, he or she takes responsibility for setting up a time to talk in the near future. (You need to decide how "the near future" is defined.)

5. We will make "couple meetings" a weekly ritual in our life. (Schedule a time now.)

6. We will ritualize time for the great things: fun, friendship, and sensuality. We will agree to protect these times from conflict and the need to deal with issues.

# 7

# The Difference Between
# Issues and Events

*To see the truth, to glimpse reality, we must learn to*
*look at our existence in a new way. By the very limits*
*of nature, ours is an "outside-in" form of observa-*
*tion. What our human instruments are able to*
*observe and experience—sensorially, intellectually,*
*and emotionally—is only an indicator of what lies*
*beneath the surface. . . . If we were to strip away*
*all those layers, we would begin to have a glimpse of*
*reality. As it is, we perceive at best a few outer layers*
*of reality, leaving the inner layers untouched.*

*Simon Jacobson[1]*

Rushing through life, we fail to look beneath the surface, beyond
the obvious. The more certain we are of the reasons for our
anger and disappointment with another, the less able we are to learn
anything new. Nursing our wounds, savoring anger, we lose interest
in the hidden hopes and fears that shape our behavior.

From Joseph and Pharaoh to Freud and his patients, Jews have
turned not only to hard-edged logic but also to the subterranean
world of dreams, images, intuition, and prayer in order to compre-
hend the incomprehensible. The Jewish notion of God is of the
One that is unknowable, yet we never stop seeking and struggling
to understand. Without this attitude of humility and curiosity, we

can never transcend conflicts that seem so insignificant and yet destroy love.

So far, we have focused on how you can manage conflict and disagreements in your marriage that arise out of everyday happenings. For some couples, this is all the help they need. But some conflicts cannot be resolved without an understanding of deeper issues that can transform everyday irritation into major problems.

In this chapter, we help you understand the difference between *issues* and *events*, how they are connected, and how important it is to deal with them separately. Then we discuss ways you can begin to identify the deeper, often hidden issues that motivate you and your partner, and look at how to use them to strengthen your relationship. The techniques and ground rules you have learned so far will be very valuable for handling both issues and events in a way that keeps you working together as a team. Read on, and you will see what we mean.

## ISSUES VERSUS EVENTS

As we pointed out in Chapter Five, most married couples say that the three major issues that cause problems are money, sex, and communication. Other issues they commonly fight about are in-laws, children, recreation, alcohol and drugs, religion, sex, careers, and housework.

Although these issues are important, we find that they are not what couples argue about most frequently. Instead, couples argue most often about the small, everyday happenings of life. We call these *events*. We want to help you separate out events from issues, and then to separate out the issues that are more apparent—such as money, communication, and sex—from the deeper, often hidden, issues that affect your relationship. An example will help you see what we mean.

Ellen and Mitch are a couple who argue a lot about money. One day, Ellen came home from work and put the checkbook down on the kitchen counter as she went to the bedroom to change. Mitch looked at the checkbook and became livid when he saw an entry for $150 made out to a department store. When Ellen walked back into the kitchen, tired after a long day at work, she was expecting— or at least hoping—that Mitch would hug her or ask, "How was your day?" Instead, the conversation went like this:

MITCH: What did you spend that $150 on?
ELLEN: *(very defensive)* None of your business.
MITCH: Of course it's my business. We just agreed not to spend so much, and here you go blowing it.

And they were off into a huge argument about the issue of money. But it happened in the context of an event—Mitch happening to look and see that Ellen spent $150. Events like this are common to all couples. In this case, Ellen had actually spent the $150 on a new sweater for Mitch because he had just received an offer for a new job. But that never even came up.

Many couples, particularly those in unhappy relationships, try to deal with important issues only in the context of triggering events. This seldom works well. Couples in conflict often end up in a vicious cycle of painful conflict and unproductive avoidance. A history of fights triggered by events leads couples to shy away from dealing directly and constructively with major issues. Hoping to avoid more conflict, they avoid dealing with important issues for too long. As tension mounts over the unresolved issues, a relatively minor event can trigger another painful explosion that only serves to further reinforce the pattern of avoidance until the next eruption.

For Ellen and Mitch, so much negative energy is stored up about the issue of money that conflict is easily triggered. They never sit down and talk about money in a constructive way; instead, they argue as checks bounce, bills come in, or other money events occur. They never get anywhere on the big issue because they spend their energy just dealing with the crises catalyzed by events.

## Avoiding the Real Problem

As in this example, events tend to trigger conflict at inopportune times—you're ready to leave for work, you're coming home from work, you're going to bed, you're out trying to relax, the kids are around, or friends have come over. These are the worst times for dealing with issues.

Yes, we are suggesting that you consider controlling your impulse to argue about an issue at the moment when an event triggers it. There are two keys to developing your ability to exercise self-control. The first is to pause for a moment and to envision the scene that will unfold if you act on your impulse to attack with angry words or contemptuous looks. (Yes, sometimes the nonverbal can be even more destructive than actual words.) Because so much conflict in marriage is predictable and ritualized, it is not difficult to imagine what will happen next. Ask yourself, "Is this really what I want to have happen right now?" If the answer to your question is, "No, I really don't want to go through that scene again," move on to the next step.

The second step is to practice soothing yourself. Try talking to yourself about the importance of self-restraint. "I don't have to deal with this right now. This isn't the right time. We can talk later." Taking a few deep breaths or turning on some music that you find soothing can help as well.

You say it's not easy to control and calm yourself. Who said creating successful marriages was easy? If it were, there would be far more of them. It takes practice and hard work, even if the work involves learning how to relax. Many Jews pride themselves on their verbal ability and spontaneity; more Jewish marriages would be successful if talent with words was balanced by the ability to remain silent (not sullen) at those times when complaints and criticism are likely to lead to unproductive conflict.

Of course, silence is not the complete answer. There are ways of using an event to identify an important issue in a respectful way that is more likely to lead to resolving it. In our first example, Mitch could have said, "I noticed that bill for $150, and it really tapped into my concern about money. How about we sit down and talk about it later." In this way, he would have acknowledged the event but left the issue for a mutually agreed-on time when they could deal with it more effectively. That's what we mean by separating issues from events. Things work a lot better when your partner does not feel ambushed.

Likewise, Ellen could have said, "Listen, let's stop the action. I can see you're upset about the bill, but let's wait for a better time to talk about the issue. We're both really tired right now. Could we talk tomorrow after dinner?" If they had been practicing the skills we have presented so far, this could have saved their evening by containing the event so that it didn't trigger the explosive unresolved issue about money at a time when they weren't prepared to deal with it.

They also could have tried to talk about the issue for a few minutes—agreeing to have a fuller discussion later. Mitch might have said, "Let's talk about what just happened for a few moments and then try to move on and have a nice evening together." Couples can use the Speaker-Listener Technique if they want to make sure that both partners feel heard, then let the subject go until later.

One reason why people are tempted to use events to deal with issues, even when they know that it is likely to lead to painful conflict, is that they don't feel that "later" will ever happen, so why wait? They use the event to desperately plunge into an issue, feeling that this is their only chance to make their point. We don't recommend that you try to talk out issues in the context of events. But if you really need to do it, make sure that you use the Speaker-Listener Technique, especially when you are trying to deal with an issue that you know has been difficult for the two of you.

Practicing the skills and techniques we have been teaching will make it more likely that you will handle events better and plan the time to deal with important issues. And you will maintain a level of control as to where, when, and how you will deal with the issues.

# HIDDEN ISSUES

Most of the time, people can recognize the issues that are triggered by events because they have almost the same content. With Ellen and Mitch, his looking at the checkbook started the event, and the issue was money. That's not hard to figure out. But you will also find yourselves getting caught up in fights around events that don't seem to be attached to any particular issue. Or you may find that you aren't getting anywhere when you talk about particular problems; you're just spinning your wheels. These are signs that you aren't getting at the real issues. The real issue isn't about money or careers or housework or leaving the toilet seat up—it is deeper and more elusive.

Hidden issues often drive the really destructive arguments. For example, Ellen and Mitch ended up arguing about a particular purchase. For Mitch, the underlying issue had more to do with his feeling that his career was not going well. He worried that Ellen didn't respect and accept him because he didn't make more money. Ellen's anger and hurt, though, was fueled by her unspoken fear that Mitch really didn't care about her anymore.

When we say that issues are hidden, we mean that they are usually not being talked about openly or constructively. Instead, the underlying key issues often get lost in the flow of the argument. Mitch was aware of feeling anxious about his career, and Ellen had interpreted Mitch's tension and criticism as a sign that he no longer cared about her. When the checkbook set off the fight, Mitch and Ellen didn't really deal with the underlying issues. Like many couples, they were missing the forest (the hidden issues) for the trees (the events).

To summarize:

- Events are everyday happenings, such as dirty dishes or a bounced check.

- Issues are the larger topics that all couples must deal with, such as money, sex, and in-laws.

- Hidden issues are the deeper, fundamental issues that can come up with any issue or event.

In our work with couples, we see several types of hidden issues—issues of control, power, and anxiety; needing and caring; recognition; commitment; integrity; and acceptance. There are surely others, but these capture a lot of what goes on in relationships.

## Control, Power, and Anxiety

Couples in all cultures struggle with issues of control and power. Especially in the past twenty-five years, as the roles and rules that governed traditional gender roles have so radically shifted, men and women are often unclear or in conflict about how the work of life should be divided. For Jews, there is an added level of historical anxiety that is superimposed on these more universal issues.

As a people, the Jews have often been powerless to resist persecution. Grasping for a sense of control often is connected to unconscious attempts to quiet a chronic sense of unease. Jews have no monopoly on suffering or anxiety, but we should not underestimate the impact of two millennia of persecution and wandering from land to land. The legendary overprotectiveness of Jewish parents is not just a stereotype that applies to earlier, less secure generations—it lives on in different forms even among Jews who have not directly experienced anti-Semitism.

Even today, it is not just the memory of the past that feeds Jewish anxiety. Recent events, such as the 1999 shooting of Jewish children at a Jewish community center in Los Angeles, tap into the ancient Jewish fear that ultimately there is *nowhere* that is safe for Jews. Although Jewish leaders understandably try to reassure the community about the rarity of these attacks, statistics cannot compete with horrifying images on the television screen of wounded children and a smirking, gloating anti-Semite. Thus, for Jews, the ordinary marital issues of control and power can be amplified in confusing ways by our collective anxiety. Overzealous attempts to control the trivial can be motivated by an unspeakable primal dread that we can actually control nothing.

In our everyday life, we usually shy away from the deeper issues. On the surface level, these control issues most often take the form of questions about who will have the most status and power. Who decides who does the chores? Are your needs and desires just as important as your partner's, or is there an inequality? Is your input important, or are major decisions made without you? Who is in charge? If you are encountering these kinds of issues, you may be dealing with hidden control issues.

Even if there are no ongoing struggles over control between you, these issues can affect your relationship when you need to make decisions—even small ones. For example, what happens if one of you really wants to eat pizza and the other feels like having Chinese food? This is an event without a lot of long-term significance. Nevertheless, if either of you is unyielding in what you want, a lot of conflict can develop over something as simple as cuisine. You may feel as though the other person is trying to control you or as though you need to be in control. A power struggle can result over just about anything.

Whatever the topic, control issues are least likely to damage your relationship when you feel that you're a team, and that each partner's needs and desires are attended to in the decisions you make. That hasn't been the case for Isaac and Naomi. They are like many couples—their different attitudes about money and children mix together. Naomi goes through the roof every time Isaac buys expensive things for their seven-year-old son, Nathan, without consulting her. She gets even more upset if she feels that Isaac buys something that she feels is not safe for Nathan. Isaac resents Naomi's insistence on being involved in every decision. Each partner feels that the other is overcontrolling.

Isaac and Naomi are locked in a struggle for power and control that is being played out over money and their child. Each of them wants control and feels as though the other is taking something away. They have little sense of being on the same team, working together. After particularly bad events, as when Isaac bought an expensive bicycle for Nathan, they live with a tense silence for days. Of course, they rarely talk about power or control. When they do talk, it is usually about particular purchases or Nathan's safety. But they never get very far in their discussions or their arguments, because they haven't found a way to address the underlying issues that fuel their conflict.

Often people are motivated to be in control because they are actually hypersensitive about being controlled by others, so control becomes a big issue. Usually these people have experienced a very controlling and powerful authority figure, often a parent, somewhere in the past. That's the case with Isaac. Isaac is trying to show— mostly to himself—that he's in control by the way he spends money. "I'm not going to let her tell me what to do!" He has the power to do what he wants—he thinks.

Isaac is the child of Holocaust survivors. He grew up in a family in which his parents rarely let him make any decisions for himself, especially if they felt he might be injured or hurt. They tried to control every aspect of how he dressed, talked, studied, and played.

When Isaac turned sixteen, he began to defy his parents in every way that he could, constantly proving to himself that he was the one who was in control. He began to stay out late, smoke marijuana, and neglect his schoolwork. He now works as a trader on the stock market, where his love of risk works quite well for him. He loves getting up very early in the morning and riding his motorcycle to work.

Naomi is a third-generation American Jew. She was raised with material comforts and suburban safety. But her younger brother had died of a rare form of cancer when she was eight years old. Her parents had always been protective of their children, but after her brother's death, they redoubled their efforts to insulate their surviving child from harm. In her teen years, Naomi never resisted her parents' control. She grew up into a competent but somewhat anxious adult.

When they met, Naomi was attracted to Isaac's energy and his love of excitement. He was drawn by her beauty and comforted by her willingness to bend to his wishes. Not surprisingly, Naomi's parents did not approve of the relationship with this somewhat unconventional young man. For the first time in her life, Naomi defied her parents' wishes; in a fateful exercise of autonomy, she married Isaac. Now, ten years later, as his wife and the mother of their child, she found his once irresistible independent spirit difficult to deal with.

As seven-year-old Nathan became more independent himself, Naomi became increasingly fearful about the dangers of his world. Instead of remembering how she had felt controlled by her own parents, she took on their anxiety in her parenting of Nathan. The cost of the expensive bicycle that Isaac had bought for Nathan concerned her. But the bicycle was a symbol of Nathan's increasing freedom to venture out into a world that Naomi sees as dangerous and unpredictable.

Isaac loves Naomi, but he has found the responsibilities of marriage and parenthood more difficult than he had imagined. If he really looked beneath the surface, he would begin to realize that it wasn't just Naomi who was trying to control him but also the life that he had chosen. He saw in Nathan a version of himself who he could again set free from the overcontrol of another Jewish mother. The couple had never found a way to discuss the underlying and deeper concerns that fueled their fights about money and Nathan.

This example shows why it is no accident that money and children are such important triggers of control issues. A great many decisions in our lives revolve around money and, if we are raising them, children. If you have significant power or control problems in your marriage, it's likely that you struggle a lot with money as well as with how to raise your children. Money and children in and of themselves are often not the deeper issues, but they certainly provide plenty of events that can trigger them.

When you disagree, either you will compromise or one of you will get your way. But it's hard to compromise or let your spouse win an argument if it will make you feel controlled, powerless, or too anxious. It's best to keep such issues from being a problem in your marriage in the first place. If either of you is struggling with too many unresolved issues of control, power, and anxiety, you may find it difficult to deal with even minor decisions. If decision making is an area of tension in your relationship, use it as an opportunity to begin looking beneath the surface.

## Needing and Caring

A second major arena for hidden issues involves caring. The main theme of these issues is the extent to which you feel loved. As we will see, such issues come up when a person feels that his or her important emotional needs aren't being met.

Jill and Jay are a couple who came to one of our workshops. They told us that they repeatedly fought over who should refill the orange juice container, but orange juice wasn't the real issue fueling their arguments. As it turned out, when Jay's mother refilled the juice container, he thought of it as demonstrating her love and care for him. Because Jill wouldn't do it, Jay felt she didn't love him. Jay was very aware of feeling uncared for, but in their arguments about orange juice he didn't talk about that feeling. Instead, he focused on what he saw as Jill's stubbornness. He complained to Jill, "I can't believe you're not willing to do such a small thing for me."

Jill would snap, "Who do you think you are telling me to make the orange juice? Where do you get off saying I have to do it?" She worried that he was trying to coerce her into the traditional wife role. That wasn't his motive, but she was very sensitive, as she had been previously married to a domineering man. Jay was acting the same way, at least around the orange juice issue, not because of control issues but because he felt a need to be cared for in a certain way. Discussing these hidden issues brought them closer, and orange juice no longer seemed especially important.

JAY (SPEAKER):   When I hear myself talking about the orange juice issue more calmly, I realize it sounds kind of weird. But for me, it's really not about wanting to control you. I've been so primed by my upbringing to connect refilling the OJ with love that I've put this pressure on you to be sure that you love me.

JILL (LISTENER):   So for you, the key issue is wanting to know I care, not wanting to control me?

JAY: (SPEAKER) (*goes on to validate her, as well*) Exactly, and I can see how you'd be feeling controlled without knowing that. (*Jay passes the floor to Jill.*)

JILL (SPEAKER):  You're right. I've really felt you wanted to control me, and that's a real hot button given what I went through with Joe.

JAY (LISTENER):  It really did seem to you that I just wanted to control you, and that's an especially sensitive area given what you went through with Joe.

JILL (SPEAKER):  You got it. I want to be your partner, not your servant.

JAY (LISTENER):  Sounds like you want us to be a team.

JILL (SPEAKER):  Yep!

As you can see from the tail end of their conversation, learning to talk about the bigger concerns paved the way for greater connection instead of alienation brought on by empty orange juice containers. This is another example of the pointlessness of trying to solve the problem about the event—refilling the orange juice container—unless you are communicating well enough to get the hidden issues out in the open. Jay and Jill finally were able to use their communication skills to talk about his feeling of being uncared for and her concern about being controlled. That's the key: talking about these kinds of deeper issues rather than letting them operate as hidden issues in arguments.

## Recognition and Appreciation

The third type of hidden issue involves recognition and appreciation. Does your partner acknowledge and value your activities and accomplishments? Whereas caring issues involve concerns about being cared for or loved, recognition and appreciation issues are more about feeling valued by your partner for who you are and what you do.

Consider Burt and Mirav, a couple who own a business together. Burt is president and treasurer of their corporation, and Mirav is vice president and secretary. Most of the time, they enjoy running their business together, but one day they were seated at a luncheon when someone asked Burt a question about the company. His quick response was, "I'm the only officer in this company." Mirav, who was sitting right next to him, was furious and embarrassed.

We can only speculate about why Burt failed at times to recognize Mirav's role in the company. Perhaps his own control issues were seeping out when he made this comment. Perhaps he thought, "I can do it all," and really did disregard her contributions to the company. Whatever his hidden motives, such events will make Mirav's involvement less and less rewarding. She may slowly pull away from him over time. She admired his drive and accomplishments, but she also felt that she had made a big contribution to the company's success. If they want to prevent further damage to their relationship, they had better talk openly about this key issue.

Such examples are common. For example, many men tell us that they don't feel that their wives place much value on the work they do to bring home income for the family. Likewise, we hear many women—whether or not they work outside the home—say that they don't feel as if their husbands appreciate what they do at home for the family. In these cases, spouses may try hard for a while to get recognized, but they will eventually burn out if their partner continually fails to express appreciation. It's OK to want your spouse to recognize and appreciate what you bring to the relationship. How long has it been since you told your partner how much you appreciate and admire the things he or she does?

## Commitment

The focus of this fourth hidden issue is on the long-term security of the relationship, expressed by the question, "Are you going to stay with me?" One couple we worked with, Amy and Danny, had huge arguments about their separate checking accounts. Whenever the bank statement arrived, Danny would complain bitterly about Amy's having a separate account. This problem wasn't related to a money or hidden control issue. For Danny, the hidden issue was commitment. He had been married once before, and his ex-wife had had a separate account. She decided to leave him after fifteen years of marriage, which was easier because she had saved up thousands of dollars in her own account.

Now, when Amy's bank statement would arrive, Danny would associate it with the thought that she could be planning to leave him. That was not her plan at all, but because Danny rarely talked openly about his fear, she wasn't given the opportunity to alleviate his anxiety by affirming her commitment. The issue kept fueling explosions of conflict during these events.

Sometimes the issue of commitment is triggered by the success of one partner. Psychologist Stephen Beach and his colleagues have suggested that in distressed relationships, people are threatened by the success of their partners. In healthier relationships, partners tend to take pride in each other's accomplishments.[2] Perhaps the commitment in distressed relationships is already threatened, and the success of one partner is seen by the other as providing more alternatives for leaving. Success can also trigger hidden recognition issues. If one partner is not feeling recognized and sees the other partner receiving a lot of recognition, this could intensify feelings of not being appreciated.

Do you worry about your partner's long-term commitment to you and the marriage? Have you talked about this openly, or does this issue find indirect expression in the context of events in your relationship? In Chapter Nine, we'll focus in much more depth on how commitment issues affect relationships.

## Integrity

The fifth type of hidden issue relates to integrity. Have you ever noticed how upset you get when your partner questions your intent or motives? These events can spark great fury. With Robert and Carol, arguments frequently end up with each being certain they know what the other meant. Most often they are sure that what the other meant was negative. Both of them are therapists, so you would think they would know better, but they have a serious problem with making negative interpretations. Here's a typical example of their interaction:

CAROL:  You forgot to pick up the dry cleaning.
ROBERT:  *(feeling a bit indignant)* You didn't ask me to pick it up; you asked me if I was going by there. I told you I wasn't.
CAROL:  *(really angry at what she sees as his lack of caring about what she needs)* You did say you would pick it up, but you just don't give a damn about me.
ROBERT:  *(feeling thoroughly insulted)* I do care, and I resent you telling me I don't.

Carol's caring issue is pretty much out in the open here, even though the couple isn't exactly having a constructive, healing talk about it. But Robert's issue has more to do with integrity. It is not as evident, but it is there. He feels insulted that she is calling him an uncaring, inconsiderate husband who never thinks about her needs. Each partner winds up feeling criticized and invalidated.

As we pointed out earlier in this book, it is not wise to argue about what your partner really thinks, feels, or intends. Don't tell your spouse what is going on inside, unless you are talking about *your* insides! To do otherwise is guaranteed to trigger the issue of integrity. And anyone will defend his or her integrity when it is questioned.

## Acceptance: The Mother of All Hidden Issues

There seems to be one primary issue that can underlie all the others we have listed so far: the desire for acceptance. Sometimes this is felt more as a fear of rejection, but the fundamental issue is the same. At the deepest level, people are motivated to find acceptance and to avoid rejection in their relationships. This reflects the deep need everyone has to be both respected and connected.

You can see this issue come up in many ways. For example, some people are afraid that if they act in certain ways their partner is going to reject them. A lowered sense of self-worth would only make such fears more intense. People may ask for what they want indirectly rather than directly, for example, by saying "Wouldn't you like to make love tonight?" rather than "I'd like to make love with you tonight." Caution squelches passion as the expression of desire is muted by a fear of rejection.

People act out hidden issues of acceptance and fear of rejection in a number of other ways. Consider Jerry and Mara's problem with Mara's yearly trip to visit her parents. Jerry and Mara have been married for ten years, and most of the time their relationship has gone very well. They have six-year-old twins, have good friends, and are financially secure. They talk regularly about the more important issues, which keeps things running pretty smoothly. However, there is one problem they have never really solved.

Every year at Christmas, Mara travels from their home in Phoenix to her parents' home in a small town in Kansas, where she grew up. Mara had been raised as a Methodist but had converted to Judaism before she and Jerry got married. She took her commitment to being a Jew seriously and was responsible for organizing their children's Jewish studies at the local synagogue. But she had always made it clear to Jerry that becoming a Jew did not mean giving up her parents, to whom she was very attached. She also insisted on taking their children to see her parents, because she felt it was important for them to feel some sense of connection to both sets of grandparents. They had moved to Arizona from Kansas City, where they had met, for Jerry's work and also to be close to his parents, who lived nearby.

Every year, usually the night before her trip, she and Jerry would argue.

JERRY:  I really hate it when you leave for this trip every year. You leave me to handle everything myself.

MARA:  *(feeling a bit defensive)* You knew when we got married that I did this every year. I don't know why you have to complain about it every time.

JERRY:  *(going on the attack)* I just don't think it's very responsible to leave for a week every year at this time. This year Hanukkah and Christmas happen to fall in the same week, and I think you're just going to confuse the kids by exposing them to all of your parents' Christmas stuff.

MARA:  *(She thinks, "Why do we have to do this every year? I hate this argument." She is getting angrier.)* I have made it very clear to my parents that my children are being raised as Jews, and they respect that. The kids' Jewish identity is strong, and being around their grandparents' celebration of *their* holiday doesn't take anything away from them. I don't see you taking the lead on doing much to make the kids feel good about being Jewish. That seems to be my job.

JERRY:  *(angrier himself)* If you cared more about me and our family, you wouldn't have this need to separate us every year at this time when all the rest of our friends are getting together.

MARA:  *(getting up to leave the room, feeling disgusted)* Yeah, you're right. You're always right, *my dear.*

JERRY:  *(yelling after her as she walks out)* I hate it when you talk to me like that. You can't treat me like your mom treats your dad. I won't stand for it.

MARA:  *(shouting from the other room)* I'm not like my mother, and besides, she's a lot nicer than you. You aren't telling me what to do. I'm going. I'll keep going every year, and you might as well just get used to it.

What's really going on here? Getting ready for the trip is the event. This nasty argument is as much a part of the tradition as the trip is. Neither of them likes it, but they haven't found a way to do it differently.

As Jerry and Mara learned in their communication workshop, many hidden issues are being triggered. Deep down, Jerry doesn't feel cared for when these trips come up. He feels lonely when Mara leaves, and this is hard to handle because he sees her looking forward to going. He wonders if she's delighted to get away from him. He feels abandoned—reflecting some commitment issues that also get triggered. His focus on the kids is a smoke screen for his real concerns.

Mara likes to be in control of her life, so that's one hidden issue being triggered here. As they argue unproductively, the issue of integrity also comes up. She feels that he is calling into question her devotion as a wife. She sees herself as very dedicated to the family and just wants this one-week trip each year to be with her parents. She doesn't think that's asking a lot, especially because she felt that moving to Arizona was a much bigger sacrifice that she had made for the marriage.

Underneath it all, you can see acceptance as the most basic hidden issue driving the issues of power, caring, commitment, and integrity in their argument. Neither of them feels totally accepted by the other, at least around this issue. Mara feels the lack of acceptance the most acutely. She sometimes wonders whether Jerry takes her commitment to helping create a Jewish family seriously. Sometimes she wonders whether any born-Jews really accept Jews-by-choice. It's an issue she has never discussed, but it bothers her, especially this time of year.

Mara and Jerry have a basically strong relationship and get along well most of the time. Yet the need for acceptance is so deep seated for all of us that it can become triggered by almost any event or issue—if we let it. In a strange way, Mara and Jerry are very organized: they limit themselves to one big fight a year, their predictable December debate. But it doesn't make the fight easy, and they do tend to get tense in the weeks approaching the trip. In this argument, Mara and Jerry aren't talking about the hidden issues in any productive way. The deeper issues aren't totally hidden, but they aren't being dealt with directly and constructively, either. Let's discuss how to do this right.

# RECOGNIZING THE SIGNS OF HIDDEN ISSUES

You can't handle hidden issues unless you can identify them. There are four key ways to tell when hidden issues may be affecting your relationship.

## Wheel Spinning

One sign of hidden issues is that you find yourselves spinning your wheels as you talk about the same problem over and over again. When an argument starts with you thinking, "Here we go again," you should suspect hidden issues. You never really get anywhere on the problem because you aren't talking about what really matters—the hidden issue. Mara and Jerry can and have argued in this manner for hours. It doesn't get them anywhere, and they both know it. It's as if they are mired in mud; in fact, they're slinging it.

## Trivial Triggers

A second clue that there are hidden issues is that trivial events are blown up out of all proportion. The argument between Jill and Jay described earlier is a great example. Failing to fill the orange juice container seems like a trivial event, but it triggers horrendous arguments driven by the issues of power and caring. You can't have a big argument about something meaningless unless there is something bigger at stake—a hidden issue.

## Avoidance

A third sign of hidden issues is that one or both of you are avoiding certain topics or levels of intimacy. If walls have gone up between you, it often means that important, unexpressed issues are affecting the relationship. Perhaps it seems too risky to talk directly about feeling unloved or insecure. But the trouble is that these concerns have a way of coming up anyway.

Quite a few of the topics couples avoid reflect hidden issues in relationships. For example, we have talked with many couples from different cultural or religious backgrounds who strongly avoid talking about these differences. We think that this usually reflects concerns about acceptance. As we saw with Mara and Jerry, the deeper question is "Will you accept me fully if we really talk about our different backgrounds?" Avoiding such topics not only allows hidden issues to remain hidden; it puts the relationship at greater risk, because such differences can have a great impact on a marriage. Other common but often taboo topics include sex, weight, money, politics, and core values. There are many such sensitive topics that people avoid dealing with in their relationships out of fear of rejection or conflict.

## Scorekeeping

A fourth sign of hidden issues in your relationship is that one or both of you start keeping score. Scorekeeping could mean that you are not feeling recognized for what you put into the relationship. It could also mean that you are less committed to your relationship. Or it could mean that you are feeling controlled and are keeping track of the times your partner has taken advantage of you. Whatever the issue, it can be a sign that important things are not being talked about—just documented.

As Jerry senses Mara's trip getting closer, he becomes focused on what looks like evidence of her distance from him. When she works a bit late or goes over to her sister's for a couple of hours, he begins to think that she isn't paying enough attention—that maybe he isn't as important to her as she is to him. He asks himself, "Why isn't she doing more for our relationship, the way I am?" Mara really does care and is interested. Most of the time Jerry knows it, but he keeps score as this yearly event approaches because it raises important issues for him.

# HANDLING HIDDEN ISSUES

What can you do when you realize that hidden issues are affecting your relationship? You can recognize when one may be operating and start talking about it constructively. This will be easier to do if you are cultivating an atmosphere of teamwork using the techniques we have presented thus far. We strongly recommend using the Speaker-Listener Technique when you are trying to explore such issues.

If you are in an argument and suspect hidden issues are taking over, call a Stop Action. Using the first ground rule in this way will help you shift the conversation to the level of the hidden issue— either right then or at an agreed-on time in the near future. Later is usually better. You are not as likely to have the time or the ability to be very skillful in the context of some event.

Make sure to deal with the issue in terms of Problem Discussion, not Problem Solution. Be aware of any tendency to jump to solutions. In our opinion, the deeper the issue, the less likely it is that problem solving will be the answer. If you haven't been talking about the real issue, how could your solution address what is really at stake? What you need first and foremost is to hear and understand each other's feelings and concerns.

This process is not just about achieving a better understanding of your partner—it is also about understanding yourself. We all struggle with many conflicting thoughts, feelings, impulses, and values. But we are so often focused on our partner that we fail to try to understand ourselves. Pay attention to both of you. Nurture a sense of curiosity, openness, and wonder.

In *I and Thou*, the great Jewish thinker Martin Buber wrote of the transformative power of deep communication between two humans. Buber's distillation of Jewish wisdom led him to the conclusion that it is *only* through a true communion between the *I* and the *Thou* that we can reach our own potential as human beings.[3] The not-so-secret agenda in our work is to help you discover this level of connection. Without greater access to your own and your mate's inner world, your relationship will never be as rich and rewarding as it can be. A related Jewish concept is that of *b'tzelem Elohim,* the creation of each of us in God's image, and the need to strive to recognize and respect this in our partners. This would nat-urally lead to changes in the way we relate to one another.

Achieving an I-Thou connection can have the greatest impact on hidden issues. We believe that such talks are so powerful because the most common root issue is the desire to be truly known by another. Couples tell us that when they finally are able to talk more openly about these issues, they experience a tremendous sense of relief, as if a weight has been lifted. Understanding does not always lead to agreement, but we have found that if you need to problem-solve, it is far easier after you each feel understood.

You also need to realize that just one talk usually won't resolve a hidden issue, because such issues often have many layers. It may be obvious that hidden issues are operating, but this doesn't mean that the issue itself is obvious. Sometimes it is clear, and sometimes it is pretty murky. You may not be able to identify the issue right away; you just know there's something uncomfortable that you need to keep talking about.

What if you can't resolve the issue? This happens more frequently than most people realize, and is easier to handle than most people real-ize, too. In Chapter Five, we talked about agreeing to disagree. With hidden issues, often the best possible solution is to communicate your feelings and fears clearly and openly and to reach a mutual agreement not to let those issues act as filters. That your family of origin or a pre-vious relationship left you too sensitive to control issues or too worried about commitment or integrity issues really may have no easy solution. What you can do is allow for the impact of those feelings and not allow them to distort important communications in this relationship. By recognizing and validating your partner around such issues, you limit the power of those issues to be destructive to your relationship.

Hidden issues are like the childhood monster that lived under the bed. We didn't want to look down to see what was there, but we knew it was important and big and probably scary. It lived there until we found the courage to look. Now we face different fears, and we don't have to face them alone. Who better to help you pierce the darkness than the person with whom you share your life?

———————

Our goal in this chapter has been to give you a way to explore and understand some of the most frustrating occurrences in relationships. You can prevent a great deal of damage by learning to give events and issues the time and attention they require. The model presented here, along with all the skills and techniques described in the previous chapters, will help you do just that.

For all too many couples, the hidden issues never come out. Instead, they fester and produce layers of sadness and resentment that eventually destroy the marriage. You don't have to let hidden issues undermine your love. When you learn to discuss deeper issues openly and with emphasis on validating each other, the issues that generated the greatest conflict can actually draw you closer together, to create a sense of I and Thou.

In the next chapter, we turn to the subject of expectations. So many hidden issues arise from deeply held expectations that we thought the topic deserved a chapter of its own. It also will help you understand what you expect from one another and where those expectations come from.

## EXERCISES

Think and write about these questions individually, on a separate piece of paper; then sit down and talk together about your impressions.

### Signs of Hidden Issues

Think through the list of signs that hidden issues may be affecting your relationship. Do you notice that one or more of these signs come up a lot in your relationship? What do you notice?

1. Wheel spinning
2. Trivial triggers

3. Avoidance

4. Scorekeeping

## Identifying Hidden Issues

Next, consider which hidden issues might operate most often in your relationship. In addition to the hidden issues listed here, there may be some big issue you would like to add. Consider each issue and the degree to which it seems to affect your relationship negatively. Also, how deeply hidden are these issues in your relationship?

Note whether certain events have triggered or keep triggering the issues. You can list these events on the right-hand side of your list of issues or on a separate piece of paper.

- Power, control, and anxiety

- Caring

- Recognition and admiration

- Commitment

- Integrity

- Acceptance

## Working Through Hidden Issues

Plan some time together to talk about your observations and thoughts. For most couples, certain hidden issues come up repeatedly. Identifying these issues can help you draw together as you each learn to handle them with care. Also, discussing these matters gives you an excellent opportunity to get in some more practice with the Speaker-Listener Technique. We recommend you set a regular couple meeting time to talk about hidden issues in the Problem Discussion format. Put the emphasis on understanding your partner's point of view as fully and clearly as possible, not on resolving some immediate, concrete concern.

# 8

# Unfulfilled Expectations and What to Do About Them

*Divorced Jewish man, seeks partner to attend shul with, light Shabbos candles, celebrate holidays, build Sukkah together, attend brisses, bar mitzvahs. Religion not important.*

*Worried about in-law meddling? I'm an orphan! Write.*

*Staunch Jewish feminist, wears tzitzis, seeking male who will accept my independence, although you probably will not. Oh, just forget it.*

*Jewish male, 34, very successful, smart, independent, self-made. Looking for girl whose father will hire me.*

*Actual personals that appeared in Israeli papers*

Judaism and Jewish history have imbued the Jewish psyche with an abundance of expectations, both positive and negative. Our ambitions and accomplishments are matched only by our angst and anxiety. Jews often suffer from a nagging sense of "not-good-enoughness." How much money or how many mitzvot does it take in order to feel fulfilled? Just as the biblical concept of chosenness has been experienced as a blessing and a burden, the heights and depths of our history have only reinforced the sense of Jewish specialness and inadequacy.

There is no simple way to assess the impact of history on Jewish relationships. Issues of self-esteem are universal, and everyone's personal and cultural history affects the way he or she approaches intimacy. But it is important to be as aware as possible of how the past affects your expectations. You may want to review your reactions to the work on Jewish identity you did in Chapter One to try to clarify how being Jewish affects the way you approach your relationship.

Our expectations about intimacy and love are the yardsticks by which we measure success in relationships. These expectations are deeply affected by our own sense of self-worth. If we deny too many of our own desires out of a sense of unworthiness, we may find beginning a relationship much easier than enjoying it. Over time, our dissatisfaction can grow with an awareness that not enough of our needs are being met. If, in contrast, our expectations (and opinion of ourselves) are too inflated, we may be constantly disappointed with our partner. If only he or she were a little taller, richer, more beautiful, less critical, more adoring, younger, older, funnier, more Jewish, or less Jewish, then, and only then, would I feel the love I yearn for.

In this chapter, we help you explore your expectations for your marriage: what they are, where they come from, and just how reasonable they are. At the end of this chapter is a very important exercise with which you will explore and share your expectations for your relationship.

In fact, this chapter is primarily designed to prepare you for the exercise—it's that important. Although some relationships fail because of unreasonable expectations, many more suffer because expectations are never made clear. It is our goal to help you, first, better understand your own expectations; second, learn to communicate those expectations with your partner; and, finally, work on negotiating your differences.

We are not so naive as to believe that simply being clear about your expectations always leads to happy endings. Perhaps your expectations are not so reasonable. And yes, there are some issues in relationships that can be too sensitive or difficult to deal with. Successful couples understand and accept that many differences cannot be resolved. But overall, we have seen far more marriages end because there was too little sharing about expectations rather than because there was too much.

Exploring your expectations will also help you understand how issues, hidden or not, are triggered in your relationship. Together with all the skills you have learned so far, exploring your expectations will give you the best shot at preventing the kind of frustrating conflict we discussed in Chapter Seven.

## HOW EXPECTATIONS AFFECT RELATIONSHIPS

*Who is rich? He who is satisfied with his portion.*
*Ethics of the Fathers 4:1[1]*

People hold expectations about every aspect of their relationships. Expectations can become powerful filters that distort your understanding of what happens in your relationship. The reason is that people tend to see what they expect to see. Also, it isn't just that filters distort or limit information: our filters shape our behavior in ways that actually elicit the behavior we expect from others. When we approach others with suspicion or hostility, our expectations that people are rejecting or angry are seldom contradicted. In many ways, we do create our own realities.

In this chapter, we focus on your expectations of the way you think things are supposed to be in your relationship. For example, you may have specific expectations about relatively minor things, such as about who will refill the orange juice container or who will balance the checkbook—the stuff events are made of. Or you may have expectations about common issues—money, housework, in-laws, and sex. You may also have expectations about the deeper, often hidden, issues: how power will be shared or not shared, how caring will be demonstrated, or what the commitment is in your relationship. Expectations affect everything!

Consider Zoey and Max. They have been married for only a year, and things have gone pretty well. However, Zoey is upset about how late Max has been working. Max is upset with Zoey for making what he thinks are impossible demands on him.

Zoey, a graduate student in psychology, comes from a wealthy Jewish family. Her parents inherited much of their wealth, and Zoey never saw either of her parents sacrifice for the comforts they had enjoyed. Her family had not offered any money to help them start out, and Max insisted that they never ask them for any.

Max is now the one who is responsible for earning the income for both of them. He is an ambitious young lawyer who is very aware that part of his drive for success came from growing up as the poorest Jewish child in his neighborhood. His father died when Max was five, and his mother supported him and his sister by working long hours as a secretary. She sacrificed her health earning the money for them to live in a middle-class neighborhood with good schools.

Like many young couples, Max and Zoey have a lot of expectations and issues to resolve about what married life is supposed to be like. Max often comes home past nine in the evening. Zoey is very angry about his late hours, and his arrival home sometimes triggers huge arguments, like this one:

ZOEY: (*feeling agitated*) I don't see why you have to come home so late every night. I didn't marry you just for a new last name.
MAX: (*obviously irritated*) How many times do we have to argue about this? I am working to support both of us. How do you expect us to pay the bills and get ahead?
ZOEY: I don't think you need to work as hard as you do. My parents would probably be willing to give us some money. I know you don't want to ask, but even now you are making enough money to work a little less.

MAX:  I don't want to ask anybody for money. I see what happens to people who are on welfare. It takes away their drive and self-respect. *(with an edge of contempt in his voice)* Your parents would love to see you beg, so that they could control our life the way they do your brothers.

ZOEY:  *(angrily)* All you care about is your damn career.

MAX:  *(stiffening)* I'm doing this for you and for me and for our future. I know how to sacrifice for what I want. I'm not so sure you do.

ZOEY:  *(resentfully)* I work hard too. And after I get finished with graduate school, I'll be able to pull my own weight. I don't need you telling me about sacrifice.

MAX:  *(turning away and walking toward the door)* A lot of appreciation I get for working so hard and taking care of us. Thanks a lot.

Zoey and Max are arguing about expectations. Max didn't expect that Zoey would complain about his long hours at work. Actually, he expected appreciation. He liked spending time with Zoey, but felt that economic security should be his—and her—first priority. Zoey expected Max to work hard, but she certainly wasn't prepared for him being home so late almost every evening. She had a lot of romantic expectations about spending evenings together, and she felt rejected by what she saw as Max's preoccupation with work.

In this example, it might be difficult to argue that any of their expectations are totally outrageous. What is much more important is that their expectations don't match, and this is fueling conflict. You can easily imagine that hidden issues of caring and acceptance are also at work. Max could be wondering if Zoey really appreciates him, considering that she is complaining about his long hours. Zoey could be feeling that Max is more concerned with work than with her. Studies show that it's more likely that relationships will develop problems when expectations are unreasonable. Do you think that Max's or Zoey's expectations are unreasonable?

# EXPECTATIONS AND HIDDEN ISSUES

When hidden issues are triggered by events, it is usually because some expectation wasn't met. Underlying *power* issues are expectations about how decisions and control will be shared or not shared. Underlying *caring* issues are expectations about how you are to be loved. Underlying *recognition* issues are expectations about how your partner should respond to who you are and what you do. Underlying *commitment* issues are expectations about the strength of the relationship bonds and, most important, about safety from abandonment. Underlying *integrity* issues are expectations about being trusted and respected. And underneath all of these expectations are core expectations about *acceptance* by your partner. *A hidden issue can't get triggered in the first place unless an expectation is violated.*

# WHERE EXPECTATIONS COME FROM

Expectations build up over a lifetime of experiences. These expectations are based in the past but operate in the present. There are three primary sources for our expectations: our family of origin, our previous relationships, and the culture we live in.

## Family of Origin

We learn many of our expectations from our families as we grow up. Our family experiences lay down patterns—both good and bad—that become models for how we think things are supposed to work when we become adults. Expectations are transmitted both directly by what our parents say and indirectly by what we observe. No one comes to marriage a blank slate.

For example, if you grew up with parents who totally avoided conflict, you may have developed the expectation that couples should seek peace at any price. If you now encounter disagreement and conflict, it may seem to you as if the world is going to end. If you observed your parents being very affectionate, you may have come to expect this would be true in your marriage as well. If your parents divorced, you may have some expectation in the back of your mind that marriages don't really last.

Elena and Mark were a couple who had constant fights about child rearing. Elena came from a home where her mother and step-father were extremely harsh in their discipline. Her stepfather would chase the kids around the house when he was angry. If they were caught, they were hit wherever his hands happened to land. Almost worse was the way both parents yelled and screamed when the children would make the slightest mistake.

In contrast, Mark came from a family where, in general, the kids could do whatever they wanted. There were limits, but they were pretty loose. Whenever Mark and Elena's five-year-old son, Joey, acted up, Mark responded by raising his voice, but he actually did nothing to set limits on Joey's behavior. Joey had learned to all but ignore Mark's angry voice. There were no real consequences.

With her background, Elena expected that when Mark raised his voice, someone was about to get hurt. Her expectation was based in the past, but it still had real power. She would even get sick to her stomach from the tension if she thought that someone was about to get in trouble. It was as if her stepfather were chasing her all over again.

At times, she saw Mark as being abusive even though he wasn't. Her expectations became powerful filters, distorting her perception of what was really going on. Actually, Mark, like his parents, was quite lenient. Sure, he could lose his temper and yell from time to time, but he was a softy.

As a consequence of their expectations, neither Mark nor Elena provided consistent discipline for Joey, who suffered because of this lack of consistency. His teacher reported that he was one of the most difficult kids in the school; for his part, Joey didn't understand why the teacher was so insistent that he observe the class rules. What kind of expectations of his partner do you think he will have when he grows up? You can see how problematic expectations might be handed down from generation to generation.

Conflicts caused by unexpressed expectations are very common. If we had the space, we could give literally thousands of examples. It is enough to say here that we each have many expectations that grew out of our experiences in our families of origin. Understanding this basic fact is the first step to dealing more effectively with those expectations and preventing increased conflict.

## Previous Relationships

We also develop expectations from all the other relationships in which we have participated—most important, from previous dating relationships or marriages. We have expectations about how to kiss, what is romantic, how to communicate about problems, how recreational time should be spent, who should initiate the first move to make up after a fight, and so on.

Suppose, for example, that in previous dating relationships, when you began to open up about painful childhood events, you were rejected. Logically, you may have developed the expectation that such a topic is off-limits with certain people. On a deeper level, you may have the expectation that people can't be trusted with knowledge of the deepest parts of who you are. If so, you will pull back and withhold intimacy in your present relationship.

Studies show that people who have come to expect that others can't be trusted have more difficulties in relationships. If you look at their entire life, their expectation will usually make sense; however, it can lead to trouble if the mistrust is so intense that they can't even allow someone they love to get close. The good news is that you can learn to change negative expectations and to make a relationship safe for intimate talking.

Are you aware of how many of the expectations you have for your partner are based on your experiences with others? It is worth thinking about, considering that your partner is a different person from those you knew, dated, or were married to in the past. It may not be realistic or fair to hold the same expectations for your partner that you had with someone else.

## Cultural Influences

A variety of cultural factors influence our expectations. Television, movies, religious teachings, and what we read can all have a powerful effect on expectations. Even more powerful in their insidiousness, advertisements constantly bombard us, creating an insatiable hunger for material goods.

But it's not just the messages we receive through the popular media that affect our expectations. The examples throughout this book reveal a lot about the diversity of Jewish love and intimacy. Before the 1970s, many more Jews, especially in the Eastern United States, lived in relatively homogeneous neighborhoods where many people were the children and grandchildren of Eastern European Jewish immigrants. Although some of these neighborhoods remain, a lot has changed.

Today, knowing that someone is Jewish gives us only limited information about the nature of the person's cultural background and how it shapes his or her expectations. Jews may be recent immigrants from Russia or Israel, sixth-generation German American Jews, children of Holocaust survivors, or African American Jews-by-choice. People raised as Protestants are today rabbis, and some Jews raised in Orthodox communities have become totally secular. The list goes on and on. And considering that in many cities in the United States there is an intermarriage rate of over 50 percent between Jews and partners from every imaginable background, "Jewish marriage" obviously has become a very culturally complex category.

Conversion of a partner to Judaism does not eliminate cultural differences in a relationship. Brad and Jane have been married for ten years. Early in their relationship, Jane, who had been raised as a Methodist, had converted to Judaism. After ten years together, they decided to have a child. They were both overjoyed when Jane gave birth to healthy girl, whom they named Arielle.

Planning for the baby naming at their synagogue, they found themselves tripping for the first time over different culturally bound expectations. Brad, who had grown up as part of a large, extended Jewish family, took it for granted that his parents would stay with them when they came from Philadelphia for the naming. Jane, who had been raised in a Protestant family that had stressed independence, felt that it was really important to have their home to themselves during this exciting and stressful time.

> BRAD: *(angrily)* I can't believe that you wouldn't want to let my parents stay with us after they come all the way across the country.
>
> JANE: *(equally angry)* I can't believe that you don't care about preserving this precious time for just the three of us.
>
> BRAD: You told me when we first met that you were really close to your family, just like I am. You call this close? What's so bad about them staying with us?
>
> JANE: I am very close with my family, and I resent you suggesting that I'm not. My parents are coming too, and they were considerate enough to get a motel room for themselves. And they don't have nearly as much money as your parents.
>
> BRAD: That's not the point. I want them to be here with us. They've waited a long time to have a grandchild, and this means a lot to them. They want to be with us as much as possible. They can only stay for the weekend. Why should their being in our home detract from our happiness?
>
> JANE: I don't understand. They could stay at the motel that is just five minutes from here. They could be with us a lot, and we could have some privacy. Is that too much to ask?
>
> BRAD: You don't understand.
>
> JANE: That's true. I don't.

When Jane and Brad first met, they both were telling each other the truth when they said that they felt very close to their families. But the cultural filters they brought to their relationship meant that they defined *close* in very different ways.

Even the most joyous life transitions are stressful, and the intensity of these moments can reveal differences that were never very obvious. For Brad and Jane, this incident helped them begin examining their different expectations about what family and being close meant to each of them.

Jewish couples often bring very different cultural expectations to their marriages, even when both partners are born Jewish. Both Sara and Ira were Jewish, but they came from families with very different emotional environments. Sara was the daughter of a German Jewish physician and was raised with her brother as the only Jewish children in a small Texas town. Her family worked hard to "fit in," and as a child she went to a public school where all her classmates were from conservative Christian backgrounds. She remembered her parents criticizing their New York relatives as "having no manners." Ira was raised in a Jewish neighborhood in New York City. His school was 85 percent Jewish, and his family looked down on the "uptight goys" who lived in an adjacent neighborhood.

Even though Ira found Sara's calm demeanor attractive, it was certainly not familiar. And as much as Sara found Ira's intensity exciting, she sometimes felt overwhelmed by him. As their relationship matured, they discovered that the same traits they found most attractive could also be at the center of their most troubling arguments. Fortunately, over time, they had learned to step back from their arguments and talk about their different emotional frames of reference.

> SARA: We were having a very intense conversation a while ago about whether to buy a new car, and to me it felt like we were arguing. I said to Ira that we shouldn't buy the car if it was going to lead to a fight.
> IRA: I said, "Who's arguing? We're having a discussion. This is not an argument."
> SARA: I don't know how I did it, but I restrained my impulse to up the ante. Instead, we ended up using this event to begin talking about how each of our families dealt with conflict when we

were growing up. I began to realize that to Ira, it really wasn't an argument, and that helped me relax. When I was growing up, raised voices and continual interruptions would have meant something really bad. Actually, I never saw my parents fight. For me knowing that we have different "codes" makes it a little easier to deal with. I don't take it so personally.

Ira:  It used to make me really uptight when Sara would tell me to "calm down." Now that we've talked more about our differences, I realize that lowering my volume a little bit won't make me a boring person.

# HOW TO PUT EXPECTATIONS TO WORK FOR YOU

Expectations can lead either to massive disappointment and frustration or to deeper connection and intimacy between you and your partner. There are three keys to handling expectations well:

1. Being *aware* of what you expect

2. Being *reasonable* in what you expect

3. Being *clear* about what you expect

## Being Aware of What You Expect

Whether you are aware of them or not, unmet expectations can lead to great disappointment and frustration in your relationship. You don't have to be fully aware of an expectation to have it affect your relationship.

Clifford Sager, a pioneer in this field, notes that people bring to marriage a host of expectations that they never make clear. These expectations form a contract for the marriage.[2] The problem is that most people have little notion of what is in the contract when they get married. Sager further suggests that many expectations are unconscious, making it very hard to be aware of them. Not all expectations are deeply unconscious, but many become such a part of us that they function automatically. Like driving a car, much of what you do is so automatic that you don't even have to think about it.

At the end of this chapter, you will have the opportunity to increase your awareness of your own expectations. One great clue to expectations is disappointment. When you are disappointed in your relationship, some expectation hasn't been met. When you are disappointed, it is a good habit to stop a minute and ask yourself what you expected. Doing this can help you become aware of the expectations that may be unconsciously affecting your relationship.

## Being Reasonable in What You Expect

Being reasonable is the most difficult task. What each of you considers reasonable may differ in many ways. What is reasonable in one relationship may not be in another; expectations that bring pleasure in one phase of life can create misery in later years. How are we to know what is reasonable? Who is to judge?

Is it reasonable to expect your spouse to never be one minute late, to tolerate your extramarital affairs, or to put up with your violent behavior? Probably not. We hope you don't think these are reasonable expectations. If your expectations are too rigid or unreasonable, you probably will not have a very happy marriage.

What about expecting that your spouse will spend a lot of time with you and your children? That sounds good. What about also expecting a very high standard of living? Why not? But if you hold both of these expectations and expect them not to sometimes clash, you may find yourself very frustrated. Jews are often raised with high expectations for both financial success and for emotional contact. Many Jewish couples, like Zoey and Max whom we met at the beginning of this chapter, find themselves having difficulties creating clear priorities.

One study made it clear that a hidden unreasonable expectation is the belief that you can have it all. Researchers studying the emotional stability of women physicians divided their subjects into three groups.

The first group comprised doctors who said that their families came first—that they were willing to sacrifice some success to have more time with their families. The second group said that their careers in medicine came first and that they would have to work in their family life around their work. The third group said that it was possible for them to balance practicing medicine and having a family.

Guess which group suffered from the most depression, anxiety, and marital problems. It was the balance group. Although the ideal of balance sounds good, these physicians tended to have much more difficulty prioritizing career and family when the two came into conflict. Like it or not, something always has to give; by making clear choices, what gives is less likely to be your health or your marriage.

## Being Clear About What You Expect

A specific expectation may be perfectly reasonable but never clearly expressed. It is not enough just to be aware of your expectations or to evaluate their reasonableness: you must be able to express them. We often assume that our model of the ideal marriage (made up of the sum total of our expectations) is the same as that of our partner. Why should we have to tell our partner what we expect? We assume that he or she already knows.

This is an unreasonable expectation. People assume that their partner knows what they want, so they don't bother to state clearly what they need. In fact, many partners feel that if they have to ask for what they need, something is wrong. Even worse, many think that if they ask and their partner responds, the outcome isn't meaningful. They say, "If I have to ask for a hug, it doesn't really mean much." We disagree! When you ask and your partner responds, that is evidence of your partner's love and commitment.

Unreasonable assumptions often occur in the sexual arena. How many people make the assumption that their partner should know just what is most pleasing sexually? We see this over and over again. One partner becomes angry because the other fails to meet a desire or expectation. But more often than not, the person has never expressed the expectation, in effect asking the partner to be good at mind reading.

Worse, when a partner fails to read key expectations, it's easy for hidden issues to be triggered. The partner with the unmet expectation may feel that the other doesn't care. We'll deal with the sexual problems this causes in Chapter Fourteen.

Unless you make your expectations clear, you will have trouble working as a team. You can't work from any kind of shared perspective if you don't share *your* perspective.

––––––––––––

You need to be aware of your expectations, be willing to evaluate them, and offer to discuss them. Otherwise, they will have the power to trigger all the biggest issues in your relationship. And if you don't deal with them openly, you will also miss an opportunity to define a mutual vision of how you want your marriage to be.

Too often, we think of expectations only in terms of what we want from someone else. We can, we hope, also hold the expectation that marriage presents us with an opportunity to deepen our own capacity for love. In this case, we can take pride in our ability to learn to be more accepting and unconditionally loving as years go by. Look for opportunities to retire some of your less necessary expectations. Expect a little more of yourself and a little less of your partner.

The exercises we are about to present are among the most important in this book. It takes time to do them well. It also takes considerable follow-up. We hope you can find the time and motivation to do the work. If you do, you will improve your understanding of mutual expectations. Combining that understanding with the skills you are learning can have a major positive impact on the strength of your relationship both now and in the future. Just remember, there is a difference between not having any issues and handling issues well.

From the standpoint of giving you a lot to think about, we would expect this chapter to be one of the most difficult in the book. In addition to going through the exercises carefully, you might want to read the chapter a few more times. Again, think through what your key expectations are and how they affect your relationship. In Chapter Nine, we move on to the concept of commitment. This is a topic of great importance for relationships, and one about which people have quite a few expectations.

# EXERCISES

Use the exercises here to explore your expectations of your relationship. Spend some time thinking carefully about each area. Then write down your thoughts so that you can share them with your partner. Each of you should use a separate pad of paper. Each of the points here is meant to stimulate your thinking. You may have expectations in many other areas. Please consider everything you can think of that seems significant to you. You won't get much out of this exercise unless you are able and willing to put some time into it. Many couples have found this type of exercise extremely beneficial for their relationship.

## Getting to Know Your Expectations

The goal is to consider your expectations concerning the way you want or expect the relationship to be, not how it is and not how you assume it will be in the future. Write down what you expect, whether or not you think the expectation is realistic. The expectation matters and will affect your relationship whether or not it is realistic. Consider each question in light of what you want for the future.

It's essential that you write down what you really think, not what sounds like the correct or least embarrassing answer. It also can be valuable to consider what you observed and learned in each of these areas in your family when you were growing up. This is probably the source of many of your beliefs about what you want or don't want.

Explore your expectations regarding the following:

1. *The longevity of this relationship.* Is it "Till death do us part"?

2. *Sexual fidelity.*

3. *Love.* Do you expect to love each other always? Do you expect the way you experience love to change over time?

4. *Your sexual relationship.* What do you expect out of sexuality? What do you expect to be sexually taboo? How often do you expect to have sex?

5. *Romance.* What is romantic for you?

6. *Children.* Do you want children? More children?

7. *Children from previous marriages.* If you or your partner have children from a previous marriage, where do you want them to live? How do you expect to share in their discipline? How do they fit into your new marriage and lifestyle?

8. *Work, careers, and provision of income.* Who will work in the future? Whose career or job is more important? If there are or will be children, will either partner reduce work time out of the home to take care of them?

9. *The degree of each partner's emotional dependency on the other.* Do you want to be taken care of? How? How much do you expect to rely on each other to get through the tough times?

10. *Basic approach to life.* What is the balance you expect between feeling like a team or being two independent individuals?

11. *Loyalty.* What does that mean to you?

12. *Communication about problems in the relationship.* Do you want to talk these out? If so, how?

13. *Power and control.* Who do you expect will have more power and in what kinds of decisions? For example, who will control the money? Discipline the kids? What happens when you disagree in a key area? Who has the power now, and how do you feel about that?

14. *Household tasks.* Who do you expect will do what? How much household work will each of you do in the future? If you live together now, how does the current arrangement match up with what you expect in the future?

15. *Religious beliefs and observances.* Be specific about where, when, or what rituals you would expect to observe. If you have no kids but plan to, how will you bring them up? You will be asked to explore such expectations in much more detail at the end of Chapter Ten.

16. *Time together.* How much time do you want to spend together? Alone? With friends or family, at work, and so on?

17. *Sharing feelings.* How much of what you are each feeling do you expect should be shared? What do you expect to be kept private?

18. *Friendship with your partner.* What is a friend? What would it mean to maintain or have a friendship with your partner?

19. *The little things in life.* Where do you squeeze the toothpaste? Is the toilet seat left up or down? Who sends greeting cards? Think carefully about the little things that might irritate you (or might be going really well). What do you want or expect in each area?

20. *Forgiveness.* How important is forgiveness in your relationship? How should forgiveness affect your relationship?

Now, with your mind primed from the work you have just done, consider again the hidden issues we described in Chapter Seven. Do you see any other ways that they may influence or be influenced by your expectations? What do you expect in the areas of power, caring, recognition, commitment, integrity, and acceptance?

List any other expectations that you feel are important about how you want things to be and that did not appear in the foregoing list.

## Reasonable Expectations

Now go back to each area just listed and rate each expectation on a scale of 1 to 10 according to how reasonable you think the expectation is. On this scale, 10 means "Completely reasonable—I really think it is OK to expect this in this type of relationship"; 1 means "Completely unreasonable—I can honestly say that even though I expect or want this, it is not a reasonable expectation in this type of relationship." For example, suppose that you grew up in a family where problems were not discussed, and you are aware that you honestly expect or prefer to avoid such discussions. You might now rate that expectation as not very reasonable after all.

Next, place a big check mark by each expectation that you believe you have never clearly discussed with your partner.

## Prioritizing Your Expectations

No, we can't have it all, in spite of the expectations that our consumer culture fosters. Before you share your expectations with your partner, it is important to reflect on how important each of them is. It is very difficult to compromise when all your expectations seem equally important. Go over your list of expectations once again and put an A next to the expectations that you feel are crucial to your having a successful relationship, B next to those that are important but negotiable, and C next to expectations whose fulfillment would be nice but definitely not necessary. How many of your expectations really deserve an A?

## Sharing Expectations

After you and your partner have had the opportunity to work on the exercise individually, plan to spend time together discussing these expectations. Please don't do this all at once. You should plan on a number of discussions, each covering only one or two expectations. Discuss the degree to which you each feel that the expectation being discussed was shared in the past. Use the

Speaker-Listener Technique if necessary to keep these discussions clear and safe for real sharing. The goal of these discussions is to develop a full and clear understanding of each partner's expectations and beliefs.

1. Talk about the degree to which you both feel the expectations are reasonable or unreasonable, and discuss what you want to do about them.

2. Talk about what your overall, long-term vision is for the relationship. What expectations do you share about your future together?

# 9

# Choosing Commitment

*Let me be a seal upon your heart,*
*Like the seal upon your hand.*
*For love is fierce as death,*
*Passion is mighty as Sheol;*
*Its darts are darts of fire,*
*A blazing flame.*
*Vast floods cannot quench love,*
*Nor rivers drown it.*
*If a man offered all his wealth for love,*
*He would be laughed to scorn.*

*Song of Songs 8:6–7*

*Love at first sight is easy to understand. It's when two*
*people have been looking at each other for years that it*
*becomes a miracle.*

*Sam Levenson[1]*

In a traditional Jewish wedding, the groom wears a ritual overgarment, the kittel, on his clothes. It is the same garment that he will wear to his grave. What could be a more powerful reminder of the power of intention that is woven into the vows of marriage? The marriage ceremony is a spiritually, existentially, and emotionally charged event when the past, the present, and the entirety of one's future are condensed into a single moment.

But in every marriage, the ordinariness of daily life and inevitable difficulties replace the freshness of new love. Even partners who continue for many years to find one another interesting and attractive must deal with the repetitiveness and restrictions of married and family life. This can be especially difficult to deal with in a culture such as ours that is obsessed with stimulation, competition, the new, and the improved.

So why is it that some couples so easily abandon their vows and divorce for what seem to be frivolous reasons, whereas other couples' marriages survive the most difficult challenges? Much of what we have looked at so far has focused on communication, conflict resolution, and expectations, but we now turn to a more complex issue that has a lot to do with whether or not marriages succeed or fail: commitment.

Most married couples consider commitment the glue that holds their relationship together. In this chapter we look at the different kinds of commitment and how you can deepen yours. We will try to help you see that commitment is not just something that happens. Every day, you make choices that have a big influence on the commitment and happiness of your relationship.

## Two Couples: Two Kinds of Commitment

We start out this chapter by discussing two couples whose marital commitments are very different. Pay attention to the similarities and the differences in these two marriages.

### Josh and Tamara Cohen: Feeling Trapped by Marriage

Josh and Tamara are a couple in their early forties who seem to have it all. Josh is a successful attorney. Tamara runs the household, coordinates their children's lives, and is involved as a member of the board of the Jewish day school their children attend. Their two children, an eight-year-old girl and a six-year-old boy, are doing well in school and are well liked by their classmates. But Josh and Tamara are both acutely aware of two things that are missing in their marriage: love and a sense of commitment.

Like most couples, Josh and Tamara started out very much in love. But the responsibilities of raising children, running a law practice, and dealing with the routine of daily life have taken their toll on the relationship. Neither Josh nor Tamara was emotionally or spiritually prepared to deal with the challenges of marriage. Success had always come easily for both of them, and they seemed to enter marriage with the expectation that life would always be fun. They found their mutual affection slowly eroding as they attended to everything else but one another. In a strange way, their image among their family and friends as the "perfect couple" made each of them feel guiltier about being so unhappy in their marriage. But they knew they were.

Tamara frequently thinks about leaving Josh and has considered divorce on more than a few occasions. Josh also feels unhappy with the marriage, but he hasn't considered divorce to be much of an option. He also hasn't thought of any ways to improve the marriage. He hopes for more but hasn't told Tamara this, and he believes that trying to get closer just doesn't work. When he does try to do something positive, Tamara never seems to respond in the way that he expects. He has become anxious over the thought that she might leave, but he believes that any energy put into the marriage at this point would be wasted effort. "Maybe things will get better when the kids get older," he thinks. "I've just got to stick with it and hope for the best."

Tamara and Josh both work with people they find attractive. Larry is a good-looking man who is on the school board with Tamara, and he has made it clear that he is unhappy in his own marriage and interested in Tamara. She has been seriously contemplating an affair and finds herself thinking about it more and more. Tamara is afraid that Josh will never be the kind of lifelong partner that she hoped for. She feels that she is putting a lot more into the marriage and family than Josh is and that she gets little acknowledgment from him for her time and effort. She is convinced that Josh expects all the appreciation, because he is the breadwinner for the family. That thought infuriates her. Like Josh, she is thinking that it is just not worth the effort to try harder.

The one thing they share in common is the idea that people who really love each other shouldn't feel miserable. This assumption leads them both to conclude that there must be something fundamentally wrong with their relationship.

As Tamara thinks about leaving Josh, difficult questions plague her. First, she wonders how the kids would respond to the divorce. Would it hurt them? Would Josh want custody? Would it be hard to get a divorce? Would Josh try to stop her? How much money would they lose if they went to war over the divorce? Who would get the house? Would Josh be reliable with child support? If she married again, would another man accept her children? She also worries about how her friends and community members would view her divorce. Would they blame her for not being loyal? How would she justify breaking up the "perfect" marriage?

As Tamara considers these questions, she decides that maybe the cost of getting a divorce is greater than she wants to bear. Sure, she's in pain, but she balances this against the pain and stress a divorce would bring. Feeling trapped, defeated, and depressed, she decides that staying is better than leaving, at least for now.

## Amira and Sal Gamze: A Different Commitment

Sal and Amira Gamze have been married for twenty-five years. Chilean Jews, they had moved to the United States as a young couple, refugees fleeing from the political terror of Pinochet's persecution. Although they were raised in wealthy families, they escaped to America with nothing. Working hard to learn a new language and create a new life, Amira found satisfaction and success as an editor of children's books, and Sal founded a thriving computer services company. They have three children: a seventeen-year-old boy, a fifteen-year-old boy, and a fourteen-year old girl. Even when they faced some very difficult challenges in their marriage, both Amira and Sal had few regrets about marrying one another.

Earlier in their marriage, Sal did occasionally become aware of attraction to women he met in his work. There was also a time after they moved to a new neighborhood when Amira was feeling very unhappy and restless in the marriage. However, because of their commitment to each other and their children as well as their moral beliefs about divorce, they both had independently decided not to dwell on "What if?" possibilities. They resisted thinking about splitting up, even when they were not getting along very well. And although there have been some chronic irritations in the marriage— Amira found Sal's forgetfulness very irritating, and Sal sometimes resented Amira's preoccupation with her work—each saw the benefits of their commitment as far outweighing the problems they have. Neither of them expects perfection, and both are generally appreciative of what they have in their marriage.

Earlier this year they faced the biggest challenge in their life together. Sal had gone to his doctor complaining of recurring heartburn. The doctor conducted some exams and told Sal that he had had a mild heart attack and that he would need to undergo angioplasty, take medication, make substantial changes in his eating and exercise habits, and reduce his stress. Neither Sal nor Amira was prepared for the news. There was no history of heart disease in Sal's family, and they both had enjoyed good health. His diagnosis led to a number of stressful changes. Sal had to reduce his work hours for six months, and that created some financial strain. Mostly, the anxiety about his health was hard on everyone, especially Amira and their daughter.

The challenges of working together to deal with their children and Sal's heart disease only seemed to deepen their commitment to one another. They both took a fierce pride in their loyalty to the marriage, and their family and friends and members of their synagogue rallied around them during Sal's recovery. The couple felt supported and connected to each other and to those who cared about them. Rather than shaking the foundation of their marriage, the Gamzes used the crisis they faced as an opportunity to deepen and strengthen their relationship by talking more deeply about what they wanted out of life.

————————

As you can see, these two couples have very different marriages. The Cohens, who seem to have everything, are miserable. The Gamzes, in contrast, take pride and pleasure in their marriage, even in really difficult times. Both marriages are likely to continue for the time being, which in itself reflects some kind of commitment. But it is not just the level of happiness that separates these two marriages. The Gamzes have a much different, deeper kind of commitment. To understand the difference, we need a broad model of commitment.

## WHAT IS COMMITMENT?

*Personal dedication* refers to the type of commitment that is motivated by an individual's need to maintain or improve the quality of the relationship for the joint benefit of both partners. Personal dedication is reflected in an intrinsic desire (and·associated behaviors) not only to continue in the relationship but also to improve it, sacrifice for it, invest in it, link personal goals to it, and seek the partner's welfare, not simply one's own.

In contrast, a commitment characterized by *constraint* is motivated by an individual's awareness of the negative consequences of ending a relationship. Sometimes people stay in marriages in which they are unhappy—or even abused—because of constraint commitment. For other couples, constraint commitment is perceived positively, as something that adds a level of stability to the relationship. Constraint commitment may arise from either external or internal pressures; in general, constraints make the ending of a relationship more economically, socially, personally, or psychologically costly.

Josh and Tamara Cohen have a commitment characterized by constraint. Tamara, in particular, is feeling a great deal of constraint and little dedication. She feels compelled to remain in a dissatisfying marriage by a host of constraints: children, money, family pressure, and desire to protect her image in the community. Josh also has high constraint commitment and little dedication, although he is less intensely dissatisfied with their day-to-day life.

Like Tamara and Josh, Amira and Sal Gamze have a good deal of constraint commitment, but they also have an abiding sense of dedication to one another, reflected in their sense of being a team. Any thriving marriage will produce a significant level of constraint over time. In fact, happier, more dedicated couples are just as likely to have considerable constraints as less satisfied, less dedicated couples at similar points in their lives. Happier couples simply don't think a lot about constraints, and when they do, they often draw comfort from them. Together, the forces of constraint and dedication create a glue that keeps couples together through thick and thin. This glue gives couples like the Gamzes a secure sense of connection as they make their way through the complexity and difficulties of life.

There are many other constraints that hold marriages together. Some people are frightened of change or aren't hopeful about finding another partner. Even when very unhappy with their marriage, some people still may care about the impact of divorce on their mate. Others believe for personal or religious reasons that divorce is wrong and should be avoided at all costs. Although constraints are important to marital stability, they aren't nearly as important to the ongoing quality of your marriage as your dedication. Constraint can keep you married, but only dedication leads to real happiness.

## THE COMMITMENT OF PERSONAL DEDICATION

We want to help you understand dedication by describing ingredients that are consistent with fully developed dedication in relationships.

*Desiring the long term* refers to wanting the relationship to continue into the future. Do you want to grow old with your partner?

Wanting to be with your partner in the future is a core part of dedication in our model. There is both an expectation and a desire for the relationship to have a future. As we discuss in detail in Chapter Ten, the long-term expectation that a relationship will continue plays a critical role in the day-to-day quality of that relationship.

*The priority of the relationship* refers to the importance that you give your relationship relative to everything else. When people are more dedicated to their partners and relationships, they live and behave in ways that show it. Many people are so involved in work, hobbies, or children that the relationship takes a back seat.

*"We-ness"* refers to the degree to which couples view their relationship as a team rather than as two separate individuals who focus mostly on what's best for themselves. This has been called we-ness because *we* transcends *I* in thinking about the relationship. It is crucial to have a sense of an identity together if a relationship is to grow and be satisfying. Without this sense of being a team, you and your partner are more likely to come into conflict as problems pit one of you against the other instead of the two of you against the problem.

We are not suggesting that you merge your identity with your partner's. Rather, we are saying that it is healthy to have a clear sense of yourselves as two individuals coming together to form a team and valuing the team's goals as important. What a difference this makes in how you view life!

*Satisfaction with and pride in sacrifice* is the degree to which people feel a sense of meaning and fulfillment in doing things that are largely or solely for their partner's benefit. The point is not to find pleasure in martyrdom but to give of yourself for your partner's benefit.

Satisfaction with sacrifice is one of the few dimensions in our studies in which we have found relatively large differences between men and women: women reported less satisfaction in sacrificing than did their partners. We believe that this is a result of cultural factors. It is expected that women in general and Jewish women in particular will place a higher priority on relationships and, therefore, will sacrifice more for their partners, so they get less recognition for the sacrifices they do make. When a man sacrifices, it may be more noticeable to both him and his partner because it is not as expected. Men get more recognition, and as a result they may get more pleasure from making sacrifices.

*Not looking for new partners* is another way of maintaining commitment. The more one is attracted to or attuned to other potential partners, the less personal dedication there is to the current partner. Do you find yourself *seriously* thinking about being with people other than your spouse? We must emphasize "seriously," because almost everyone is attracted to other people from time to time. Dedication is in jeopardy if this attraction to others has become intense, especially if you have a particular person in mind. One study showed that people who are highly dedicated actually tend to mentally devalue attractive potential partners.[2]

Are you seriously thinking about being with someone else? If your relationship is about to end or if your partner is leaving you, it would be perfectly logical for you to wonder "What if?" If you are planning on keeping your marriage strong, maintain your focus on tending your own lawn rather than yearning for the grass on the other side of the fence.

## HOW DOES COMMITMENT DEVELOP?

Dedication in relationships is believed to develop mainly from the couple's initial attraction and satisfaction. Think back on the beginning of your relationship. Because you liked being together, you began to be more dedicated to staying together. As your dedication became more apparent, you may have noticed that you became more relaxed about the relationship. In most relationships, there is an awkward period during which the desire to be together is great, but the commitment is unclear. The lack of clarity produces anxiety about whether or not you will stay together. As your mutual dedication becomes clear, it seems safer to invest in the relationship.

Because of your dedication, you did things that increased constraint. Essentially, *today's dedication becomes tomorrow's constraint*. For example, as dedication grows, a couple will decide to move from a dating relationship to an engaged relationship. As dedication grows further, they decide to become married, then perhaps to have children. Each of these steps, taken as a result of dedication, adds to the constraint. You may have taken some of these steps in your relationship.

It is natural for levels of constraint to grow in marriage, and constraints can help stabilize you during rough times. Ultimately, though, a high sense of dedication tends to lead to higher satisfaction with marriage. The relationship between satisfaction and dedication is reciprocal. Greater dedication will usually lead to greater satisfaction, and dedication grows out of satisfaction in the first place. Also, when people are truly dedicated, they are more likely to behave in ways that protect their marriage and please their partner, so the effect on satisfaction is positive. It is very nice to see that your partner really cares about you and protects the relationship from all the other alternatives in life.

## HOW DOES DEDICATION DIE?

Studies show that most couples have high levels of dedication early on, when they are engaged or early in their marriage. What happens to kill this dedication for some couples over time? For one thing, if couples don't handle conflict well, their satisfaction with the marriage will go down steadily. Because satisfaction partly fuels the dedication, the dedication begins to erode along with the satisfaction. With dedication in jeopardy, the desire to give to one another is eroded further, and satisfaction is likely to decline rapidly.

But that isn't the whole story. Dedication isn't just about happiness. It is also related to personal choices, values, and confidence. Some people may find it easier than others to sustain the kind of commitment reflected in the dimensions of dedication we discussed earlier. Perhaps even more important, we think that dedication erodes when people begin to feel that their effort doesn't make any difference. This is another way in which poorly handled conflict kills a marriage. The partners begin to believe that no amount of dedication matters, and it gets hard to keep trying. When this happens, they are well on the road to a high-constraint, low-dedication, low-satisfaction marriage—if not divorce. That isn't where most of us want to be.

The secret to satisfying commitment is to maintain not just constraint but high levels of dedication. Although constraint commitment can add a positive, stabilizing dimension to your marriage, it can't give you a great relationship. Dedication, in contrast, is the side of commitment that is associated with healthy, satisfying, and growing relationships. In fact, dedicated couples report not only more satisfaction with their relationships but also less conflict about their problems and greater levels of self-disclosure. Are you just existing in your relationship, or are you making it what you hoped it would be?

How to make your marriage a high priority is your choice. It is your choice to sacrifice more at times for your partner. It is your choice how to protect your relationship from attractive alternatives. It is also your choice how long you wait before you share your concerns and how you express them. Fundamentally, these are matters of the will. We recognize that in some relationships, increasing your dedication to your partner will not make much appreciable difference. Nevertheless, far more often, your partner will respond very positively—and in kind—to evidence of your dedication.

In the next chapter, we discuss important implications of commitment and show what you can do to build a stronger marriage. But before we move on, we want to give you the opportunity to assess your commitment to your relationship.

## THE IMPORTANCE OF A LONG-TERM VIEW

*All the things in our lives, all the complicated structures we spend so much time and energy creating, are*

> *built on sand. Only our relationships to other people*
> *endure. Sooner or later, the wave will come along*
> *and knock down what we have worked so hard to*
> *build up. When that happens, only the person who*
> *has somebody's hand to hold will be able to laugh.*
>                                  Rabbi Harold Kushner[3]

When people are committed, they have a long-term outlook on their relationship. In a healthy relationship, dedication and constraint combine to produce a sense of permanence. This is crucial for one simple reason: *no relationship is consistently satisfying.* What gets couples through tougher times is the long-term view that commitment brings. They have the expectation that the relationship will make it through stormy seas.

We want to be very clear about one thing before we go on: sometimes it is wise to bring a relationship to an end. We are not saying that everybody should always make a Herculean effort to save a relationship, no matter how abusive or destructive it is. However, for the great number of couples who genuinely love each other and want to make their marriage work, a long-term perspective is essential for encouraging each partner to take risks, disclose his or her inner self, and trust that the other person will be there when it really counts.

In the absence of a long-term view, people are prone to focus on the immediate payoff. This is only natural. If the long-term benefit is uncertain, people naturally concentrate on what they are getting in the present. Essentially, the short-term view says, "Give it to me now and give it to me quick. There's no certainty in any future here."

The hidden issue of commitment, which we discussed in Chapter Seven, is easily triggered when the future of the relationship is uncertain. When the commitment is unclear, there is pressure to perform, rather than acceptance—a core issue for everyone. One partner may subtly convey to the other, "You'd better produce, or I'll look for someone who can." Most of us resent feeling we could be abandoned by the person from whom we most expect to find security and acceptance. Not surprisingly, people usually won't invest in a relationship with an uncertain future and rewards. If you believe that your effort won't pay off now and you have no hope for the future, why invest at all?

The Gamzes' long-term view allows each of them to give the other some "slack," leading to greater acceptance of each other's weaknesses and failings over time. The depth of their commitment also makes them more likely to pay more attention to opportunities to appreciate small things about one another. Whereas the Cohens experience anxiety or resentment over the core issue of acceptance, the Gamzes feel the warmth of a secure commitment, in which each conveys the powerful message "I will be here for you." That's the essence of commitment.

# SELFISHNESS

*A young child once asked a rabbi why man was created with two eyes instead of one, like the nose and the mouth.*

*"With the left eye, you should look at yourself, to see how you can improve yourself. And with the right eye, you should look at others lovingly, always seeking out their best qualities."*

Simon Jacobson[4]

Rather than following the rabbi's advice, we too often use our left eye to look inside ourselves and ask "What do I want?" and our right eye to find fault with what our partner is giving or not giving us. Our culture encourages devotion to the self. Notions of sacrifice, teamwork, and placing a high priority on the partner and on a dedicated relationship have not enjoyed much positive press lately. In fact, our society seems to glorify the individual and vilify whatever gets in the way. We all pay for these attitudes.

In contrast, we suggest that dedication is fundamental to healthy relationships and that selfishness is fundamentally destructive. Self-ishness may sell, but it doesn't help create lifelong happy unions. Do you want to get your way all the time or have a great relationship?

Selfish attitudes and behavior can and will kill a relationship. Such attitudes aren't compatible with dedication. Dedication reflects we-ness and, at times, sacrifices; in contrast, our culture asserts individual rights and the need to protect ourselves from all insult and criticism. But in our view, you can't have a great marriage when each partner is primarily focused on what is best for himself or herself. In a culture that reinforces the self, it is hard to ask, "What can I do to make this better for both of us?" It is a lot easier to ask, "What should my partner do to make me happier?"

We are *not* advocating martyrdom. In the way the term is commonly used, a martyr does things for you not out of concern for what is best for you but to put you in debt. Martyrdom is not dedication; it is usually insecurity and selfishness masquerading as doing good.

A successful relationship is based not only on what you do for your partner but also on how you do it. Do you do things with an attitude that says, "You'd better appreciate what I'm doing"? Do you often feel that your partner owes you? There's nothing wrong with doing positive things and wanting to be appreciated, but there is something wrong with believing that you are owed, as if your positive behavior is building up a debt for your partner.

## CODEPENDENCY OR COMMITMENT?

Every culture's notions of sickness and health are rooted in its values. American culture is the most individualistic that has ever existed. It should come as no surprise, then, that many American mental health professionals are vigilant in their search for signs of the dreaded disease of overdependence, but seem far less concerned about the emotional isolation of the individual. Separation and individuation are important, but so, too, is connection. In the manual of official psychiatric diagnoses, there are descriptions of "diseases" of dependence, but none that really address the inability to love.

We sometimes forget how much the American sense of individualism—each person for himself or herself—stands in contrast to traditional Jewish ideals. In this century we moved from being part of an interdependent, interconnected people—a group for which individual, marriage, and community were inextricably intertwined—to being part of the mainstream of a culture that worships the individual. Fritz Perls, a German Jewish psychiatrist and developer of Gestalt therapy, celebrated this lonely American dream.

> I do my thing, and you do your thing.
> I am not in this world to live up to your expectations
> And you are not in this world to live up to mine.
> You are you and I am I,
> And if by chance we find each other, it's beautiful.
> If not, it can't be helped.[5]

We define codependency as behavior that keeps another dependent on you, in the guise of helping or supporting that person. Such behavior often reflects the need to be a caretaker—and in control of the other person. It may look like dedication, but it isn't. In fact, it is destructive to both people involved.

The problem in our culture is that people have been labeled codependent for giving of themselves in truly constructive ways. When being giving is labeled as codependency, it is difficult to feel good about being emotionally generous. Unfortunately, the elevation of individual happiness over long-term shared goals undermines the ability to make sacrifices that are crucial to successful marriage.

Sure, you *can* give too much in ways that harm the relationship and yourself. Does it really show dedication to tolerate a spouse's impossible demands or temper tantrums? No. This is not dedication. Does it show dedication not to confront a partner's alcoholism? No. It shows far more dedication to constructively confront the behavior that threatens to destroy you, your partner, or the marriage. Having acknowledged the dangers of codependency, we still suggest that too many people are too self-centered too much of the time to be able to create the kind of relationship they deeply desire.

## HOW CAN YOU INCREASE COMMITMENT?

*I was always obsessed with women who had beautiful bodies. I have never married, but I've been involved in four relationships, each of which lasted about two or three years. Each time I had initiated the breakup, and each time I silently focused on some physical imperfection that bothered me. I was not proud of this, but figured I should go for what I wanted.*

*I have a friend who I envied for having a wife who was so incredibly beautiful. I would think that if I had someone who looked like that, I would finally be happy. When my friend's wife was diagnosed with breast cancer last year, I watched how tenderly he took care of her. She struggled long and hard with her treatment. She had a mastectomy, lost her hair during chemotherapy, and looked drawn and exhausted. I was really surprised that I found myself envying him for something that I had never really considered before—his capacity for love.*

> Bob, forty, a member of a therapy group
> for Jewish men and women

Yes, you can develop the ability to love more completely and deepen the commitment in your marriage. If you are a volatile person, you can *choose* to learn how to restrain your emotions more effectively. If you find it difficult to make your needs known, you can learn to be more expressive. Your choices are crucial to the kind of commitment you develop in your relationship.

One couple, Liz and Lloyd, told us how they reinvigorated their marriage at the seven-year point. They had been so busy building a home and family that they both were feeling distant in their relationship. Their long-term view was still intact, but they had lost something they had had at first. They went along this way, thinking that feeling distant was the price of being responsible parents and professionals, until the evening Liz got a phone call from a distraught friend, Evelyn. She told Liz that she and her husband, Alan, had just separated and were getting a divorce.

Liz and Lloyd were in shock. They knew Evelyn and Alan well, and they were particularly disturbed by the fact that they had never suspected that the couple's marriage was at risk. In the weeks that followed, as they learned more about the reasons for the divorce, they became more upset, not only because they felt for their friends but also because they realized how much they had in common with them. There had been no affair, no violent arguments, no betrayals. Alan and Evelyn had just decided that they didn't love one another any more.

Liz and Lloyd decided to discuss their reactions to their friends' separation, and, even though it had been difficult to decide to talk about it, each of them felt relieved to hear the other's concerns. They risked by sharing about their own sense of emotional estrangement from one another—an act that in itself is evidence of dedication:

LIZ:  (catching Lloyd after dinner one night, while the kids played outside) You know, I've been thinking.

LLOYD:  What about?

LIZ:  About how our marriage might be at risk too, like Evelyn and Alan's, if we don't put enough into it. It really struck me one night when Evelyn said to me that she and Alan "had put everything into their kids and nothing into their marriage." I'm scared. Let's give us more time and energy.

LLOYD:  I see that, too. It's like we put so much time into the house, the kids, and work that there really hasn't been a lot left for us.

LIZ: It's been painful for me when I take the time to think about it. I never thought I could feel so separate from you.

LLOYD: *(moving closer, looking at Liz)* It's really been worrying you, hasn't it?

LIZ: Yeah. This isn't the way it was supposed to go for us.

LLOYD: I know what you mean. I had sort of grown used to feeling separate, but when I see a couple being affectionate in public like we used to be, it hurts.

LIZ: I'm glad to hear you say that. I was afraid that you hadn't noticed.

LLOYD: *(putting his arms around her)* I have. I'm glad you brought it up. We have too much going for us to let the distance grow any further. Let's sit down and talk about what we can do about it.

LIZ: I'll get some tea.

This talk ignited a positive chain reaction in their marriage. Lloyd and Liz renewed their dedication to one another in several ways. They made time together a greater priority and followed through. Each of them began to look for ways to do more special things for the other. They doubled up on their efforts to handle conflicts and disagreements with respect. They also talked more openly about plans for the future, developing a greater sense of the long term and of being a team again. Essentially, they each decided to work on strengthening their dedication. It's not so hard when you both really want to do it.

To repeat, *it is your choice*. You can't make your partner do anything. But, assuming that you both want to make your marriage work for the long haul, you will be most successful by reflecting on how *you* can boost or maintain your dedication. As with Liz and Lloyd, the bottom line was action. If your dedication is strong, keep it that way—and act on it.

Instead of asking, "What have you done for me lately?" ask yourself what you are doing to improve and strengthen your relationship. Too many people in unhappy marriages nurse their pain and refuse to be the first one to reach out. But you have the greatest control over your own dedication and behavior, not your partner's. In most relationships, positive behavior is reciprocated, so do your best to encourage your partner to be more positive by taking the risk of being more loving yourself. *It is your choice!*

# EXERCISES

On the basis of what you have read so far, you should have some idea of your levels of dedication and constraint. The following exercises will help you refine your impressions.

In our research, we ask couples a large number of questions to help us assess their commitment. You can get a good idea of the quality of your commitment by answering the questions that follow. We suggest that you keep your answers to these first two assessment exercises to yourself. These are best done individually, for your own reflection. Only in the last exercise are you asked to compare notes.

## Assessing Constraint Commitment

Answer each item by assigning a point value between one and seven to indicate how true the statement seems to you. Use the following scale for your answers: 1 = Strongly disagree, 4 = Neither agree nor disagree, and 7 = Strongly agree.

1. The steps I would need to take to end this relationship would require a great deal of time and effort.
2. A marriage is a sacred bond between two people that should not be broken.
3. I would have trouble finding a suitable partner if this relationship ended.
4. My friends or family really want this relationship to work.
5. I would lose valuable possessions if I left my partner.
6. My partner would be emotionally devastated if I left, so even if I wanted to leave I might not.

7. I couldn't make it financially if we broke up or divorced.

8. My lifestyle would be worse in many ways if I left my partner.

9. I feel trapped in this relationship.

10. It is important to finish what you have started, no matter what.

Your answers to these few questions can tell you a lot. We can't give you an average score on these items because we don't use them in quite that way in our research. But it is obvious that the higher the score, the greater the level of constraint. In any case, we want you to use your responses for reflection. Are you aware of constraints? How great do they seem to be? What kind of constraint seems the greatest?

Most important, do you feel trapped? Almost everyone does from time to time, and this is normal. You might be more concerned if you frequently feel trapped. Having a good deal of constraint but not feeling trapped is normal in a healthy marriage. The best marriages have two partners who are both dedicated to one another and who feel comfortable with the stability implied by constraint.

## Assessing Dedication Commitment

The following items will help you gauge your level of dedication. Use the same seven-point scale for your answers: 1 = Strongly disagree, 4 = Neither agree nor disagree, and 7 = Strongly agree.

1. My relationship with my partner is more important to me than almost anything else in my life.

2. I want this relationship to stay strong no matter what rough times we may encounter.

3. It makes me feel good to sacrifice for my partner.

4. I like to think of myself and my partner more in terms of "us" and "we" than of "me" and "him [or her]."

5. I am not seriously attracted to anyone other than my partner.

6. My relationship with my partner is clearly part of my future life plans.

7. When push comes to shove, my relationship with my partner comes first.

8. I tend to think about how things affect us a couple more than how things affect me as an individual.

9. I do not often find myself thinking about what it would be like to be in a relationship with someone else.

10. I want to grow old with my partner.

We can give you an idea of what your score means on these dedication items. To obtain your score, simply add up the numbers. In our research—with a sample of people who were mostly happy and dedicated in their relationships (including everyone from those who had been dating for a few months to those married for over thirty years), the average person scores about 58 on the items on this scale. If you scored at or above 58, we would bet you are pretty highly dedicated in your relationship. By contrast, your dedication may be quite low if you scored below 45. However you scored, consider what it may mean for the future of your relationship.

## Exploring the Power to Choose Commitment

Reflect on the questions that follow. We recommend that you think about your answers individually, then meet and talk about your reflections. You will notice that we ask you to focus more on your own behavior and perspectives than about your partner's. What is your point of view, and what are you doing in this relationship?

1. What is your outlook about your relationship? Do you have a long-term view? Why or why not? If you have a long-term view, are you comforted by it, or do you feel trapped?

2. To what degree do you engage in scorekeeping? Do you notice the positive efforts your partner makes for you and

the relationship? Can you try to notice the positive efforts more? Do you think that some things are unfair and feel the need to confront your partner about them? Will you do that constructively?

3. Does your basic orientation in your marriage reflect more self-ishness or more team-centered sensitivity? What kinds of things do you do that express selfishness? What things do you do that demonstrate a desire to meet your partner's needs?

4. Think about the priorities in your life (for example, work, your partner, children, hobby, extended family, religion, education, travel, pets, television, sports). List your five biggest priorities in order of their importance to you. Now list what you think are your partner's priorities. Do you think that your relationship would benefit if you changed any of your priorities?

5. Has the dedication between the two of you eroded to dangerously low levels? If it has, what do you want to do about this?

6. If your relationship is going well, what do you think is the most important factor in keeping it that way?

Now schedule some time to talk. These talks should be handled carefully. We suggest that you use the Speaker-Listener Technique to share some of your most important impressions. Take this as an opportunity to come together, rather than as an excuse to get defensive and angry. Talk openly about where you want to go and how you are going to get there.

# 10

# The Importance of Core Belief Systems
## Judaism, Intermarriage, and Community

JED: *If only we lived alone on an island, we would
be so much happier.*
MARY: *Maybe, but we might be a lot lonelier too.*
    *Jed and Mary, a Jewish man and a Christian woman*
                *in an interfaith couples group*

Over the years, we have heard many different versions of the
sentiment expressed by Jed and Mary. Islands seem especially
attractive when couples are struggling with differences about religion, community, and family. The intensity of new love often conceals differences; time reveals them. The mythic island provides
relief from the pressures of having to make difficult decisions about
what is really important in life. Whether or not two partners in an
intimate relationship are from similar religious backgrounds, differences in what we call core values eventually emerge. No two people are identical.

In this chapter, we focus primarily on how religious and spiritual issues tend to affect the overall quality of relationships.
Although we have been looking at issues that are relevant to all intimate relationships—communication, conflict, and commitment—
we have also been exploring how being Jewish can affect couples.
No matter how religious you consider yourself, and whether or not
you are in an interfaith marriage or a marriage in which one or both

partners have converted to Judaism, there are important issues in this chapter that have relevance for your relationship.

What is meaningful about being Jewish for you? How should Judaism be practiced? If you were raised as a Christian, what does Christianity mean to you now? If you are a Jew-by-choice, how has the process of conversion changed your ideas about spirituality? What do you mean when you talk about the importance of community? What religious and spiritual values do you want to pass on to your children?

Your core values affect many aspects of your life, but they have one thing in common: they often don't lend themselves to simple right and wrong answers when you and your partner disagree about them. You may be perfectly clear about your personal answers to these questions, and your partner may be equally certain about answers that are different than your own. What's important from our perspective is *how* you communicate your beliefs and *how* you work out your differences with your partner.

If you aren't very interested in Judaism or another religion, you may be skeptical about the relevance of what we have to say. Or if you are very observant, you might see this chapter as watered down or too secular. Wherever you stand, we still invite you to explore the effect these dimensions can have on relationships. We want to show how you and your partner can participate in intimacy-enhancing discussions about these core issues.

We start with a focus on religion and look at how differences in your religious orientation can affect your relationship. We also explore the implications of interfaith marriages and of religious conversion. Most important, we help you understand the nature of your differences and how to deal with them. This can be an important process for you whether you consider yourself a Conservative, Orthodox, Reform, Renewal, agnostic, or atheist Jew. It is also relevant for you if you are Christian, from some other religious background, or a Jew-by-choice.

Religious participation affects many aspects of a relationship. Among other things, in religion, people find codes and rituals that guide them in life. Hence, for many people, their religious faith embodies central, core beliefs about the meaning of life and how it should be lived. Furthermore, for many people, issues of the spirit are considered primarily from within the religious domain, whereas others hold views of spirituality quite apart from any particular religious tradition. And as we have seen for Jews, a strong sense of Jewish identity can shape values and behavior even in the absence of formal religious observance.

Most of the research we describe is based on religious beliefs and practices rather than on spirituality. That is because you can't conduct research on things you can't measure, and although it isn't hard to measure religious activity or even core beliefs, it is extremely difficult to measure spirituality. We are not saying that spirituality isn't important; it is just that most of the research is on religious behavior.

# THE IMPACT OF RELIGION ON MARRIAGE

The impact of religion on marriage has been studied for years, because many religions codify core beliefs, values, and practices that promote stability and health in relationships. Most of this research has been conducted with those involved in traditional religious systems, particularly within the Judeo-Christian spectrum. Our goal here is to decode these findings and highlight key implications for all couples, whether they are religious or not.

Numerous studies suggest that religion has a favorable impact on marriage. These were not studies that focused on one religion, but we believe their findings may be relevant for all marriages. Couples who are more religious seem to be a bit more satisfied in their marriages. They are also less likely to divorce. In one of our studies, married subjects who rated themselves as more religious showed somewhat higher levels of satisfaction, lower levels of conflict about common issues, and higher levels of commitment.

Those who were more religious were also more likely to say that divorce is morally wrong, especially those who are more observant.

They also were more likely to believe that if they had problems, they would encounter significant social pressure to stay together and make their marriage work. And they were more likely to report being satisfied with sacrificing for one another and having a stronger sense of an identity as a team. These findings make sense, given the values that are emphasized by traditional religious groups.

A major survey of women from all religious groups by Tavris and Sadd (1975) found that more religious women reported greater sexual contentment in terms of both orgasmic frequency and openness of communication about sex with their husbands compared to non-religious women. These same women also reported greater overall marital satisfaction.

More recent research suggests that the greatest benefit of religious involvement is for couples who are involved in it together. It's not that more religious couples always have substantially better marriages or better sex. The effects we are talking about are consistent and statistically significant, but the differences are also often rather small. It would be accurate to say that something about the factors associated with religious involvement gives religious couples an edge in keeping marriages strong. Before we look at this in more detail, let's consider research on a topic of major relevance for an increasing number of couples: interfaith marriages.

## INTERFAITH MARRIAGES

The once unimaginable has become commonplace: in the United States, intermarriage among Jews now exceeds marriages between Jews. Usually forbidden by the church or the nations of the Diaspora and strongly condemned by Jews as well, intermarriage throughout most of Jewish history was very rare. Even with the freedom and openness of America, the intermarriage rate was only about 10 percent or lower just forty years ago.

The rate of intermarriage today varies considerably from city to city, but overall, approximately 50 percent of all marriages taking place today involving a Jew are intermarriages. The rates in the western United States tend to be higher than in large urban centers in the East. But even though intermarriage is no longer unusual or stigmatized as it had been, couples who bring together different religious, cultural, ethnic, or racial backgrounds face special challenges.

There are a number of factors that explain the dramatic increases in Jewish intermarriage. One is that religion probably has less of an overall impact in our culture than it used to have, so people are less likely to take it into account when picking a mate. Also, with our society becoming more and more mobile, connections with religious communities become harder to maintain, and intermarriage and divorce become more likely. In contrast, people who grow up with more religious education are more likely to marry within their faith. Finding someone who matches your faith probably becomes a higher priority when you are strongly grounded in it.

## When the Honeymoon Is Over

Whatever the reasons for intermarriage, research consistently shows that partners from different religions are more likely to divorce. Although no nationally representative studies have looked at this subject, various studies suggest that an increased risk exists for interfaith marriages. It seems likely that these effects would be related to the degree of commitment individuals have to their faith. When people of different backgrounds marry and have little allegiance to those backgrounds, we would assume that the risks for divorce are lower.

Many interfaith marriages start out just fine, with couples thinking that they can beat the odds and that love will conquer all. Although love can conquer a lot (especially if it is translated into loving and respectful behavior), the more there is to conquer, the greater the risk of failure. As is true of all couples, the way interfaith couples handle differences in their relationships is the most critical factor that predicts how they will get along in the future.

There are two key reasons why early optimism in an interfaith marriage may give way to problems later on. First, people tend to get more religious or spiritually inclined as they age, perhaps because death gets closer. Also, the challenges of life can change our perspective on religious or spiritual issues, so that what looks unimportant early in life can become more of an issue with age.

The issue of children, however, seems to stir up the strongest feelings about different faiths in a marriage. For many people, a child is their ultimate legacy. At our core, we are concerned with passing on more than our genes; we want our spirit and our values to live on in our children.

The need to define the spiritual and group identity of children seems to be almost a primal urge, an impulse that is often not very clear to interfaith couples before their first child's birth. And although the initial conflict about the identity of children is often fought out around the rituals surrounding their birth, this is just the beginning. Children are natural theologians, even if we are not. They want answers to questions about our core values and our view of the nature of reality, about God, death, and the meaning of life. Easy questions!

Often, early in a relationship, interfaith couples honestly believe that these kinds of issues will not be very important. Sometimes they are surprised when issues that seemed so insignificant suddenly become important enough to threaten the foundation of a relationship. What new love conceals, time reveals.

## Coping with the December Dilemma

Janet and Ken are an interfaith couple, but they have made their marriage work. They have two boys, who are now seven and ten years old. Janet was raised as a Reform Jew, and Ken grew up as an Episcopalian. Both had some commitment to their faiths, so it wasn't easy to work through the issues. The key for them was making their expectations very clear and using a lot of skill in dealing with the issues.

Most of the time, they didn't find their religious differences very difficult to deal with. They felt the most tension around the December Dilemma—the time when Christmas and Hanukkah seemed in competition for the hearts and souls of their children.

KEN: It's really hard for me to think about not being able to share Christmas with my children. My family wasn't that close, and Christmas was the one time in the year when I really felt like we were really connected.

JANET: We celebrated Hanukkah with the whole mishpocha— my aunts, uncles, cousins, and grandparents. It was always a lot of fun. I really liked the potato latkes. But our family was really close, and we got together at least once a month, so this definitely wasn't the only time we felt close as an extended family.

KEN: I remember asking my dad what Hanukkah was, because there were a few Jewish kids at my school, and he told me it was the Jewish Christmas.

JANET: I knew what Christmas was—it was the enemy. My father always acted like we were under siege in December. Like he had to protect us from feeling like we were missing out on something. I remember him going on and on about it being a pagan celebration of stuff. My father would take us home from my grandparents using a longer route so that we didn't have to go through a neighborhood that was famous for its Christmas decorations.

KEN: It was also the one time in the year when I felt a spiritual connection. We would go to Midnight Mass, and I always felt inspired.

JANET: To me, celebrating the miracle of the oil lasting eight days gave me a sense of pride—like no one could force us to give up being Jews.

Ken and Janet were an articulate and basically happy couple. They dealt well with their differences, even when the issues were difficult. Part of what they found helpful, as you can see from their conversation, was their ability to acknowledge just how different the two holidays were for them. They were able to acknowledge the very different meanings attached to being a Christian and being a Jew. Unlike many couples, they didn't try to hide from the contrasts in their experiences. In particular, they were able to separate three different aspects of how they reacted to the holidays.

1. *Family meaning: the significance of the holiday in terms of what it meant to their particular family.* For Ken, part of the importance of Christmas was the sense of connection that he felt was missing in his family throughout most of the year. Janet's family was very close, and although she enjoyed the Hanukkah celebration, it certainly wasn't the one time during the year when she felt connected.

2. *Sense of belonging: the meaning of the holiday in terms of feeling connected through a sense of peoplehood.* For Janet, it was clear that there were positive and negative aspects of this. She had pride in the Jewish determination to maintain their faith, but also felt her father's tension and resentment about Christmas. Ken had not grown up with any sense that Hanukkah represented any kind of threat. Also, Christmas for Ken did not evoke any sense of peoplehood about being a Protestant.

3. *Religious meaning: the religious significance of the holiday.* For Ken, Christmas was the one holiday where he got a sense of a spiritual experience. Janet did not really experience Hanukkah as a religious holiday, and saw Christmas mostly through her father's eyes, as a materialistic orgy.

Ken and Janet's ability to express and understand the real differences in their experiences and feelings about the holidays didn't always make it easy for the couple to deal with them. They always approached December as a kind of complicated question with many answers. Over the years, they had tried dealing with December in a number of different ways, including celebrating both Christmas and Hanukkah and then alternating the two celebrations on different years. One year, they decided to go on a vacation to a beach house in Hawaii, and celebrated the season by going to a big luau to avoid having to make any decisions. But they always talked about their differences with respect, humor, and a deep commitment to making their marriage work.

## Making It Work

As Ken and Janet's marriage demonstrates, couples can make mixed-faith marriages work. They saw being an interfaith couple as a more complex project than a same-faith marriage, and felt that it was their job to do the extra work that it required. They never pretended that being Christian and being Jewish were just two different flavors of religion, and they didn't blur the distinctions by talking about Judeo-Christian commonalties. They understood and respected the deeper differences between them about what it meant to be a Jew and to be a Christian.

For most interfaith couples, their success in working things out depends a lot on how committed each partner is to his or her own religious traditions as well as the couple's skill at dealing with their differences. If one or both partners in an interfaith marriage are not strongly religiously committed and if they don't become more committed later as a result of changes in their life, such differences in background will have much less potential to produce friction and conflict.

We are not suggesting that you sweep religious differences under the rug for the sake of the marriage, a process that Paul and Rachel Cowan described as spiritual gridlock.[1] Although compromise can sometimes work, ignoring strong feelings usually doesn't, at least in the long run. What is important is that you face your differences openly and honestly.

# CONVERSION

*Wherever you lodge, I will lodge. Your people shall be my people, and your God, my God.*

*Ruth 1:16*

Conversion has been an integral part of Jewish history. The biblical Ruth, in her eloquent pledge to her mother-in law, Naomi, makes clear through her words that she is choosing to become part of the Jewish people as well as accepting the Hebrew God. Ruth's importance to Jewish history is seen in her lineage—her descendant is the great King David. Ruth's words are used to this day in conversion ceremonies.

In the book *The Jewish Family and Jewish Continuity*, Sylvia Fishman reported that in recent years, as the rate of intermarriage has increased, the rate of conversion has been decreasing. Intermarriage is 500 percent higher among Jews eighteen to thirty-four years of age than for Jews over fifty-five years old. In the 1970s, almost one-third of the partners who were raised as Christians converted to Judaism when they married a Jew. In the 1980s, that number decreased to 13 percent.[2] Research shows that conversion of one partner to the religion of the other increases marital stability.[3]

It is important to stress that conversion is a complex emotional and spiritual process. It changes not only a person's religious identity but also his or her relationship to spouse, family of origin, and community. In order for it to be meaningful, conversion requires study, introspection, and sacrifice. Going through the motions of conversion to quiet in-laws' concerns or a partner's guilt can hurt a relationship more than it helps.

One man, Ed, studied earnestly with a conservative rabbi for over a year in order to prepare to convert. When the day came to complete the process, the rabbi asked him to say the words, "I am a Jew." Ed was shocked more than the rabbi or anyone else when he found himself unable to say the words. He had been intellectually prepared, but he still doubted his ability to truly feel and be Jewish.

Fortunately, the rabbi and Ed's wife were very supportive and understanding. He spent another six months studying, talking with the rabbi, and attending services before he felt that he was ready. The next time, he had no difficulty going through the ritual that led to his adopting Judaism. The rabbi remarked that he wished more born Jews took Judaism and being a Jew as seriously as Ed did.

## Dealing with Jewish Ambivalence About Converts

*I go to services once a year, on the High Holidays.*
*This year when I went, I really had a hard time with*
*feeling comfortable. I looked to the left, and there was*
*an Asian woman, and to the right, there was a black*
*man. It's not that I'm racist or anything, but when I*
*go to temple, I just want to be around other Jews.*

Debra, a thirty-six-year-old Jewish woman

Debra never considered the possibility that the Asian woman or the African American man might actually be Jewish and might even be far more involved in Jewish life than she was. Debra's statement, while disturbing to those who take Judaism seriously, is not surprising. As we saw in Chapter One, many Jews define their identity ethnically rather than religiously, and they tend to have a hard time feeling comfortable with others embracing a Judaism that seems somehow alien to them. For Jews-by-choice married to born Jews, dealing with the discomfort and sometimes the hostility of some Jews can be difficult. It's important for the born-Jew married to a Jew-by-choice to listen carefully when their mate describes unpleasant situations. Although some people may be overly sensitive and see rejection when there is none, it's a fact of life that people who have converted are sometimes not accepted as real Jews. This is a stress that can be minimized when couples deal with this as an unpleasant reality.

One Jew-by-choice, Elizabeth, told a story about an acquaintance, who, upon finding out that Elizabeth was Jewish, remarked, "That's funny, you don't look Jewish." Elizabeth responded by saying, "Well, isn't it funny how Jews look these days?" She went on to describe herself as a WASJ, a white Anglo-Saxon Jew. She explained that she had no interest in concealing her cultural background as a

Mayflower descendant, of which she was very proud. For her, being a Jew was a choice, not an accident of birth.

Sometimes the discomfort about the process of conversion is a lot closer to home. Many people who have gone through the process of conversion have talked about the difficulties that their partners have experienced as a result of their decision to become Jewish. One woman, Anne, talked about her experience with her Jewish husband, Al: "Sometimes I think that my conversion was more difficult for Al than it was for me. He had always told me that being Jewish was important to him, but he never did much to define his Jewishness. Now I'm becoming Jewish in the only way I feel I can—through studying Judaism. I don't think he had any idea of how much my decision to convert challenged his own ambivalence about being a Jew himself."

Another man, Jorge, actually had a complete circumcision before converting prior to his marriage to Stacey. He had been raised as a devout Catholic, and he approached becoming Jewish with the same commitment to religion he had always had.

> I did take becoming Jewish very seriously, but it hasn't been easy. You don't get circumcised when you're twenty-five unless you are serious, believe me. Even though Stacey said that it was very important to her for me to convert, sometimes I think she just wanted to be able to say to her parents and to her community that I was Jewish, but didn't want to bother with the implications.
>
> We've been married for eighteen years now, but we got into an argument about our daughter going out with a Christian boy. Stacey said that it was fine with her. It wasn't with me. Being a Jew is important, and I didn't convert so that my kids could intermarry.

The best way to approach conversion is as a couple. It is clear that the process of conversion catalyzes a process of change for all who are involved—not just the partner who is converting.

# STABILIZING INFLUENCES

We believe that it is clear, both from research on marriage and from our clinical experience, that resolving your religious differences is important for the success of your marriage. Couples who are able to agree about the role of religion in their marriage are more likely to benefit from two key factors: (1) the value of social support for their relationship and (2) the effect of having a shared worldview. We focus on these two factors because we believe that whether or not you share religious beliefs, strong social supports and a similar worldview are very important to the success of relationships.

## Social Support

No matter what else they may do, religious and spiritual beliefs bring groups of similarly minded people together. There is a clear benefit for most people in being part of a social group—religious or not—as long as they have a clear sense that they belong or fit into the group. In fact, research by our colleague Ken Pargament has found that church and synagogue members who fit well into their religious community have higher levels of mental health than those who don't.[4]

Studies have consistently shown that people who are more isolated are at greater risk for emotional problems such as depression and suicide, health problems, and poverty. Many studies in the field of stress management demonstrate how much more vulnerable you are if you have significant stressors but no social support system to help you. It is just not healthy for most humans to be isolated.

Religious involvement brings ready-made social structures. Religions specify codes of behavior and rituals, many of which create natural points of connection between those involved. For example, most religious and spiritual groups meet regularly for numerous activities. Spiritual activities include worship, prayer, reading, study, and discussion groups. Social activities can include picnics, group outings, get-together dinners, softball leagues, and about anything else you can think of. Service activities are also common, including food drives, visits to shut-ins, service to disadvantaged groups, community outreach services, volunteer work, and support groups. Social links to a community are important for couples, no matter how those links are created.

Of course, there are other ways for people to get together in our culture, such as neighborhood get-togethers, political groups, interest groups, sports events, support groups, and clubs. Our key point is that it is important for all couples to have a strong support system for their relationships. Are you socially connected to a group that supports and somehow helps your relationship? If not, do you want to be? These are important questions for you and your partner to address directly.

## A Shared Worldview

When you consider the spiritual or religious realm, you are dealing with core beliefs about your worldview—in other words, how you make sense of life. Everyone has some explanation for the big questions, whether it is simple or complex, religious or not. Hence, everyone has some core belief system. When you, as a couple, share such a belief system, you have a shared worldview.

Fran Dickson, a communication expert at the University of Denver, has shown in her studies that couples who have stayed together for fifty years have a shared vision that includes personal dreams and goals for the future. A shared belief system—including mutual understanding about the meaning of life, death, and marriage—makes it easier to develop a vision of life. In turn, a shared belief system supports the long-term view of commitment.

Most religions have a common understanding and language system for thinking and talking about core beliefs. So another explanation for the benefit of religious involvement is that religiously involved couples have a belief system that facilitates developing and maintaining a shared worldview.

One important factor for all couples to consider is the impact of their worldviews on the marriage. Do you share a core belief system? How do the two of you handle the similarities and differences in your views? Think about these questions as we look at two specific areas where your worldview can have an effect on your marriage: expectations and core relationship values.

## Expectations

One way in which your worldview can significantly affect your marriage is in shaping your expectations in such areas as child rearing and discipline, intimacy, dealing with in-laws, and marital roles. These aspects of your worldview have significant implications for how well the two of you negotiate the myriad decisions of daily life.

As we have seen, expectations often change over time. Common understandings that work well in one phase of life sometimes need to be renegotiated later on.

A fifty-seven-year-old Jewish man, Arthur, who had been married for twenty-five years to his Jewish wife, Sharon, had recently lost a good friend to cancer. His friend's death had stirred up a lot of emotions and soul searching, as well as some tension in his own marriage. "I'm very healthy," Arthur said, "but for the first time in my life, I can see my own mortality on the horizon. It's made me think a lot about how I use the time and energy I have." Although he and Sharon had always shared a lot in common, including their Judaism, Arthur's self-examination led to a number of changes.

In particular, he became preoccupied with the idea of tzedakah: ethical giving. He told Sharon that he wanted to give substantially more money and time to a number of Jewish causes he felt were important. Although they had always contributed some money to charity, it had not been a high priority in their marriage. Sharon's process of aging had actually led her to think a lot about saving more money for retirement, so that she and Arthur would be able to have more fun traveling in a few years. She was initially upset when he said that he wanted to give more money away.

Although they were both reacting to aging, their responses were quite different. The existential and spiritual reevaluation stimulated by their aging and by the death of Arthur's friend led to several arguments and, eventually, to a number of deep and challenging conversations between Arthur and Sharon. Their common roots in Jewish life probably made the compromises they eventually reached somewhat easier, but it still took a lot of work on both of their parts.

The potential for differences in expectations to spark conflict is so great that we spent all of Chapter Eight encouraging you to make such expectations clear, no matter where they come from. When two people share a perspective on key relationship expectations, they are going to have an easier time negotiating life. Shared expectations lead to shared rituals and routines that guide couples more smoothly through the transitions and trials they must confront every day. But as we have seen, even in relationships in which partners have a lot in common, it is important to recognize the need for renegotiations and renewal.

### Core Relationship Values

Let's focus on four key values that are emphasized in many belief systems, values with obvious positive implications for relationships such as marriage: commitment, respect, intimacy, and forgiveness. When you and your partner have similar core belief systems, it is likely that you will have a similar understanding of these values and of how you can give life to them in your marriage. We see the need for all couples to have some way to reinforce such values, regardless of their core beliefs.

*Commitment* in its various aspects is strongly emphasized in many belief systems, in terms of both dedication and constraint. Although there are great differences among belief systems about the morality of divorce, there is wide agreement across systems about the value of commitment. Long-term relationships need a sustained sense of commitment.

*Respect* is a core value emphasized in most religious or spiritual groups. Although various religions hold to specific beliefs that others may reject, most systems emphasize respect for the value and worth of others. Respect is a core need of all people; as a couple, you need to share a value system that has a strong emphasis on respect for each other.

We believe that even if you have significant disagreements and differences, you can show respect for one another by the way that you communicate. This is validation. You show interest in and respect for your partner even when you see things quite differently. You can't have a good relationship without basic respect.

*Intimacy* is prized in most religious and spiritual systems. Although various systems may understand it differently, intimacy is usually emphasized and encouraged, especially in marriage. All of the traditional religious systems in Western cultures value marriage and the relationship between the two partners.

One way to think about everything we say in this book is that couples need to have clear ways to maintain and enhance intimacy. Furthermore, poorly handled conflict can do great damage to all that is intimate. All couples seeking long-term, satisfying marriages need to value intimacy and the importance of preserving and protecting it.

*Forgiveness* is a core theme for relational health. Long-term, healthy relationships need the capacity for forgiveness. Otherwise, emotional debts can be allowed to build in ways that destroy the potential for intimacy and teamwork. Forgiveness is so crucial that we spend an entire chapter dealing with that topic. Marriages need forgiveness to stay healthy over the long term.

We hope that you can see how the four core values discussed here are reflected in the skills and attitudes we encourage. Judaism has been emphasizing these values for thousands of years in ethics, codes of conduct, and standards for dealing with others and its focus on the importance of commitment, respect, intimacy, and forgiveness. Our understanding of marital success and failure leads us to emphasize these same values. In essence, this book teaches ways of thinking and acting that enable couples to put these values into action. They are relevant for every couple. As you practice and put into effect the kinds of strategies and structures we advocate, you are building positive relationship rituals for the future health of your marriage.

---

In summary, you and your partner may have different perspectives, even if you were raised similarly. When you think about religious and spiritual differences, a lot is at stake. The same is true for any core belief system, such as a philosophy of life. Everyone has beliefs, and it is highly unlikely that a couple exists in which both partners line up perfectly on all dimensions. The point is that you need to grapple with the effects of differences in your beliefs on your relationship. The exercises for this chapter are designed to help you do just that—grapple. We want you to explore your beliefs on religious or spiritual dimensions and talk them over together.

# EXERCISES

Use these two exercises to explore your own religious beliefs and core values and to share them with your partner. It can be an enriching experience in your relationship. Talking about these issues with respect can lead to a very intimate encounter. Try it and see what we mean.

## Exploring Core Values and Religious Beliefs

The following questions are designed to get you to think about a broad range of issues related to your values and beliefs. There may be other important questions we have left out, so feel free to answer questions we don't ask as well as those we do. Jot down an answer to each question as it applies to you. This activity will help you think more clearly about the issues and will also help you when it comes time to talk with your partner about them. *As you think about and answer each question, it can be especially valuable to note what you were taught as a child versus what you believe or expect as an adult.*

## Questions for Reflection

1. What is your core belief system or worldview? What do you believe in?

2. How did you come to have this viewpoint?

3. What is the meaning or purpose of life in your core belief system?

4. What was your belief growing up? How was this core belief practiced in your family of origin? In religious practice? Some other way?

5. Do you make a distinction between spirituality and religion? What is your view on these matters?

6. In your belief system, what is the meaning of marriage?

7. What marital vows will you or did you make? How do they tie in to your belief system?

8. What is your belief about divorce? How does this fit in with your belief system?

9. How do you practice, or expect to practice, your beliefs as part of your relationship? (This could mean religious involvement, spiritual practices, or other behaviors, depending on your belief system.) How do you want to practice your beliefs?

10. What do you think should be the day-to-day impact of your belief system on your relationship?

11. How do you observe or expect to observe religious holidays? Think about the family meaning, the sense of belonging, and the religious meaning of different holidays as you were growing up and at different points in your life, up until today. What do you feel about religious holidays like Christmas, Hanukkah, Rosh Hashanah, Passover, and Easter?

12. If you have or plan to have children, how are they being raised, or how will they be raised with respect to your belief system? What about religious schooling? Parochial or public

school? Sunday school? Hebrew school? What about bar and bat mitzvahs, confirmations, dedications, and so on?

13. Do you have a brit to have a baby boy circumcised, or is it done by a doctor in the hospital, or not at all? Is it important to have your baby baptized? Dedicated? Does baptism happen later, at the age of accountability and personal belief, or now?

14. Do you give, or expect to give, financial support to a religious institution or other effort related to your belief system? How much? How will this be determined? Do you both agree?

15. Do you see potential areas of conflict regarding your belief systems? What are they?

16. What do you believe about forgiveness in general? How does forgiveness apply in a relationship such as the one you have with your partner?

17. In your belief system, what is your responsibility to other human beings?

18. Are there specific views on sexuality in your belief system? What are they? How do they affect the two of you?

19. What is the basis in your beliefs for respecting others?

20. Are there any other questions you can think of and answer?

After you and your partner have finished the entire exercise, schedule time to discuss these expectations together. These are not easy issues, so you should plan on having a number of discussions. Discuss the degree to which you each felt that the expectation being discussed had been shared clearly in the past. Use the Speaker-Listener Technique if you would like some additional structure to deal with these sometimes difficult issues. If any new expectations come up, talk about the degree to which you both feel that they are reasonable or unreasonable and discuss what you want to do to deal with any differences between the two of you.

# Tzavaah: Write an Ethical Will

*Come together, that I may tell you what is to befall*
*you in the days to come.*

Jacob (Genesis 49:1)

In common usage, a will is a legal document that instructs how one's material wealth will be distributed after death. In Judaism, however, there is also a tradition of writing an *ethical will* for one's children, which is a moral document. An ethical will is designed to communicate a person's values, beliefs, and wishes for those who are living. It is a way of passing on to the next generation your accumulated wisdom—what you believe is truly meaningful in life. The *Book of Deuteronomy* is seen as Moses' ethical will. Realizing that he would not survive the journey to the Promised Land, he made three speeches that instructed the Israelites he had led for forty years about how they were to live after he was gone.

Of course, writing an ethical will can benefit the author as well as those who will someday read it. Even if you don't have children, and even if you are not elderly or anticipating death in the near future, writing such a will for younger family members, friends, and your partner can be a meaningful exercise. There is nothing like contemplating one's own mortality to focus attention on what is truly important.

Just as legal wills need to be modified periodically because of life's changing circumstances, consider working on your ethical will as an ongoing process as well. And finally, consider sharing with your partner what you have written, thought, and felt during the process of making an ethical will. Sharing at this level can be a powerful and enriching experience.

# 11

# Atonement, Forgiveness, and the Restoration of Intimacy

*The gates of repentance are always open, and he who wishes may always enter.*

*Shemot Rabbah 19:4*

Jewish tradition teaches that on the most solemn of Jewish holidays, Yom Kippur (the Day of Atonement), if you are truly repentant, God can forgive you for sins committed against God. But for harm that you have done to another human, you must go directly to the injured person to seek forgiveness—preferably before Yom Kippur. Causing emotional or physical pain to another, intentionally or even accidentally, requires that you face the person whom you have hurt. The concept is both simple and profound: it requires that we strip away the rationalizations we use to justify our bad behavior and then work to make things right. Only then can healing and forgiveness begin.

Judaism does not share with Christianity the idea of original sin. But Jewish tradition is quite clear that human failings are inevitable and that we should constantly strive for a perfection that we will never reach. Unless you have very unrealistic expectations, you are aware that both of you will commit sins of omission and commission over the course of your marriage.

Minor infractions are normal: expecting perfection is a great enemy of happiness. Learning how to deal with the inevitable (and often frequent) bumps and bruises of intimate relationships is crucial to their success. For these smaller failures, Hebrew uses the word *chet*, a term from archery that means "missing the mark." If you want to hit the bulls-eye, you must keep practicing. A more forgiving word than sin, *chet* implies that if you keep trying, you will get closer to the bulls-eye.

Some couples will deal with more intense disappointments and devastating betrayals. *Aveira*, which can be translated as "crossing the line," is a conscious act that a person commits knowing that it is wrong. When there has been an aveira, it takes a lot more effort to mend trust that has been broken. The more significant the issues or events that cause harm, the more likely you will need some of the specific steps we recommend in this chapter.

## THE NEED FOR ATONEMENT AND FORGIVENESS

Let's look at two couples who demonstrate the importance of dealing with forgiveness in their relationships. You will see that the intensity of pain that the two couples must deal with is very different—one minor and one major—with very different implications for the process of atonement and forgiveness.

### Oops, I Forgot: The Levensons

Hannah and Norm Levenson had each been married once before, and each had primary custody of their children from the first marriage. Nothing has been remarkable about their marriage and blended family except that they have done a great job of it. They have handled the myriad stresses of bringing two sets of children together, and they have become a family. They have their ups and downs, but they handle with respect and skill the problems that arise.

Norm was chosen to be honored as Employee of the Year at an annual luncheon at his company. He was happy about the award and happier still to receive a substantial bonus for his heads-up work.

Norm asked Hannah to attend the luncheon, and she said she would be glad to come. Because the company is very family oriented, most of the employees brought their spouses and significant others to the function. Norm told his fellow workers and his boss that Hannah would be coming. A place was kept for her at the front table, right beside Norm.

Hannah worked at a fast-paced high-tech company, and on the day of the event, she got so focused on a project she was working on that she completely forgot about the luncheon. While she was gazing into a computer screen, Norm was at the luncheon feeling very embarrassed. He was also a little worried, as it was unlike Hannah to miss anything. So he fretted and fumed and made the best of the situation.

As soon as Norm walked in the door that evening, Hannah remembered the forgotten luncheon:

HANNAH: *(distressed)* Oh no! Norm, I just remembered.
NORM: *(cutting her off)* Where were you? I have never been so embarrassed. I really wanted you there.
HANNAH: I know. I know. I'm so sorry. I wanted to be there with you.
NORM: So where were you?
HANNAH: I was at work. I completely spaced out about your lunch. I feel terrible.
NORM: So do I. I didn't know what to tell people, so I made something up about you maybe being at the doctor's office with one of the kids.
HANNAH: Please forgive me, dear.

Should Norm forgive Hannah? Of course. What does it mean for him to forgive in this context?

Now consider a very different example, one in which the same questions have much more complicated answers.

## Broken Trust: The Mansoors

Mordecai and Ariel Mansoor had been together for ten years. They met in Israel, where Ariel spent a year immediately after graduating from college in Boston. Ariel fell madly in love with Mordecai. He had served as a lieutenant in the Israeli army. He came from a large, warm Sephardic family that Ariel really enjoyed.

Mordecai was ambitious, extroverted, and a risk taker. He was as drawn to Ariel as she was to him. He used to complain about how demanding and tough Israeli women were, and he liked that she was American and more willing to follow his lead.

He told Ariel that he saw tremendous opportunities for them in the United States and that he wanted to live there for at least a few years while he started a telecommunications business. He had been a communications officer in the army, and he was convinced that he could turn his skills into fortune. Ariel was relieved that being with Mordecai didn't mean giving up the familiarity of home, and she readily agreed to return to the United States.

They had a huge wedding in Israel and shortly afterwards moved to the Boston area that Ariel knew well and enjoyed. Mordecai's brother also moved to Boston, and they became partners along with an American. Mordecai began working long hours to get their new business off the ground. Ariel got a job as the business manager of a small publishing company. After three years they had their first child, a delightful girl named Malka. Two years later they had another girl, Eva, who was serious, very bright, and a real handful at times. After Eva was born, Mordecai's business was doing well enough for them to decide that Ariel could leave her job and concentrate on the home and the girls.

Everything sailed along just fine until about the eighth year of their marriage, when Ariel began to notice that Mordecai was gone more and more and that they were spending very little time together. She knew he was passionate about his business and that he drove himself much harder than any boss could. Ariel wanted to be supportive of Mordecai's work, but she began to feel more and more lonely in the marriage. She began to wonder if he really needed to be gone so much, and her loneliness started to turn to suspicion. Without much time or open communication together, it was hard to know what was going on.

She began to feel as if she didn't know Mordecai anymore. She knew other women found him as attractive as she did, and she became obsessed with the idea that he was cheating on her. She would make phone calls to the office when he was supposed to be working late, but he was rarely there. When she asked him about this, he would say that he must have been talking with his brother or meeting with a client. She didn't believe him.

Ariel got sick and tired of being suspicious. One night she followed Mordecai to an apartment complex, noting the door where he went in. She sat for a very long three hours; then she got out to look at the name on the mailbox—Sally something-or-other. When she knocked and asked for Mordecai, the woman denied all knowledge of him. Ariel screamed, "I know you're here" as the woman slammed the door shut. Ariel drove home sobbing and full of rage and pain.

Mordecai rolled in to their home an hour later. He denied everything for about three days, but Ariel wasn't about to back down. She told Mordecai to get out: "An affair is bad enough, but if you can't even admit to it, there's nothing left for us to talk about."

As Mordecai's denial crumbled, his sense of shame was so great that he was afraid to deal with Ariel head-on. He just stayed away from home. "She told me to get out, anyway," he told himself. Yet it really bothered him that Ariel was being so hard on him. He wondered if it were really over. In a way, though, he found new respect for her. No begging or pleading for Ariel, just toughness. He liked Sally, but he didn't want to spend his life with her. He missed Ariel, and the idea of not being with his children was terrifying. It became clear to him that he wanted to save his marriage.

Of course, Ariel didn't feel tough at all. She was in agony. But she was very certain about what she had seen. There was no chance that she would go on with Mordecai unless he dealt with her honestly, and even then she wasn't sure whether she wanted to stay or leave. She came home one night to find Mordecai sitting at the kitchen table with a terrible look of pain on his face.

MORDECAI: (*desperately*) Please forgive me, Ariel. I'm not sure how it happened. I know it was wrong. I'll get help.

ARIEL: (*cool outside, raging inside*) I'm not sure what happened either, but I think you know a lot more than I do.

MORDECAI: (*looking up from the table*) I guess I do. What do you want to know?

ARIEL: (*icily, controlling her rage*) I'd like to know what's been going on, without all the lies.

MORDECAI: (*tears welling up*) I've been having an affair. I met Sally through work, we got close, and things sort of spun out of control.

ARIEL: I guess they did. How long?

MORDECAI: What?

ARIEL: (*voice raised, anger coming out*) How long have you been sleeping with her?

MORDECAI: Five months. Since the New Year's party. Look, I couldn't handle things here at home. There's been so much distance between us.

ARIEL: (*enraged*) So what! I wasn't happy with how things were going, either. But I didn't go looking for someone else. I don't want you here right now. Just go. (*turning away, heading into the next room*)

MORDECAI: If that's what you want, I'll go.

ARIEL: (*as she walks away*) Right now, that's what I want. Please leave me alone. Just let me know where you'll be for the kids' sake.

MORDECAI: (*despondent*) I'll go to my brother's. That's where I've been lately.

ARIEL: (*sarcastically*) Oh, thanks for telling me.

MORDECAI: I'll leave. Please forgive me, Ariel, please.

ARIEL:  I don't know if I can. (*goes upstairs as Mordecai slips out the back door*)

At this point, Ariel had some big decisions to make. Should she forgive Mordecai? Could she forgive him? She had already decided that she might never be able to trust him again, not fully. He clearly wanted to come back, but how could she know that he wouldn't do this again the next time they had trouble together?

What do you think? Has Mordecai really tried to atone for what he has done? Should Ariel forgive Mordecai, and what does it mean for her to forgive him?

## WHAT IS ATONEMENT?

> They [the rabbis] even debated whether it was better
> to have sinned and repented than never to have
> sinned or had the impulse to sin at all. Some believed
> that a person who never had to undergo teshuvah was
> inferior to the person who successfully confronted his
> mistakes and temptations, but overcame them: "In
> the place where the penitents stand, even the wholly
> righteous are not permitted to stand."
>
> David Ariel[1]

Atonement is the process of taking personal responsibility for missing the mark. Although some people may be uncomfortable with the religious connotations of the word *atone*, it is clear that trying to make amends for one's errors, whether or not you see it in theological terms, is one of life's most difficult moral challenges. Open the Bible or today's newspaper and you will read story after story of individuals trying to escape the consequences of their actions. Taking responsibility for our mistakes requires overcoming the very powerful human need not to feel at fault. Sometimes it seems almost as difficult as overcoming our need to breathe.

Atonement requires the desire to make things right, the determination to make amends, and the humility to find healing words, and to engage in healing actions. The path of atonement, of taking responsibility, opens up the possibility not only of repairing and restoring your relationship but also of deepening it. It also gives you the chance to become a better person. A crisis in your relationship presents real dangers, but it also may provide you with an opportunity to create a stronger and deeper love.

## What Atonement Isn't

Atonement isn't looking for ways out of taking total responsibility for one's actions. Of course there are always at least two sides to every conflict or situation. But the fact that there are mitigating circumstances, as a lawyer might say, does not absolve an individual of his or her responsibility. Atonement also is not wearing your recovery from sin like some merit badge. A too-quick "I'm sorry" may not be a real sign of atonement but instead an attempt to shut down an important dialogue that needs to take place. Making excuses, blaming others, and not making behavioral changes are all not atonement. And certainly, repeating the hurtful acts is a sure sign of a failure to try to right wrongs. And because it requires humility and self-discipline, atonement is by definition difficult. If it is easy, it is probably not atonement.

# WHAT IS FORGIVENESS?

Forgiveness is a decision to give up your perceived or actual right to get even with, or hold in debt, someone who has wronged you. A good metaphor for forgiveness is that of a canceled debt. *Forgive* is a verb; it is an action you have to decide to take! If one of you is unable to forgive the other, it will be very difficult for you to function as a team, because one of you is kept "one down" by being indebted to the other. We are not suggesting that every hurt can be healed or that you *should* forgive your partner. We are saying that you can choose to be active in trying to find ways to forgive.

The opposite of forgiveness is expressed in statements (or thoughts) such as these:

"I'm going to make you pay for what you did."

"You are never going to live this down."

"You owe me. I'm going to get even with you."

"I'll hold this against you for the rest of your life."

When you fail to forgive, you act out these kinds of statements, or even state them openly. Remaining in a relationship where forgiveness seems impossible usually leads to more misery. A lack of forgiveness can result in a kind of scorekeeping, with the message being "You are way behind on my scorecard, and I don't know if you can catch up." In that context, resentment builds, conflict increases, and, ultimately, hopelessness sets in. The real message is "You can't do enough to make this up." People often walk away from debts they see no hope of paying off.

## What Forgiveness Isn't

You hear the phrase "forgive and forget" so often that it seems that to forgive requires one to forget. This is one of the greatest myths about forgiveness. Can you remember a very painful wrong that was done to you for which you feel you have forgiven the other person? We bet you can.

Just because you have forgiven another person and given up your wish to harm that person in return doesn't mean you have forgotten that the event ever happened. Fortunately, when people say "forgive and forget," they usually mean that it is necessary to put the infraction in the past. There can be value in putting a hurt in a box labeled the past, but amnesia is not a prerequisite for forgiveness. What is important is that you have given up holding the incident over your partner's head.

Another misconception is the belief that if a person still feels pain about what happened, he or she hasn't really forgiven the one who caused the pain. You can still feel pain about being hurt in some way yet have fully forgiven the one who harmed you. Ariel Mansoor may come to the point of completely forgiving Mordecai. She may work through and silence her rage and desire to hurt him back. However, in the best of circumstances, what happened will leave a scar and a grief that may take years to fully heal. In the case of the Levensons, the way in which Hannah hurt Norm was far less severe, with fewer lasting consequences. As it turned out, he did quickly forgive her. He didn't dwell on her forgetfulness the day of his award, and he didn't need to grieve about his embarrassment. However, when he is reminded of it, for example, at company events, he remembers and feels a twinge of the humiliation he felt on that day. This doesn't mean that he is holding it over Hannah or trying to get even. He has forgiven her. The incident is just a small painful memory along the path of their marriage.

Another misunderstanding about forgiveness is the idea that it removes the responsibility of the person who hurt you. When you forgive, you are in fact saying nothing about the responsibility of the one who did wrong. The one who did wrong is responsible for the wrong, period. Forgiving someone does not absolve that person of responsibility for his or her past and future actions. It does take the relationship out of the mode where one punishes the other, but forgiving in no way diminishes the responsibility for the wrong that was done.

If your partner has wronged you, it is up to you to decide if you can forgive. Your partner can't do this for you. It is your choice. If you want your relationship to move forward, you need to have a plan for forgiving. Even if you don't want to forgive—perhaps because of your own sense of justice—you may still need to do so for the good of your marriage. We understand that this is often a very difficult process.

The Levensons dealt with their hurtful event in an ideal way. Hannah took complete responsibility for missing the luncheon by apologizing and asking Norm to forgive her. He readily forgave her and had no intention of holding it against her. Their relationship was even strengthened by the way they handled this event. Norm gained respect for Hannah's total acceptance of responsibility, and Hannah appreciated Norm's love and his ability to forgive and move on.

For the Mansoors, Mordecai's affair was a much more serious betrayal; it also took awhile for Mordecai to fully apologize and ask for forgiveness. His patience and persistence in working on the marriage will be the real test of his sincerity. For them to move forward, he will have to be very understanding about Ariel's need to build trust slowly. Ariel will have to decide if she is willing to take the risks involved in opening her heart again. She will also need to learn to be more assertive about making her needs known.

Before we move on to specific steps you can take to help the process of healing, we want to discuss the crucial distinction between forgiveness and restoration in a relationship.

## What If You Have Been Wronged, But Your Partner Can't or Won't Take Responsibility?

Anger, guilt, and loneliness are the bitter fruits of betrayal, misunderstanding, and conflict in relationships. Usually forgiveness and what we call *restoration*—the re-establishment of openness and intimacy in a relationship—go hand in hand. Norm and Hannah, for example, quickly restored their connection because they placed no barriers in the way. They both handled their own responsibility without complication, and restoration naturally followed.

But what do you do if you have been wronged in some way, yet your partner does not take responsibility in a way that you feel good about? Do you allow restoration to occur even though your partner seems unrepentant? It may be possible if you are open to examining the possibility that your partner really didn't intend to do anything wrong, even though you felt hurt by what happened. There can be a sincere difference in the interpretation of what and why a troubling event happened.

Nina and Charles Barker, for example, went through a troubling event, and neither initially acknowledged what they each had done wrong. They had been married fifteen years, and the relationship was generally satisfying. Although they weren't handling conflict very well, their dedication remained strong.

On one occasion, when Nina was out of town for a few days, Charles decided to surprise her by cleaning out the garage. He threw out all sorts of old boxes, and thought he had done a great job, too. The garage hadn't looked so good in years, and he knew that the mess had always bothered Nina. When she returned, she was very pleased, just as Charles had thought she would be. The problem was that he had thrown out a box containing mementos from her bat mitzvah. It was an accident. He had even noticed the box and thought he had put it aside to protect it. Perhaps his daughter, who was helping him, put it with the other boxes by mistake. Anyway, it was gone for good.

When Nina realized that the box was gone, she went into orbit. She was enraged. She accused Charles of being stupid, insensitive, and domineering. Then she went on to say, "You never really accepted that I'm Jewish, and I don't believe throwing it away was a mistake."

What Charles did was unfortunate. Nina had every right to be upset; the mementos meant a lot to her. But it really had been a mistake. With her acceptance issue triggered as well as some hidden issues about her Jewish identity, Nina was being unfair in accusing Charles of intentionally hurting her. This was a very negative interpretation. In reality, he was trying to do something he knew she would like. They both felt hurt and angry and invalidated.

When you are harmed in the way Nina was, it is OK to expect an apology—not because your partner intended to hurt you but because a mistake did hurt you. Charles can apologize to Nina, but she has a long wait ahead if she needs to hear him say, "You're right. I threw out your things because I'm a control freak and I think I can do whatever I want with anything in our house, and I also hate the fact that you're Jewish. I'll work on it." Not likely!

In fact, at this point he may feel that he's the one who is owed an apology. Although he is sorry about the mistake he made, he is also quite hurt and angry about Nina's accusations. In fact, what could have been a minor incident ended up creating bitterness and anger for several days, because Charles refused to apologize for accidentally throwing the box away, and Nina had trouble apologizing for her harsh interpretations.

Whether or not you both agree on the nature or the seriousness of what happened, you can still move ahead and forgive. Doing so may be hard, but if you don't, you and the relationship will suffer added damage. In fact, there is good reason to believe that when you hang on to resentment and bitterness, you put yourself at risk for psychological and physical problems, such as depression and high blood pressure. That's no way to live.

Now for the really difficult case: suppose it is very clear to you that your partner did something very wrong and isn't going to take any responsibility, as initially was the case in Mordecai and Ariel's situation. Until Mordecai was able to admit to and take responsibility for his affair, there was no chance of moving forward. Sure, both of them were responsible for letting their marriage slip. They had grown distant, and neither was more to blame than the other for that. However, in response to this distance, Mordecai chose to have the affair. He was responsible for that action, not Ariel.

When Mordecai showed up in the kitchen asking for forgiveness, the worst thing Ariel could have done would be to instantly try to forgive and forget and go on as if everything had returned to normal. It hadn't. You can't sweep things like this under the carpet, and we don't believe she would be likely to succeed in truly forgiving him without a deeper, more complete process of atonement and forgiveness.

When Mordecai came back to the house that night, Ariel didn't know what level of responsibility he would take for the affair. She wondered, "What if deep down he really blames me for it? What if he thinks it's my fault for not being more affectionate?" If she thought that he felt his behavior was justified or that he wasn't serious about changing, why should she allow any restoration of the relationship? It would be a great risk to take him back. Still, she could try to forgive him.

Here is what actually happened. Before Mordecai acknowledged what he had done, they had some very nasty talks on the phone. With so much tension in the air, it was easy for arguments to escalate. Even after he admitted to the affair, he tried to use the distance in the relationship and Ariel's lack of support as excuses for his behavior. It was very difficult for Ariel not to back down and start to blame herself, but she got a lot of support from her sister and her mother, and decided to hold her ground. Mordecai would have to honestly face his actions and their consequences.

Mordecai was surprised by how firm Ariel was being, and he felt a growing respect and desire for her. Like many Israelis, Mordecai was deeply connected to traditional Jewish values, even though he didn't consider himself religious. He found himself thinking a lot about *teshuvah*, the idea of turning, of changing for the better. He began to look more honestly at himself and started to be much clearer about his responsibility for his behavior. In their phone conversations, he began to persistently state his desire to rebuild the marriage. He wanted to turn things around.

One night, Ariel asked Mordecai to come to the house for a talk, and she arranged for the children to be with her parents for the evening. When she met with Mordecai, she poured out her anguish, pain, and anger. He listened. She focused on how his behavior had affected her, not on his motives and weaknesses. He took responsibility to the point of offering a sincere apology and saying that he didn't blame anyone but himself for the affair. Now she thought there was a chance that they could get through this. Their talk concluded this way:

MORDECAI: I've had a lot of time to think. I believe I made a very bad choice that hurt you deeply. It was wrong of me to begin the relationship with Sally.

ARIEL:  I appreciate the apology. I needed to hear it. I love you, but I can't pick up where we left off. I need to know that you'll get to the root of this problem.

MORDECAI:  What do you want me to do?

ARIEL:  I'm not sure. I've got so many questions that I don't know which way is up. I just know that I needed to hear you say you'd done something very wrong.

MORDECAI:  Ariel, I did do something very wrong. I know it. It's also clear to me—clearer than it's been in a few years—that I want this marriage to work. I want you, not someone else.

ARIEL:  I'd like to make it work, but I'm not sure I can learn to trust you again.

MORDECAI:  I know I hurt you very deeply. I wish I could take away your pain.

ARIEL:  That's what I want. I hope I can forgive you, but I need some way to believe that it won't happen again.

MORDECAI:  Ariel. I'd like to come back home.

ARIEL:  All right, but I need to know we'll go and get help to get through this.

MORDECAI:  Like a therapist.

ARIEL:  Yes, like a therapist. I'm not sure what to do next, and I don't want to screw this up. If you'll agree to that, I can handle having you come back home.

MORDECAI:  I will do whatever it takes.

ARIEL:  Don't expect me to go on as if nothing's happened. I'm very, very angry with you right now.

MORDECAI:  I know, and I won't pressure you to act like nothing happened.

ARIEL:  OK.

As you can see, Ariel really opened up, and Mordecai validated her pain and anger. He didn't get defensive or blame her. If he had, she was prepared to end the marriage. She gained hope from this talk. Ariel knew she could forgive—she's a very forgiving person. But she also knew it would take some time—she's no fool. And she knew they needed help. The future looked uncertain, and there was a lot to work through if they were going to restore their relationship.

Mordecai did the best he could under the circumstances. The next day, he began calling around to find a good therapist. His doing so showed Ariel that he was serious about repairing their marriage and provided evidence of long-unseen dedication. She was glad that she resisted her own impulse to find the therapist, something that in the past she probably would have seen as her job to take care of. It meant a lot to her that he took the initiative, because she knew Mordecai was a very proud and private man and that getting help from a stranger was not an easy thing for him to do.

The relationship couldn't be restored until they got to work. It took time, but they did the work. Ariel remembers—she won't be able to forget—but the ache in her heart continues to grow fainter as they have moved forward through forgiveness and on to restoration of their relationship.

## WHAT ABOUT REGAINING TRUST?

We are often asked how one can regain trust when an incident has seriously damaged it. The question is not as important for minor matters of forgiveness; for example, there is no real loss of trust between the Levensons. But the Mansoors have experienced a great loss of trust. Whatever the incident, suppose that forgiveness proceeds smoothly, and you both want restoration. How do you regain trust? It is not easy. We will make four key points about rebuilding trust.

1. *Trust builds slowly over time.* As we said in Chapter Nine, trust builds as you gain confidence about your partner's commitment. Although research shows that people vary in their general level of trust for others, deep trust only comes from seeing that your partner is there for you in a consistent way over time.

Ariel can only regain her trust in Mordecai slowly, and he has to be patient to earn her trust. The best thing that can happen is for a considerable amount of time to go by without a serious breach of trust. That takes commitment and new ways of living together. The couple can't afford to let the same kind of distance build up again. And if Mordecai has another affair, it may be impossible for Ariel ever to trust him again.

2. *Trust has the greatest chance of being rebuilt when each partner takes appropriate responsibility.* The best thing Mordecai can do to regain Ariel's trust is to take full responsibility for his actions. If Ariel sees Mordecai doing all he can do to bring about serious change without her prodding and demanding, her trust will grow, and she will gain confidence that things can get better—not perfect, but better. As we said in Chapter Nine, it is easier to trust when you can clearly see your partner's dedication to you.

Ariel can also help rebuild Mordecai's trust. For one thing, he will need to see that she doesn't plan to hold the affair over his head forever. Can she ever really forgive him? If she reminds him about the affair, especially during arguments, he won't be able to trust her statement that she wants them to get closer and move ahead.

3. *If you have damaged your partner's trust, it is easier to further damage it than to regain it.* It takes a long time to regain trust but only a moment or two to crush it. If Mordecai comes home on time tonight to be with Ariel, still trying, she will gain a little more trust. If instead he comes home two hours late without a good excuse, Ariel's trust will take a big step backward. Mistakes are going to happen, but the commitment to change must remain clear. The commitment says that you have the motivation to rebuild trust.

4. *Surveillance doesn't increase trust.* You can't gain trust by following your partner around every moment of the day to make sure he or she doesn't do anything wrong. It won't add to Ariel's trust to follow Mordecai wherever he goes or to call up friends and ask what he has been up to. Sure, if he has an affair again, she might find it

out sooner. Otherwise, all she will know for sure is that Mordecai doesn't get off track when he knows she is watching his every move.

The exception to this is when you both agree that some checking up is acceptable. Ariel and Mordecai could agree that, for a time, he will call frequently or that she will call him to touch base more often than usual. But over the long term, for both of them to relax in their relationship, Ariel will have to come to trust Mordecai again. Let's hope that her trust will not be misplaced. To trust again is a risk. Your partner could let you down again, and there is no way to be sure that this won't happen. That's why they call it trust.

## UNDERSTANDING THE DIFFERENCE BETWEEN EXPLANATION AND EXCUSE: SHELLEY AND ARNIE STEIN

Although modern psychology has helped alleviate much human suffering, sometimes it is misused and creates problems of its own. When therapists apply their understanding of human motivation as a way to explain away personal responsibility, it can create a false sense of unaccountability. One woman, Shelley Stein, who had endured several violent outbursts by her husband, Arnie, excused his behavior by saying that he had had a terrible childhood and that his therapist had told her that Arnie had an impulse control disorder that sometimes made self-restraint impossible. Shelley lived in fear of his outbursts but tried to comfort herself with the fact that he was seeing a therapist and that his explosions were far less frequent. "He's making progress," she would say to herself.

Her friend Sylvia urged her to stop putting up with his threats and violence and to call the police if he were ever physically abusive again. Shelley finally found the courage to tell Arnie that he had to control his temper and that she would press charges if he ever hit her. Of course, he didn't believe her, as she had never followed through on any of her past ultimatums. Three months later, he did hit her; she did call the police, and he was taken to jail.

Sylvia discovered that when she really set a limit and followed through, Arnie's "impulse control disorder" suddenly disappeared. She finally realized that she had contributed to his violence by excusing it. As terms of his probation, he entered a group treatment program offered by the local domestic violence center, and he began for the first time to take serious steps toward assuming personal responsibility for his temper.

Yes, you may very well have played a role in the events leading up to some major betrayal, and it is important for you to look at your part of the problem. Perhaps you were too forgiving of bad behavior. Maybe you lived with too much distance in your marriage for too long without actively dealing with it. You might have failed to do your share in earning enough income for the family, yelled too much at the kids, drank too much alcohol, or not taken good enough care of your body. The list of possible human shortcomings is long. *Always remember, though, that your imperfections did not cause your partner to betray or to hurt you.*

You are responsible for dealing with your own problems; blaming your partner for your behavior won't help the situation, nor will using your own failings to justify your partner's sins. Two of the most difficult tasks in life are taking responsibility for our own actions and insisting that those we love do the same. Good relationships are built on two seemingly contradictory capacities: compassion and confrontation. We need to be able to forgive, but sometimes forgiveness can only begin when we are willing to take the risk of setting limits. Develop both abilities!

# STEPS TO FORGIVENESS AND RESTORATION

We now want to give you more specific and structured advice on how to move toward forgiveness and restoration in your relationship. In suggesting specific steps, we don't mean to imply that forgiveness is easy. But we do want you to use these steps to get through the toughest times. The steps are similar to those in the problem-solving process we described in Chapter Five. They can work very well to help you rebuild your trust when you have a specific event or recurring issue to deal with. We can't give you the motivation, courage, or humility required, but we can help you set the conditions that lead to taking responsibility and to forgiveness.

Each step has some key points. We summarize many of the points made in this chapter, as well as draw a road map for handling forgiveness. As with other strategies we have presented, our goal here is to provide specific steps that can help couples handle difficult issues well.

## Step 1: Schedule a Couple Meeting to Discuss the Specific Issue Related to Broken Trust

If an issue is important enough to focus on in this way, do it right. Set aside a time when you will be without distractions. Prepare yourselves to deal with the issue openly, honestly, and with respect. As we said in Chapter Six in discussing ground rules, setting aside specific times for dealing with issues makes it more likely that you will actually follow through and do it well.

## Step 2: Set the Agenda to Work on the Issue in Question

Identify the problem or harmful event. If you can't agree on what issues should be part of your agenda, wait for a better time.

## Step 3: Fully Explore the Pain and Concerns Related to This Issue for Both of You

The goal in this step is to have an open, validating talk about what has happened that harmed one or both of you. You shouldn't try this unless each of you is motivated to hear and show respect for your partner's viewpoint. The foundation for forgiveness is best laid through such a talk or series of talks. Validating discussions go a long way toward dealing with the painful issues in ways that bring you closer together. This would be a great time to use the Speaker-Listener Technique. If there is ever a time to have a safe and clear talk, this is it.

## Step 4: The Offender Asks for Forgiveness

If you have offended your partner in some way, an outward appeal for forgiveness is not only appropriate but also very healing. Because it validates your partner's pain, a sincere apology would be a powerful addition to a request for forgiveness. "I'm sorry, I was wrong, please forgive me" is one of the most healing things one person can say to another. Apologizing and asking for forgiveness is a big part of taking responsibility for having hurt your partner. (This doesn't mean that you sit around and beat yourself up for what you did. You have to forgive yourself, too!)

But what if you don't think you have done anything wrong? You can still ask your partner to forgive you. Remember, forgiveness is a separate issue from why a hurtful event occurred. So even if you don't agree that you did anything wrong, your partner can choose to forgive. It is harder, but it is doable. Listen carefully to your partner's pain and concern. Even if you feel that you aren't at fault, you may find something in what your partner says that can lead to a change on your part to make the relationship better.

Here's an additional word of advice: *don't* enter into discussions about forgiveness expecting or demanding some kind of quid pro quo for your apology. If you have hurt your partner and intend to try to rebuild your relationship, saying (or even thinking), "OK, I'll apologize for what I did if you apologize too" is a recipe for disaster. Don't do it.

## Step 5: If Applicable, the Offender Makes a Commitment to Change Patterns or Attitudes That Give Offense

This step depends on your agreement that there's a specific problem with the way one of you behaved. It also assumes that what happened is part of a pattern, not just a one-time event. For the Levensons and the Barkers, this step isn't very relevant. For the Mansoors and the Steins, it is critical.

If you have hurt your partner, it also helps to make amends. This is not the same as committing to make important changes. When you make amends, you make a peace offering of a sort, not because you owe your partner but because you want to demonstrate your desire to get back on track. It is a gesture of goodwill. One way to make amends is by doing unexpected positive acts. This shows your investment and ongoing desire to keep building your relationship.

## Step 6: If Possible, the Offended Agrees to Forgive

There is a Jewish tradition that when a person is asked for forgiveness three times and still refuses to forgive, the person who has offended has no more obligation to ask for forgiveness. Although this does not mean that the injured party *must* forgive anything, it does reinforce the idea that forgiveness is a process that involves both partners: one to take responsibility and to ask for forgiveness, and one to look within to find if it is possible to erase the emotional debt and truly forgive.

Ideally, the one needing to forgive clearly and openly acknowledges his or her desire to forgive. This may be unnecessary for minor infractions, but for anything of significance, this step is important. It reinforces the idea that forgiveness is a process that involves both of you, and that you are working together to heal your relationship.

This step has several specific implications. In forgiving, you are attempting to commit the event to the past and agreeing that you won't bring it up in the middle of future arguments or conflicts. You both recognize that this commitment to forgive doesn't mean that the offended will feel no pain or effects from what happened. But you are moving on. You are working to restore the relationship and repair the damage.

## Step 7: Expect Healing to Take Time

These steps are potent for getting you on track as a couple. They begin a process; they don't complete it. These steps can move the process along, but you may each be working on your side of the equation for some time to come. Even when painful events come between you, your relationship can be healed. It is your choice to work on healing it.

---

We hope that you are encouraged by the possibility for atonement, forgiveness, and reconciliation in your relationship. We also hope that you see that if you are successful, you can not only repair damage but also ultimately have a deeper and more satisfying relationship. If you have been together for only a short time, this may seem more like an academic discussion than a set of ideas that are crucial for your relationship. If you have been together for some time, however, we are sure you understand the importance of the process of forgiveness. We hope that this process will occur naturally in your relationship. If it does, keep at it. Do the work of prevention. The rewards are great. If you need to work on resentment or hurt that has built up walls, begin tearing them down. You can do it. These steps will help you get started.

In the three chapters that follow, we turn to the sublime, shifting direction to talk about how you can enhance the most wonderful aspects of marriage: fun, friendship, and sensuality. We have literally saved the best for last. If you have been working on what we have presented thus far, you are now ready to experience, or return to, the wonders of marriage.

# EXERCISE

There are two parts to this assignment, one to do individually and one to do together. Use a separate pad of paper to write down your thoughts.

## Individual Work

First, spend some time in reflection and writing about issues or events about which you may harbor resentment, bitterness, and lack of forgiveness. How old are these feelings? Are there patterns of behavior that continue to offend you? Do you hold things against your partner? Do you bring up past events in arguments? Are you willing to push yourself to forgive?

Second, spend some time reflecting and writing about situations in which you may have really hurt your partner. Have you taken responsibility? Did you apologize? Have you taken steps to change any recurrent patterns that hurt your relationship? Just as you may be holding onto some grudges, you may be standing in the way of reconciliation on some issues if you have never taken responsibility for your own actions in creating the problem.

## Working Together

As with everything else we have presented, practice is important for really putting positive patterns in place. Therefore, we recommend that you plan to sit down at least a couple of times and work through some issues using the model presented in this chapter. To start, pick less significant events or issues just to get the feel of things. This helps you build confidence and teamwork. Remember to use the Speaker-Listener Technique.

If you have identified more significant hurts that haven't been fully dealt with, take the time to sit down and tackle these more complex issues. Doing so may feel risky, but if you do it well, the resulting growth in your relationship and in your capacity for intimacy will be well worth it.

# 12

# Preserving and Protecting Friendship

*I knew nothing of books when I came forth from the
womb of my mother, and I shall die without books,
with another human hand in my own. I do, indeed,
close my door at times and surrender myself to a
book, but only because I can open the door and see a
human being looking at me.*

*Martin Buber[1]*

In these last chapters of the book, we want to help you preserve
and enhance the really great things in your relationship. Like
flowers without sunlight and water, many marriages wither and die
from a lack of attention to the best parts of the relationship. We
want to help you prevent that from happening. To start, we focus
on friendship.

As we have discussed, partners bring a whole array of expectations to their relationships, and one of the most positive is that they
will be good friends. Having a strong friendship is one of the best
ways to enjoy your relationship and to protect it for the future. Let's
look at some important principles for keeping friendship alive and
well in your marriage, or for rebuilding friendship if it has weakened
from lack of attention.

Several years ago we conducted a study on the goals that partners had for their relationships. We asked couples in all stages of a

relationship, from those who were planning marriage to couples in long-standing marriages of twenty years or more, to rank a list of possible goals, such as financial security, satisfying sex, and raising a family. What do you think that most people—both men and women—told us? It turned out that the single most important goal for marriage was to have a friend in one's mate.

How would you answer this question? When we have asked people, they have said that a friend is someone who supports you, is there for you to talk with, and is a companion in life. In short, friends are people we relax with, open up to, and count on. We talk and have fun with friends. In this chapter, we focus on the talking side of friendship, and in the next two chapters, we will focus on the role of fun and sexuality in building and maintaining your relationship and your friendship.

Unfortunately, many couples who start out as friends don't stay friends. They fail to preserve and protect friendship, one of the best aspects of the relationship. Falling short of the expectation of being friends can lead to strong feelings of disappointment and sadness. To get an idea of what can happen over time to friendship in marriage, let's look at some common problems couples have in creating and maintaining friendship.

## BARRIERS TO FRIENDSHIP

*When a friend makes a mistake, the friend remains a*
*friend and the mistake remains a mistake.*
                                        *Shimon Peres[2]*

Despite our high hopes and best intentions, barriers to friendship in marriage inevitably appear. Here are some of them.

### Between Careers and Kids, There's No Time

We all lead busy lives. Between work, the needs of the children, the upkeep of the home, exercise, paying bills, and sleeping, who has got time for friendship? Friendship, the very core of a relationship, often takes a back seat to all these competing interests. Too often, we neglect our most precious relationship, taking for granted that it can wait until we have the time.

For example, Emma and Joseph are a dual-career couple who have been together about five years. Their daughter, Rose, was two years old at the time we met them. Although they were happy with their marriage and life together, they felt as if something was slipping away:

JOSEPH: We used to sit around for hours just talking about things. You know, like politics or the meaning of life. We just don't seem to have the time for that any more.
EMMA: You're right. It used to be so much fun just being together, listening to how we each thought about things.
JOSEPH: Those talks really brought us together. Why don't we do that anymore?
EMMA: We don't take that kind of time like we used to. Now, we've got Rose, the house—not to mention that we both bring too much work home.
JOSEPH: It seems like we're letting something precious slip away. What can we do about that?

Joseph asks a great question: "Why don't we do that anymore?" and Emma has an answer that many of us can relate to. All too often, couples don't take the time just to talk as friends. The other needs and cares of life crowd out this time to relax and talk. But that's not the only reason friendship weakens over time.

## We've Lost That Friendship Feeling

Many people have told us that they were friends with their spouses to begin with, but not now—they're *just married*. It is as if once you are married, you can't be friends anymore. You can be one or the other, but not both. Well, that's a problematic belief.

The strongest marriages we have seen have maintained a solid friendship over the years. Take Dede and Paul, who have been happily married for over forty years. While they were at one of our workshops, we asked them what their secret was. They said that it was commitment and friendship. They started out with a great friendship and never let it go. They have maintained a deep respect for one another as friends, and they freely share thoughts and feelings about all sorts of things, in an atmosphere of deep acceptance. That has kept their bond strong and alive.

Don't buy into an expectation that says that because you are married—or planning to be—you can't stay friends. You can!

## We Don't Talk Like Friends Anymore

Think for a moment about a friendship you enjoy with someone other than your partner. How often do you have to talk with that person about problems between the two of you? Not often, we'd bet. Friends aren't people with whom we argue a lot. In fact, one of the nicest things about friendships is that we don't usually have to work out a lot of issues. Instead, we're able to focus on mutual interests in a way that we both enjoy.

Friends talk about sports, religion, politics, philosophy of life, guys, women, sex, love, fun things they have done or will do, dreams about the future, and thoughts about what each of them is going through at this point in life. Friends talk about points of view and points of interest. In contrast, what do many couples talk about most after they have been together for years? Let's list some of the common things: problems with the kids, problems with money and budgets, problems with getting the car fixed, concerns about who has got time to finish some project around the home, concerns about in-laws, problems with the neighbor's dog, concerns about each other's health—the list goes on and on.

If couples aren't careful, most of their talks end up being about problems and concerns—not points of view and points of interest. Problems and concerns are part of married life, and they must be dealt with, but too many couples let these issues crowd out the other, more relaxed talks they once shared and enjoyed. And because problems and concerns can easily become events that trigger issues, there is much more potential for conflict in talking with a spouse than with a friend. That brings us to the next barrier.

## We Have Conflicts That Erode Our Friendship

One of the key reasons couples have trouble remaining friends is that friendship-building activities and discussions are disrupted when issues arise in the relationship. For example, when you are angry with your partner about something that has happened, you are not going to feel much like being friends right then. Or worse, when you do have the time to be friends, conflicts come up that take you right out of that relaxed mode of being together. We believe that this is the chief reason that some couples talk as friends less and less over the years.

When couples aren't doing a good job of keeping issues from erupting into their more relaxed times together, it becomes hard to keep such positive times going in the relationship. The worst thing that can happen is that time to talk as friends becomes something to avoid. As we said earlier in the book, couples in conflict start to feel that talking leads to problems. This is one of the chief reasons some couples give up on friendship over time. But as we will see, you can prevent that from happening.

## I Already Know My Partner Very Well

It is too easy for people to assume that their partner doesn't change much over time. Couples begin to assume that it is not going to be interesting to talk as friends. They think they already know how their partner thinks about almost everything. But is this really true? We don't think so. Everyone goes through changes all the time. New events happen, new ideas replace old, and we are touched by many of the things that happen to us. Haven't you changed over the years?

Sharing reactions to life as you live it can be a very rewarding part of your friendship together. You can't know what new thoughts and ideas your mate is having unless you are able to talk as friends.

## We're Victims of the Boomerang Effect

One of the major barriers to friendship in marriage is created when thoughts that couples have shared at tender and intimate moments are used as weapons in fights. When partners do this, it is incredibly destructive to friendship.

Through positive, intimate experiences as friends, we learn things about our partners that, if we aren't careful, can be used later when we feel more like enemies. When we are mad at our partner, many of us have a tendency to say things that really hurt. Using shared intimacies as weapons is very damaging to a relationship. Who is going to share vulnerabilities and self-doubt if they might later be used against him or her in a fight?

## We Were Never Friends

What if friendship wasn't there in the beginning? If this is your situation, you may not be sure how to be friends now. In the days of *Fiddler on the Roof* and arranged marriages, people felt lucky if love and friendship developed in a marriage. Today, most couples start out with big expectations about friendship in marriage, yet some couples do miss this important stage of development in their relationship.

---

Now that we have covered some of the common barriers to keeping friendship alive, we want to share some tips to help you protect this vital part of your relationship. The ideas we suggest can work for building, rebuilding, or maintaining friendship in marriage. They work because they capture what couples do to nurture friendship in the first place.

# PROTECTING FRIENDSHIP IN YOUR RELATIONSHIP

In our work with couples, we have discerned some core principles that help protect and enhance friendship. If you have a good friendship going, these principles will help prevent your friendship from weakening over time. If you have lost something in terms of being friends, use these ideas to regain what you have been missing.

## Make the Time

Although it's great to be friends no matter what you are doing, we think that you can benefit by setting time aside specifically to talk as friends—and that means making the time. Otherwise, all the busy stuff of life will keep you occupied with problems and concerns. We mentioned how Dede and Paul had preserved and deepened their friendship over the forty years they had been married. One of the things they did to keep friendship alive was to plan time to be alone together. They would take long walks together and talk as they walked. They would go out to dinner. They would take weekend vacations from time to time, without the kids. They made the time, and it has been paying off for many years.

Of course, the issue of time always should direct us toward examining our priorities. We live in a fast-paced culture where almost everyone seems to be trying to do too much. The strong value Jews place on both achievement and children makes the Jewish marriage particularly vulnerable to being put last on the list of "to do's." Let's try a little guilt on you. All of your achievements will turn to dust if you allow your love to die. And if you really are concerned about your children, you will take better care of your marriage, because that's the real foundation their lives rest on. Feeling a little guilty about not paying enough attention to keeping your marriage strong? Good! Go out and do something about it.

## Protect Your Friendship from Conflict

In earlier chapters of this book, we focused on skills and techniques you can use to handle conflicts well, such as the Speaker-Listener Technique, good problem-solving skills, and ground rules. In Chapters Seven through Eleven, we added to these skills by presenting the issues-and-events model as well as concepts relating to forgiveness and core values. All these strategies are powerful tools for dealing with conflict, but you didn't become a couple only to handle conflict well; it is something you have to do if you want to protect the more wonderful aspects of intimacy from the damage of mishandled conflict. So one key to keeping friendship alive is protecting your friendship times from conflict.

One last point about protecting your friendship from conflict: avoid the tendency to use thoughts shared in moments of intimacy as weapons in a fight. Nothing adds fuel to the fire like betraying a trust in this way. As we said earlier, this is incredibly destructive and creates huge barriers to future intimacy. If you are getting so mad that you are tempted to do this, you probably aren't handling issues effectively enough in your relationship. This means that you may need to work harder—and together—on all of the principles and techniques we have taught. It takes a lot of skill and practice to get to the point where you can handle conflicts with respect, but it's worth the work. You work hard in other areas of your life, don't you? Why not with the one who matters the most?

## Talk Like Friends

Now let's move on to discuss how you can talk like good friends. We want to highlight some points about the way friends talk that can help you protect and enhance your relationship.

### Listen Like a Friend

Good friends listen with little defensiveness. You don't have to worry as much about hurting friends' feelings or offending them. That's because friends care about what you think and feel, and relationship issues are rarely at stake. "A friend is a person who's glad to see you and doesn't have any immediate plans for your improvement" (attributed to Mark Twain). When you are talking as friends and neither of you is trying to change anything about the other, you can relax and just enjoy the conversation. Even when you find yourself talking about some really serious issues, you often don't want a friend to tell you what to do. You just want someone to listen. It feels good to know that someone cares. Friends often provide that kind of support, and you can do this for each other in your relationship.

If you really want to push your listening skills, try using the Speaker-Listener Technique. Although we mostly think of the structure as benefiting couples when they have difficult issues to talk about, the emphasis on good listening can be a plus when you are talking as friends. Whether you use the technique or not, paraphrasing key points your partner makes can boost the intimacy of friendship talks. That's because good listening skills tend to open people up. Active listening invites the speaker to go on, to say more, to be vulnerable or silly or whatever. It feels great to have a friend who really wants to know more about you. Listening in this way is a gift you can give to your partner.

### Friends Aren't Always Focused on Solving Problems

Most of the time, when you are with a friend, you don't have to solve a problem. There may be a limited amount of time, but there's no pressure to get something done. As we said in Chapter Five, when you feel pressed to solve a problem, you cut off discussions that can bring you closer together. That's why it is so important not to talk about relationship issues when you are spending time together as friends; there is too much temptation to solve problems and give advice.

Even when you are talking about problems that have nothing to do with your relationship together, giving too much advice can throw a wet blanket on the conversation. It can appear as though you are saying, "If only you'd see the wisdom of what I'm telling you to do, we could move on and talk about something more interesting." People don't usually want advice from a friend as much as they want to know that someone cares. Don't give in to the temptation to give too much advice or solve too many problems in your time together as friends. Try to keep the avenues of discussion open so that you can learn more about each other.

### Try It

We recommend that you set aside times to talk as friends. Let's summarize the ways to make this happen:

1. Ban problem issues and relationship conflicts from these times.
2. Find some time when you can get away from the pressures of life. Don't answer the phone. For example, leave the kids with a baby-sitter and go out to dinner.
3. Focus on topics of personal or mutual interest.
4. Listen to each other in ways that deepen the sharing between you.

We have found that these methods can help couples to preserve and protect friendship. As we said at the start of this chapter, friendship is a core expectation people have for modern marriage. If you set the basic conditions for it to happen, it will blossom and continue to grow throughout your marriage.

Like much else you have learned about in this book, maintaining friendship is a skill. To keep your friendship strong, you may have to work on it a bit, but we can't think of anything of greater importance for the long-term health of your marriage than to stay friends. In this chapter, we have tried to outline some of the strategies that really make friendships work, especially those that help you communicate. As we move to the next chapter, we'll change the focus to fun. This is another key area of intimacy and friendship in marriage that is often taken for granted. Most people want to have fun with their partners. We hope you do, too, because we have some specific ideas about how you can preserve pleasure and joy in your relationship.

# EXERCISES

We often mistakenly assume that we know more about our mates than we actually do. These exercises can help you learn more about each other's joys and fears, hopes and dreams. Uncritical curiosity about your partner is a great gift that can deepen your friendship and love.

## Take Turns Choosing Topics to Talk About

Plan a quiet uninterrupted time to talk as friends. Take turns picking topics that are of interest to each of you. Ban relationship conflicts and problem solving. You might consider some of the following topics.

- Some aspect of your family of origin that you have been thinking about.

- Personal goals, dreams, or aspirations.

- A recent book or movie. Pretend that you are professional critics, if you like.

- Current events, such as sports or politics.

## Practice Active Curiosity

Take turns pretending to be your favorite television interviewers, and interview your partner about his or her life story. This can be a lot of fun, and it is very much in the spirit of listening as a friend. The best interviewers on TV are experts at listening and drawing out their guests. Your genuine, nonjudgmental curiosity about your partner is one of the greatest gifts you can give.

## Ritualize Time Together

Talk together about how you can build time for friendship into your weekly routine. If you both believe that it should be a priority, you need to sanctify time for your friendship.

# 13

# Overcoming the Fear of Fun

*The Hebrew language is flush with synonyms for joy*
*(deetza, reena, simcha, chedva, sasson, etc.). It has,*
*of course, at least as many words for suffering.*

Joshua Halberstam[1]

Although lots of people find Jewish humor funny, that is not the same as saying that Jews are always comfortable with fun. Jewish humor is built on irony, self-deprecation, anger, anxiety, and lament. Funny, yes; fun, not exactly. Maurice Sendak, author of the famous children's book *Where the Wild Things Are*, remembered spending a lot of time with his Italian neighbors in the building where he grew up. When he was a child, however, he didn't realize that they were not Jewish. He just thought that they, unlike his family and the other Jews he knew, just happened to be happy Jews.[2]

As we will see in this chapter, Maurice Sendak's parents were not the only Jews who were less than comfortable with fun. Even the word *fun* sounds somehow trivial to many Jews and tends to make them a little uncomfortable. It's all right to engage in meaningful activities: learning, earning, helping, achieving, making, getting, analyzing, and preparing. Even exercising and recreation are acceptable, as long they are in the service of improving or protecting one's health. But fun—is it really kosher? We think it needs to be in order to create successful relationships.

In Chapter Twelve, we talked about the importance of being friends with your partner. Now we build further on the theme of enhancing your relationship by focusing on how to preserve and increase fun in your relationship. You will notice many similarities between this chapter and Chapter Twelve. In fact, it will seem as though you have read many of the key points before. Nevertheless, fun is such an important aspect of your connection together that we think it deserves its own chapter. Fun is kosher!

Couples are often surprised that we include a focus on fun in our workshops; they ask, "Why is fun so important?" In general, fun experiences are another key way for couples to connect and to achieve intimacy. Here we will discuss the value of fun and also offer you some methods for keeping it alive in your relationship. So let's take on the serious topic of *fun*. Don't worry; it won't hurt too much.

## THE IMPORTANCE OF PRESERVING FUN

Fun plays a vital role in the health of family relationships. In the early versions of PREP, fun was a very small part of the program.

However, as a result of a study conducted in Denver several years ago, we learned that we weren't paying enough attention to the role of fun in marriage. It always had seemed like common sense to believe that fun was important, but this research highlighted that fact. In a study of strong marriages, couples were surveyed using over fifty questions on all aspects of their relationships, including satisfaction, commitment, communication, and just about anything else you could think of. We were very surprised to find that, among all the variables, the amount of fun these partners had together emerged as the strongest factor in understanding their overall marital happiness. That is not to say that other positive things weren't going on in these relationships, but good relationships become great when you are preserving both the quantity and the quality of your fun times together.

In contrast to the couples in these strong marriages, many couples don't continue having fun with much consistency as time goes on. What makes this so puzzling is that fun plays a critical role in the development of most relationships during courtship. Time spent playing together provides a relaxed kind of intimacy that strengthens the bond between two people. So why does fun go by the wayside for many couples when it is such a large part of developing the relationship in the first place? You would think it would be easy for couples to maintain something that is so pleasurable. Let's look at some barriers to fun in marriage; we'll then show you how to protect and enhance enjoyment in your relationship.

## BARRIERS TO FUN

Most couples have a great deal of fun early in their relationships, but for too many, it fizzles out as time goes on. What follow are some of the most common reasons that we hear from couples for why the fun fades away. Although some of these issues affect all couples, you will also see that Jews sometimes face special challenges in allowing fun to be kosher in their relationships.

### Fun Is Wrong When There Is So Much Suffering in the World

The traditional Jewish commitment to *tikkun olam*—to healing the world—is a core value in Jewish life. Central to Jewish identity is the idea of our deliverance from slavery and of our identification with the suffering of others. This has led to a remarkable history of Jewish involvement and achievement in areas such as health care and human rights. We aren't saying that all Jews are great humanitarians, but it is clear that Judaism and the experiences of Jewish history have led a great number of Jews into professions that give them the ability to make a difference in the world.

But we have noticed the tendency for many Jews, especially those in the helping professions, to have difficulty knowing when they have done enough. The "wounded healer" syndrome seems particularly prevalent among rabbis, therapists, and physicians. Doing good is good, but being revered as a healer and helper can become a dangerous addiction if you have difficulty setting boundaries. Remember the quotation from *Ethics of the Fathers* (1:14): "If I am not for myself, who will be for me? And if I am only for myself, what am I? And if not now, when?" Balance your need to help others with taking time for pleasure in your own relationship.

## Fun Is Dangerous

> *I remember my grandmother, who immigrated from Russia in 1910 at the age of eighteen. Whenever she would say anything pleasurable, like "What a beautiful child," she would always spit out the words "ken ahora" immediately afterwards. It means "against the evil eye."*
>
> Dan, a forty-five-year-old Jewish man

"Ken ahora" was a constant refrain among the Jews of the immigrant generation, because life had taught them never to put down their guard. To relax and totally enjoy the pleasure of the moment was too anxiety provoking for a generation that knew that danger was never far away. Ken ahora served as a magical preemptive strike against the possibility of loss. An incantation designed to appease the perverse power of evil, loss, and death, it was a way of saying "Don't worry, I know that you can snatch my pleasure from me without warning, so you don't have to prove your power to me right now." In muted forms, the anxiety of the past was passed on to the more secure generation of the present and still can inhibit the full enjoyment of pleasure.

In the Introduction to this book, we talked about the breaking of a glass at the end of the wedding ceremony as a reminder of the fragility of marriage or of the destruction of the Second Temple in Jerusalem. Regardless of the interpretation, it is a striking example of how Jewish tradition serves to restrain us from fully relaxing with the joy of the moment. Most Jewish ritual celebrations—even the most joyous—include some remembrance of sadness and loss. We always need to be prepared.

## We're Married Now, So We Don't Have Time for Fun

> *My parents were members of a Reform synagogue when I was growing up, but they weren't very involved. They were really surprised when I joined a modern Orthodox shul after finishing medical school. I chose to become observant not only because I really enjoyed Judaism but also because I knew that keeping Shabbat would force me to stop working and be with my family and friends. I knew myself well enough to know that without really clear boundaries, I would never know when to stop.*
>
> *Noah, a forty-two-year-old physician*
>
> *In the future world, a man will have to give an accounting for every good thing his eyes saw, but of which he did not eat.*
>
> *Palestinian Talmud, Kiddushin 4:12*

One of the unspoken expectations people sometimes hold about marriage is that it isn't supposed to be fun for very long. Many of us vowed to love and honor, but where is fun mentioned in the wedding vows? It is as if once you get married, you have to be an adult, and adults don't or shouldn't have fun. Work and responsibilities are often emphasized over and above legitimate needs for rest and relaxation. There is nothing wrong with being a responsible member of society. In fact, we encourage it. But you also have to let your hair down sometimes and enjoy each other.

We were recently talking about fun and marriage when one husband, Bob, mentioned that his wife was just too busy at work to plan for pleasure. Jeanne worked all the time. She would feel guilty if she hadn't finished her projects at work, but there were so many projects that she was never done. Bob would ask her if she could go for a walk or go out to eat, but she would always feel that she had to work late. It wasn't that Jeanne didn't like to have fun, but her sense of responsibility to her work was so great that she and her marriage were suffering.

Does this sound like you or someone you know? These anti-pleasure ethics may be a combination of the legacy of Jewish suffering and the Puritan ideals that remain a part of the Anglo American psyche. There are examples of Jewish rebellion against these attitudes. The Chassidic movement, which celebrated dancing, singing, and drinking in the celebration of God, certainly went against the more austere notions of traditional rabbinical Judaism. Also, as Hermann Cohen, the famous Jewish philosopher of the early twentieth century, remarked about Zionists, "Those fellows want to be happy."[3] But a focus on happiness and pleasure is often the exception rather than the rule in the American Jewish psyche.

"Work hard and rewards will come," the saying goes. And, in fact, certain rewards do tend to come from hard work. But you also have to look at your overall priorities. How many couples do you know who worked hard their whole lives to build a home, send their kids to college, and have a retirement nest egg but weren't able to reap the benefits because of death or divorce? At the end of life, when people are asked what they wish they had done differently, hardly anyone says, "I wish I'd worked harder, sold another car, completed more projects." People usually wish they had played more with the kids or spent more time with their spouse. Don't wait. Make sure that fun and play are an essential part of your relationship—now.

## Play Is for Kids

Many child development experts have observed that play is the work of childhood. Through play, children develop important social, emotional, and cognitive abilities. We believe that the developmental importance of play doesn't stop after childhood, but continues throughout life. Fun and play allow release from all the pressures and hassles of being an adult.

The relaxed togetherness of playful times is important in the initial development of the bond between two people. That's because when we are having fun through play, we are often relaxed and more ourselves. It is under these conditions that people fall in love—when one sees in the other the relaxed self in the context of fun times together. You rarely hear someone say, "I really fell in love with him when I saw how much he loved to work."

## Conflict Prevents Us from Having Fun

As is the case with friendship, mishandled conflict is a real killer of fun times together. In Chapter Fourteen, we make the same point about sensuality. Poorly handled conflict can ruin the most enjoyable aspects of any relationship.

The tendency to let conflict interrupt fun times can be especially troublesome for couples who are working their way back from an unhappy time toward a more satisfying relationship. It takes self-discipline not to let old conflict seep into new attempts to build love. When you slip, don't get too discouraged. Keep trying.

# TAKING FUN SERIOUSLY

> *Go eat your bread in gladness, and drink your wine*
> *in joy; for your action was long ago approved by*
> *God. . . .*
> *Enjoy happiness with a woman you love, all the fleet-*
> *ing days of life that have been granted to you under*
> *the sun—all your fleeting days. . . . Whatever it is in*
> *your power to do, do with all your might.*
> *Ecclesiastes 9:7–10*

Is fun work? It depends on your point of view. It certainly takes time and energy. We believe that part of the commitment you make to your relationship should include dedicating regular time together for enjoyment, pleasure, and fun. Take the initiative in finding ways to nurture your love.

# EXERCISES

The following exercises can help you overcome any barriers to fun that exist in your relationship.

1. Brainstorm and create a list of activities that you both find pleasurable and fun. Be creative. Anything goes, so have a good time coming up with ideas.

2. Write these ideas out on index cards to make a "fun deck." It will come in handy when you don't have much time to decide what to do but are ready for some good times. We recommend doing something enjoyable together on a daily basis, even if it is just cuddle time or laughing at jokes together.

3. Set aside time for bigger chunks of fun. Pick out three things from the deck that you would enjoy doing and hand them to your partner. Each of you should take responsibility for making one of your partner's three things happen in the time you have set aside. Go for it!

# 14

# Thou Shalt Enjoy Sex

*Why, when talking about sex, do I need to add that*
*we were more European than Jewish? Simply because*
*if our attitudes were more Jewish than European, we*
*would have been more open and adventurous about*
*sex than most people think possible, including many*
*Jews who are unfamiliar with their tradition.*

Dr. Ruth Westheimer[1]

Sexuality and marriage are inseparable, according to Jewish tradition. Not only that, sexuality is seen as holy. In *Igeret HaKodesh*, Rabbi Nachmanides (Ramban) taught, "When sexual intercourse is done for the sake of Heaven, there is nothing so holy and pure." Sex on Shabbat, the day of rest, is considered a mitzvah. Many traditional commentators have noted that pleasurable sexuality is an obligation, based on talmudic teachings that "On the Day of Judgment, a person will be required to give an accounting for all 'permissible enjoyments' that his eyes beheld and he did not partake of."

Jewish tradition also makes it quite clear that both women's and men's sexual pleasure in marriage are crucial to a successful union. Women are seen as sexual beings whose needs are important to fulfill. The *Mishna* (Sotah 3:4) states, "A woman prefers little food and sexual indulgence to much food and continence."

The *Mishna* even legislates the sexual responsibility of men to their wives, depending on the man's profession and how often he had to be away from home. For example, men of independent means were obligated to provide their wives with sex every day; laborers, twice weekly; donkey drivers, once a week; camel drivers, once every thirty days, and sailors, once every six months. A wife had the right to prevent her husband from changing his work if it meant that she would be sexually deprived.

But positive Jewish traditions and beliefs do not necessarily prevent couples from having sexual concerns. In fact, all couples commonly report that sexual issues are among their top three problem areas. Therefore, it is important to work toward preserving and enhancing the quality of the physical intimacy between the two of you. In this chapter, we show you how you can enhance and protect your sexual relationship in three important ways: (1) separating sexuality from sensuality, (2) protecting physical intimacy from anxiety and conflict, and (3) communicating clearly about sensual and sexual desires.

## SEPARATING SEXUALITY FROM SENSUALITY

*How sweet is your love,*
*My own, my bride!*
*How much more delightful your love than wine,*
*Your ointment more fragrant*
*Than any spice!*
*Sweetness drops*
*From your lips, O bride;*
*Honey and milk*
*Are under your tongue;*
*And the scent of your robes*
*Is like the scent of Lebanon.*

*Song of Songs 8:6*

Think about sexuality. What comes to mind? For many, the first thought is of sexual intercourse and all the pleasurable acts that may come before and after. Anything else? Perhaps thoughts about what arouses you or your partner, or feelings you have when you want to make love with your partner.

Now think about sensuality. What comes to mind? Usually, some pleasant experience that involves touching, seeing, smelling, or feeling—for example, walking on the beach or being massaged with sweet-smelling oil. How about the roughness of a beard or the silkiness of hair? The smell of your partner after a shower? Chocolate? You get the idea. These are memories of sensual experiences, which are not necessarily goal oriented or directly connected with sexuality.

Sensuality includes physical touch or other senses but is not always associated with making love. We would include hugging, affectionate cuddling, and nonsexual massages—all acts that provide physical pleasure in nonsexual ways. This distinction between sensuality and sexuality is important.

In the early stages of a relationship, touching, holding hands, hugging, and caressing are common. Unfortunately, over time many couples tend to bypass the sensual areas and move more exclusively to goal-oriented sexual behavior. They pay less attention to the kinds of touching and sensing that were so delightful before. This leads to problems, because such touching is a basic, pleasurable part of overall intimacy.

For example, Leah and Gene have been married for eight years. Like many other couples, they used to spend a lot of time just cuddling and caressing each other. As the years went by, they got busier with children, work, and home, and after a year or two of marriage, they had settled into a pattern of having sex about twice a week. Because of time pressures and the other cares of life, the couple devoted less and less time to sensuality. At night, in bed, one or the other would initiate sex, and they would quickly have intercourse.

Leah and Gene had become quite efficient at making love—or, rather, having intercourse. They didn't have or make a lot of extra time, so they made do. In fact, they were making do rather than making love. Their focus on sexual intercourse instead of sensuality led to dissatisfaction for both of them. "What happened to all those times we'd lie around for hours together?" Leah wondered. "It seems like Leah used to be a lot more responsive when we made love," Gene mused. We will come back to Leah and Gene in a little while.

The fact is that there needs to be a place for sensual touching in your relationship—both in and out of the context of making love. This is similar to the distinction between Problem Discussion and Problem Solution. Just as the pressures of life lead many couples to the problem-solving stage prematurely, too many couples shortchange their sensuality and prematurely focus on sex, an approach that leads to sex that may lack tender touching and real intimacy. As we learned from the classic studies of psychologist Harry Harlow, baby chimps are at risk for dying without enough physical contact—and without touching, so are marriages.

Therefore, it is important to make sensual experiences a regular part of your relationship, apart from sexuality. Furthermore, sensual experiences set the stage for better sexual experiences. The whole climate for physical intimacy is better when you have preserved sensuality. Talk together about what is sensual for each of you. What do you enjoy? Make the time for sensual experiences, like massages, that don't necessarily lead to sex.

It is also important to keep sensuality as a regular part of your lovemaking. Keeping a focus on a variety of ways of touching preserves and elevates the importance of the whole sensual experience. Most couples prefer this broader sensual focus to a narrow focus on sex. It fosters a fuller expression of intimacy in your physical relationship. We give you some specific suggestions for preserving and enhancing sensuality in the exercises at the end of the chapter.

## BARRIERS TO PLEASURABLE SEXUALITY

Before suggesting ways you can enhance your sensuality, we are going to discuss some obstacles that may stand in the way of your mutual pleasure. Satisfying sexuality requires arousal, the natural process through which we are stimulated to sensual or sexual pleasure. Although just about everyone is capable of being aroused, this pleasurable feeling can be short-circuited by anxiety. Numerous studies suggest that anxiety is the key factor inhibiting arousal. We would like to discuss two kinds of anxiety in this context: performance anxiety and the tension created by conflict in your marriage.

## The Barrier of Performance Anxiety

Those who have studied the sexual relationship most extensively, such as William Masters and Virginia Johnson, have described a particular type of anxiety that is virtually incompatible with good lovemaking. Performance anxiety is anxiety about how you are performing when you make love. Anxiously asking yourself questions such as "How am I doing?" or "Is my partner enjoying this?" on a regular basis reflects performance anxiety.

When you are keeping an eye on your performance, you put distance between yourself and your partner. You are focused on how you are doing rather than on being with your partner. Many people report feeling distant when making love, as if they were just watching what is going on instead of participating. This kind of detachment can lead to a variety of sexual problems. The focus is no longer on the pleasure you are sharing; instead, you feel as though your self-esteem is at stake. In these situations, the event of making love has triggered issues of acceptance and the fear of rejection rather than creating pleasure and a sense of connection.

The focus on performance interferes with arousal because you are distracted from your own sensations of pleasure. This distraction leads to many of the most common sexual problems people experience—premature ejaculation and problems with keeping erections for men, and difficulty lubricating or having orgasms for women. You can't be both anxious and pleasantly aroused at the same time. And you can't relax and enjoy being with your partner if you are concentrating on not making mistakes.

Let's go back to Gene and Leah again. Gene became aware over time that Leah was less and less pleased with their lovemaking. Without a focus on sensuality and touching throughout their relationship, Leah began to feel as if Gene were just using her sexually. This feeling was intensified because he had orgasms every time they made love, but hers were less frequent. As unsatisfying as their lovemaking had become for both of them, it seemed to Leah that it was nevertheless better for Gene, so her resentment grew.

Gene knew that Leah was resentful, and he wanted to make things better. But instead of talking it out and working on the problem together, he decided he would just try to do a better job of making love to Leah. This wasn't all bad as ideas go. However, it caused him to be more and more focused on performing, and his anxiety increased. Thoughts about performance became his constant companions during their lovemaking: "How's Leah doing? Is she getting excited? Does she like this? I wonder if she thinks I'm doing this right? Man, I'd better try more of this for a while; I'm not sure she's ready."

Pretty soon he was pleasing Leah more, but he was growing tenser and tenser about what he was doing when they made love. Sure, he was meeting some of her needs, but he wasn't feeling at all connected with her or satisfied in their lovemaking. He was performing! Leah knew there was a change in Gene's attention to her arousal, which pleased her to a degree. But she also had a growing sense of unease—she felt that Gene was somewhere else when they made love. She was having more orgasms and feeling less satisfied.

The key for Leah and Gene was to rediscover the sensual side of their relationship by sharing their feelings about what was going on. They had a great deal of love and respect for each other, and they each decided to take the risk of talking directly about sex. Once they were able to begin to deal with the issues, things quickly got better. Here's how they began:

LEAH: (*bringing up the subject after the kids were asleep and she and Gene were relaxed and reading in bed*) Can we talk for a minute about something?

GENE: Sure. What's up?

LEAH: I've been thinking that our lovemaking just isn't like it used to be.

GENE: *(He feels a twinge of anxiety but decides to listen nondefensively. He turns toward Leah to show his interest.)* I agree. I'm really glad you're bringing it up. What's it been like for you?

LEAH: Well, lately, it seems like you're trying harder to please me, but for some reason I don't like what's going on that much more than before. I was reluctant to talk about it, because I didn't want to hurt your feelings.

GENE: It's OK. I can handle it. And I know what you mean. It's just not relaxed like it used to be. I'm tense half the time we're together in the bedroom.

LEAH: I wonder why that is. Are you trying too much? It almost seems to me like you're not there with me.

GENE: Well, yes. I am trying hard to please you. I knew you weren't happy with what we've been doing, so I was trying to make things better for you. But that's been a drag. Now I'm worried so much about doing things right that it's no fun to make love.

LEAH: I appreciate that you've been trying to make things better for me. And I've sensed what you're saying about you working so hard at it that you're not having any fun. That's partly why I'm not happy with the whole thing. It's not like it used to be, when the two of us really enjoyed being together in bed.

GENE: It's pretty clear that what I'm doing isn't getting us back to the way things used to be. We used to enjoy our time in bed together so much, like that time in San Diego where it was just the two of us, alone, for the whole weekend. We used to spend more time touching and kissing, and I think that made the whole thing better.

LEAH: It sure did. That's what I really want more of, not what we're doing now. Like you say, we used to spend the time for it to be like that. I think time is our biggest problem here. Most of the time, now, it seems like we're in a hurry, like making love is something to get over with rather than something to enjoy. That's frustrating to me.

GENE: Me too. When there's time pressure, we don't spend the time to just caress each other and relax. I think that sets us up for having a frustrating time when we jump into making love.

As you can see, they didn't try to fix the problem prematurely. Each of them listened to the other's frustrations and desire to improve their sexual relationship. They agreed that they had been giving too little time to this important aspect of their marriage. As they moved on, they decided to make more time for lovemaking, and they pursued sensuality together in and out of the context of lovemaking. They began to spend time just touching and massaging each other, as they used to do. These changes made a difference. It took some time, but they were able to eliminate a lot of their fears about performance and reestablish a full and pleasurable physical relationship.

## The Barrier of Relationship Conflict and Anxiety

> When our love was strong, we could have made our bed
> on the blade of a sword. Now that our love is no longer
> strong, a bed sixty cubits wide is not large enough.
> Babylonian Talmud, Sanhedrin 7a

Mishandled conflicts can destroy your physical relationship by adding tension both in and out of the bedroom. Let's face it, when you have been arguing and angry with each other, you usually don't feel like being sensual or making love. Some couples find that their sexual relationship is temporarily enhanced by the "making up" following conflict, but for most people, poorly handled conflict adds a layer of tension that affects everything else in the relationship, including sexuality.

There is probably no area of intimate connection that is more vulnerable to the effects of conflict and resentment than your physical relationship. If you are experiencing conflict in other areas of your relationship, it can be difficult to feel positive about sharing an intimate physical experience. Worse, for couples with a lot of unresolved issues, conflicts can often erupt in the context of lovemaking.

Even though touching sensually and making love are powerful ways to connect, destructive conflict builds barriers. If you can protect your times for physical intimacy from conflict, you can do a great deal to keep your physical relationship alive and well. To do this, you must work to handle conflict effectively—for example, by using the ground rules and the other techniques we have been stressing. *It is critical to agree to keep problems and disagreements off-limits during times you reserve to be together to touch or make love.* We can't think of anything more powerful for preserving your ability to enjoy physical intimacy.

Sometimes the conflicts affecting the physical relationship are about sensuality or lovemaking. Consider Don and Melissa, who felt stuck in a sexual impasse. They had been married just a few years and were worried that their closeness was slipping away. Their conversation went something like this:

DON: When I come home from work, I'd like to be able to hug and kiss you as part of saying "hello." That doesn't seem too unreasonable, does it?

MELISSA: No, it isn't, but that's not what I see happening. You start putting your hands all over me without seeing if I'm in the mood or busy. I feel like I'm not even a person sometimes.

DON: But it's like that in bed, too. I want to snuggle up to you, and you pull away. I like to touch a lot, and you don't seem to anymore.

MELISSA: I'd really like to, but it seems like we need to slow down, with you being more aware of what I want. And if you yelled at me earlier in the day, I'm not going to feel like touching or making love later on.

Don and Melissa had a positive relationship. They were at our workshop to learn how to keep it that way. Their physical relationship was one area where they were having trouble, and we were able to make some suggestions that helped them before real resentment built up.

We would like you to notice several things in this example:

1.  Don and Melissa had fallen into a pursuer-withdrawer pattern in regard to physical intimacy. It is not uncommon for men to withdraw from conflict but be the pursuer in the arena of physical intimacy. Any time there is a strong imbalance with one pursuing and one withdrawing with regard to sex, the situation is ripe for conflict.

2.  What each of them did in this pattern was affected by the other. As Don pushed more, Melissa pulled back, and as she pulled back, he pushed more—just as we described in discussing gender differences in Chapter Three. One partner's actions are rarely independent of the other's.

3.  They each had developed some negative interpretations about what all this meant, which they hadn't been talking about constructively. Melissa started to believe that Don was just interested in sex, which turned out not to be the case, and he started to think that she wasn't interested in any touching, whether or not it led to sex. As we discussed earlier in the book, even though men and women may have different preferences regarding how they approach intimacy, we feel that both sexes want to connect in a variety of positive ways. Don and Melissa were both interested in talking, touching, and making love, but barriers were creeping into their marriage. They needed to start talking about what was going on, and that is what we encouraged them to do.

Obviously, a lack of communication about your physical relationship can create barriers. If Don and Melissa hadn't been interested in preventing this pattern from going further, real problems with conflict could have developed in their relationship. In turn, the resulting anxiety and tension could have led to decreased arousal and interest in the physical relationship. When a couple allows that to happen, sex and sensuality can lead to despair rather than delight. Sex becomes something to "get over with," because it stirs up anxiety about potential conflict.

Physical intimacy is an area that's particularly ripe for triggering hidden issues of control, caring, and acceptance. For example, the way your partner pursues lovemaking may lead you to feel controlled. That's what Melissa was feeling when Don would touch her when she wasn't ready or interested. Or perhaps one partner avoids sex as a way to gain some control in the relationship. Likewise, it is very easy to feel uncared for if your partner doesn't show an interest in touching or making love in the ways that interest you the most. Don was beginning to believe that Melissa didn't care, because she rebuffed his attempts to hug her when he came home. To be rebuffed physically or sexually is particularly stinging to most people. It is often experienced as a deep rejection.

You can't prevent or repair such patterns unless you are handling conflict well and communicating openly and safely. It is just too easy to let resentments build if you don't open up about your concerns, especially when hidden issues are being triggered. Don and Melissa told us later that they had a great discussion about their problem and were able to develop real solutions for handling their concerns about physical intimacy. In their discussion, Melissa learned that Don wasn't just trying to use her sexually and that he truly cared a lot about keeping their physical relationship strong. He learned that she was interested in their physical relationship but wanted some changes to make it better. She wanted him to take her needs and state of mind into account in his physical advances.

Melissa felt that Don heard her concerns, and she was relieved when she saw his genuine desire to work on this part of their relationship. Don felt that he was being heard when he expressed how important the physical relationship was to him, not just for the sake of sex but because this was an important way to feel an intimate sense of emotional connection.

After having such a good discussion, they went on to some problem solving that really got them on track. For one thing, they decided to reemphasize their sensuality by planning times for touching when the focus wasn't on sex. This helped Melissa to relax about touching again and allowed her to see that Don wasn't only focused on sex. They also agreed to some ground rules of their own about when and where certain kinds of touches were OK. They planned for a way to enjoy the pleasures of a long hug at the end of the workday, without either of them feeling any pressure to have sex.

Don and Melissa were able to feel much more connected by having a really good Problem Discussion followed by a Problem Solution session. They cleared the blocked emotional pathways that were causing pain and distress in their intimate relationship, and doing so allowed their love to flow more freely. Because they were able to do this, they could also agree to plan times to make love that allowed for more sharing, verbally and nonverbally, about what they really liked. And that brings us to our last major point in this chapter.

## COMMUNICATING DESIRES

*I would say that the sexual organs express the human soul more than any other part of the body. They are not diplomats. They tell the truth ruthlessly.*

Isaac Bashevis Singer[2]

The Bible uses the word *la'da'at*, "to know," for having sex. This is not just a biblical fig leaf, modestly concealing explicit sexuality. It is consistent, though, with the constant repetition in Jewish tradition of the connection between intimacy and sexuality. *Knowing* requires communication, and open communication can involve taking the risk of making yourself vulnerable.

It is critical for you to communicate about your physical rela-tionship in ways that protect and enhance this important way of being intimate. This need for good communication applies not only to handling potential conflicts about physical intimacy but also to letting each other know what you desire. We are talking about real communication here, not mind reading. Mind reading can cause many serious conflicts throughout a relationship, including conflicts about sensuality and sexuality. The problem is that people too eas-ily assume that they know what their partner wants, and when. It can be even worse when they assume that their partner should know what they want without being told.

## You Should Know What I Like!

It is a mistake to assume that your partner will like whatever you like or that you can read each other's minds. Would you go out to a restaurant and order for your partner without talking about what he or she would like? Maybe once in a while it might be fun, but most people want to order their own food. It is also too easy for some people to assume that their partner won't like the things they like. In either situation, you are making assumptions. And because many couples have trouble communicating about their physical relationship, it is very easy for these assumptions to take control. You don't know what your partner's expectations are until you ask.

Of course, because of your previous experiences together you can often assume correctly, and things can work out fine based on those assumptions. However, keep in mind that people change, so check-ing in with each other about desires and expectations is valuable for a good sexual relationship. We can't tell you how many couples we have talked with in which one partner expects the other to "know" what she or he likes most when making love. It is as if peo-ple believe that "it just isn't romantic or exciting if I have to tell you what I want. You should know!" That's an unreasonable expec-tation. If you hold this fantasy, you should probably challenge it for the health of your relationship.

Couples who have the best sexual relationships usually have ways of communicating both verbally and nonverbally about what they like. Furthermore, they usually have a genuinely unselfish desire to please one another. There is a strong sense of teamwork, even in lovemaking.

We recommend that you communicate clearly about what feels pleasurable to you while you are touching or making love. Your partner won't know unless you say something. We aren't suggesting that you have a Speaker-Listener discussion in the middle of making love, though if it excites you, let us know!

Finally, look for ways to give to your partner in your physical relationship. If you are keeping conflict out of the bedroom, handling conflict well in the rest of your relationship, and taking the time and energy to preserve sensuality, this kind of sharing will be much easier to do.

## Taking a Risk

Many people also have to overcome the fear of rejection that can occur when they ask for what they want. Your desires say something about who you are, so to express them is to risk feeling rejected. But unless you take risks, you will settle for less in your relationship. Again, don't expect your partner to read your mind. Just as important, don't take it as a terrible rejection if your partner isn't interested in some kinds of lovemaking that interest you. That's normal in any marriage. As in other areas, you must be sensitive to each other's needs and desires. Although there may be some behaviors one of you would enjoy but the other wouldn't, there are probably many others that you are both very interested in and that you would both enjoy, including some you may not have tried or talked about before.

Communication is the key to getting to know your partner more deeply. It also helps to try some new ideas to break out of ruts. Read a book on massage or sex together. This might help you talk about these issues. Agree to surprise each other one night. Try something new, even if just once. Exploring both the sensual and sexual sides of your relationship may relieve concerns about performance and help you find even more pleasure and create a deeper connection.

We are not saying that every couple can have a wonderful physical relationship. You both have to want it, protect it, and nurture it. If things are going well in your physical relationship, keep them that way. If problems have developed, the ideas we are emphasizing here can help you get back on track.

———————

Before we finish this chapter, we want to offer a word of caution. It is important to rule out any underlying physical or emotional barriers to satisfying sexuality. Untreated or undiagnosed diseases, including depression or diabetes, can hurt every aspect of your relationship, including the sexual. The side effects of certain prescribed medications (such as antidepressants) or too much alcohol can also impair sexual performance, even if you are great communicators. If you are having sexual problems, you should consult with your physician to make sure that medical problems requiring physical interventions or medication are not getting in the way of satisfying sexuality.

———————

In this chapter, we have discussed several ways to keep your physical relationship growing and vibrant. Now it is up to you. We don't intend this chapter to be a substitute for sex therapy if you have a history of significant sexual difficulties. If you do, we encourage you to work together and with professionals to overcome the problems. Working with an experienced sex therapist can usually accomplish a great deal. Our focus here has been on helping couples with satisfying physical relationships to keep things that way—and to make them even better.

We want to help you maintain and increase physical intimacy. As with so many areas we have discussed, working wisely on this aspect of your marriage can produce great benefits. Physical intimacy isn't all that marriage is about, but it is one of the areas, like fun and friendship, where you can develop a lasting, satisfying ability to connect. To close this chapter, we offer exercises that can help you enhance your abilities to connect sensuously and sexually.

# EXERCISES

The exercises we describe have been used successfully for years by many couples. If you are ready for sensual and sexual enhancement, read on.

## Make Sex a Ritual

Even if you are a camel driver or a sailor, you need to have time set aside for being sexual. And whether you are religiously observant or not, creating your own Shabbat, a time when you expect to be sexual and sensual with each other, can be very positive for your relationship. Ritual is not the same as routine. Routine saps vitality from life; ritual can imbue it with meaning and depth.

## Sensate-Focus Exercise

Years ago, William Masters and Virginia Johnson began studying the various ways in which problems develop in sexual relationships. They created an exercise that can benefit you whether or not you are having problems with your physical relationship. This exercise is called the Sensate-Focus. It has two purposes: (1) to keep you focused on sensuality and touching in your physical relationship and (2) to help you learn to communicate more openly and naturally about what you like and don't like in your lovemaking.

This isn't the time for sexual intercourse. That would defeat the purpose, because the focus is on sensuality. Don't be goal oriented, except toward the goal of relaxing and doing this exercise in a way that you each enjoy. If you want to make love following the exercise, that's up to you. But if you have been having concerns about feeling pressured sexually, we would recommend that you completely separate these practice times from times when you have sex.

In fact, you shouldn't have sex unless both of you fully and openly agree to do so. No mind reading or assumptions!

The general idea is that you each take turns giving and receiving pleasure. The first few times, you are either the Giver or the Receiver until you switch roles halfway through the exercise. When you are in the Receiver role, your job is to enjoy the touching and to give feedback on what feels good and what doesn't. Your partner can't know this unless you say how you feel. You can give either verbal or hand-guided feedback. Verbal feedback means telling your partner what actions feel good, how hard to rub, or what areas you like to have touched. Hand-guided feedback consists of gently moving your partner's hand around the part of the body being massaged to provide feedback about what feels good.

As the Giver, your role is to provide pleasure by touching your partner and being responsive to feedback. Ask for feedback as often as necessary. Be aware of changes in how your partner is reacting: what feels good one minute may hurt or tickle the next. Focus on what your partner wants, not on what you think would feel good.

To start out, choose roles and take turns massaging your partner's hands or feet for about ten or twenty minutes, asking for and giving feedback. We recommend massages of areas like the hands, back, legs, or feet the first few times to get the hang of the technique. This also helps you relax if either of you is tense about sexuality. Then switch roles. Repeat as often as you like, but also remember to practice these roles in other aspects of your sensual and sexual relationship.

We recommend that you try the Sensate-Focus exercise over the course of several weeks, several times a week. As you practice the exercise and become more comfortable, you can add in variations of the technique. Assuming that all is going well with your exercises, begin to move to other areas for touching. Wherever you want to be touched, including sexual areas, is great.

As you continue with this exercise, you can drop the rigid emphasis on the Giver and Receiver roles and work on both of you giving and receiving at the same time, while still keeping an emphasis on sensuality and communication of your desires. Or you can vary the degree to which you stay in these roles as you wish. Through practice, it will become easier for you to communicate openly about touch. It will also be easier for you to work together as you continue to keep physical intimacy vibrant and alive.

## Exploring the Sensual

In addition to the Sensate-Focus exercise, set aside a specific time for sensual activities together. This works for all couples, regardless of whether or not they are engaging in sexual activity. Be sure you won't be interrupted. (This is the time for baby-sitters or answering machines.)

At the start of this exercise, talk about what is sensual for each of you and what you would like to try doing to deepen sensual experiences in your relationship. Here are some ideas:

- Give a massage to your partner, using the Sensate-Focus technique.

- Share a fantasy you have had about your partner.

- Cuddle and hug as you talk to your partner about the positive things you love about him or her.

- Plan a sensual or sexual activity for your next encounter.

- Plan a wonderful meal together. Prepare it together and sit close to each other. Share the meal.

- Wash your partner's hair.

- Spend some time just kissing.

# 15

# Ancient Wisdom and Modern Insights

*A season is set for everything, a time for every experi-
ence under heaven. A time for being born and a time
for dying.*

*Ecclesiastes*

The psychological wisdom of Judaism is revealed in its use of
time to nurture and balance the full range of human experience: a time for mourning and joy, for restful reflection and sensual
abandon, for atonement and forgiveness. All of Jewish tradition
revolves around rituals of renewal that ensure that such a time is set
for every experience under heaven.

Jewish tradition also accepts the inevitability of conflict in
human life as well as the need for its regulation. We are heirs to
ancient guidelines, values, and rules about how to treat others, especially when anger flares. Our traditions teach us how to use dialogue, debate, and even argument in ways that deepen
understanding and commitment between people.

Our modern research into what makes marriages succeed and
fail is a rediscovery of the truths that Jewish tradition never forgot.
We have learned that the commitment to a relationship can be
measured by the dedication of time to nurture it. The chapters of
this book have focused on how couples need a time for facing their

differences, a time for creativity, and time for rest and renewal, friendship and fun, and sexuality and pleasure.

Misunderstanding, anger, and disappointment are inevitable in the best of marriages. Closeness creates friction as well as warmth. We talk about fighting *for* your marriage because both ancient wisdom and modern science reveal the importance of finding ways to deal with conflict in intimate relationships. Conflict is not the problem—but poorly handled conflict is. True to Jewish tradition, we have tried to show how to ritualize and structure the ways we deal with our differences.

Love, devotion, loyalty, and commitment to the ideals of marriage and family don't just happen—they take work. If you are willing to take the time to practice the rituals of emotional and spiritual engagement, you can integrate them into your daily life. And if you also nurture your connections to family, friends, community, and the Jewish traditions that you find meaningful, you can sanctify and strengthen your relationship.

Just as the person who has sinned and truly atoned can be seen as more righteous than the person who has never erred, we believe that couples who have learned to deal with conflict in their marriages can have more resilient and satisfying marriages than those who avoid facing their differences. There is no more meaningful legacy for our children—and no more important way to nurture the promises we have made to one another—than to be warriors for peace. In this book, we have shown you ways to transform anger into the energy that deepens love. Jewish tradition teaches the importance of *tikkun olam*—of repairing the world. We believe that practicing the skills that lead *to shalom bayit*—peace in the home— is a wonderful place to begin.

# Notes

## Introduction

1. Levav, I., Kohn, R., Golding, J. M., & Weissman, M. M. (1997). Vulnerability of Jews to affective disorders. *American Journal of Psychiatry, 154*, 941–947.

## Chapter One

1. Roth, P. (1969). *Portnoy's complaint*. New York: Bantam Books, pp. 133–134.

2. Telushkin, J. (1992). *Jewish humor: What the best Jewish jokes say about the Jews*. New York: Morrow, p. 33.

3. Patai, R. (1977). *The Jewish mind*. New York: Scribner, p. 223.

4. Crohn, J. (1995). *Mixed matches: How to create successful interracial, interethnic, and interfaith relationships*. New York: Fawcett, p. 195.

5. Klein, J. W. (1980). *Jewish identity and self-esteem: Healing wounds through ethnotherapy*. New York: The American Jewish Committee. Also see Frondorf, S. (1988). *Death of a Jewish American princess: The true story of a victim on trial*. New York: Villard Books. This book reports on the horrifying results of projection of negative stereotypes onto the opposite sex. Steven Steinberg, a Jewish man from Phoenix, Arizona, was acquitted by an all-Gentile jury for murdering his Jewish wife. Using the so-called JAP (Jewish

American Princess) defense, the defense portrayed his wife, Elena, as materialistic, sexually withholding, and bitchy, and not only won Steinberg's freedom but his right to inherit her property. One juror who spoke to a reporter said, "He should have won a medal."

6. Crohn, J. (1995). Op cit.

7. Crohn, J. (1995). Op cit, pp. 34–35.

## Chapter Two

1. Zborowski, M., & Herzog, E. (1978). *Life is with people: The culture of the shtetl.* New York: Schocken Books, p. 301.

2. Patai, R. (1977). *The Jewish mind.* New York: Scribner.

3. Kushner, H. R. (1987). *When all you've ever wanted isn't enough.* New York: Pocket Books, p. 187.

4. Markman, H., Stanley, S., & Blumberg, S. L. (1994). *Fighting for your marriage: Positive steps for preventing divorce and preserving a lasting love.* San Francisco: Jossey-Bass, p. 24.

5. Graetz, N. (1998). *Silence is deadly: Judaism confronts wife beating.* Northvale, NJ: Aronson.

## Chapter Three

1. Telushkin, J. (1992). *Jewish humor: What the best Jewish jokes say about the Jews.* New York: Morrow, p. 84.

2. Zborowski, M., & Herzog, E. (1978). *Life is with people: The culture of the shtetl.* New York: Schocken Books.

3. Meyerhoff, B. (1978). *Number our days.* New York: Simon & Schuster, p. 244.

4. Cantor, A. (1995). *Jewish women/Jewish men: The legacy of patriarchy in Jewish life.* San Francisco: Harper San Francisco.

5. Crohn, J. (1986). *Ethnic identity and marital conflict: Jews, Italians, and WASPs.* [Monograph]. New York: American Jewish Committee.

6. Levav, I., Kohn, R., Golding, J. M., & Weissman, M. M. (1997). "Vulnerability of Jews to affective disorders." *American Journal of Psychiatry, 154,* 941–947. It is also interesting to note that this

study found that Jewish men's rates of alcohol abuse was half that of non-Jews. It also found that Jewish men in more assimilated environments had somewhat lower rates of depression and higher rates of alcoholism than other Jewish men. The study found that Jewish women were no more likely to be depressed than non-Jewish women.

7. Sowell, T. (1981). *Ethnic America: A history*. New York: Basic Books, p. 5.

8. Klein, J. W. (1980). *Jewish identity and self-esteem: Healing wounds through ethnotherapy*. New York: American Jewish Committee.

9. Rosen, G. "The impact of the women's movement on the Jewish family." In S. Bayme & G. Rosen (Eds.), *The Jewish family and Jewish continuity*. Hoboken, NJ: KTAV Publishing House, 1994, p. 281.

10. Fishman, S. B. (1994). The changing American Jewish family faces the 1990s. In S. Bayme & G. Rosen (Eds.), *The Jewish family and Jewish continuity*. Hoboken, NJ: KTAV Publishing, pp. 3–52.

11. Schwartz, J. C., Sharpsteen, D. J., & Butler, J. M. (1987). *Regulation of intimacy in conversations between same-sex close friends*. Unpublished manuscript, University of Denver, Denver, CO.

12. Levinson, R., & Gottman, J. M. (1983). "Marital interaction: Physiological linkage and affective exchange." *Journal of Personality and Social Psychology, 45*, 587–599.

13. Gottman, J. M, & Krokoff, L. J. (1989). "Marital interaction and satisfaction: A longitudinal view." *Journal of Consulting & Clinical Psychology, 57*, 47–52.

## Chapter Four

1. Ben Shea, N. (1995). *The word: A spiritual sourcebook*. New York: Villard Books.

2. Levenson, S. (1979). *You don't have to be in Who's Who to know what's what*. New York: Simon & Schuster.

3. Blech, B. (1999). *The complete idiot's guide to understanding Judaism*. New York: Macmillan, p. 159.

## Chapter Five

1. Rabbi Harold Schulweis, personal communication, 1998.

2. Patai, R. (1977). *The Jewish mind.* New York: Scribner.

3. Pogrebin, L. C. (1996). *Getting over getting older.* New York: Little, Brown.

4. Telushkin, J. (1996). *Words that hurt, words that heal: How to choose words wisely and well.* New York: Morrow, pp. 79, 83.

## Chapter Six

1. Telushkin, J. (1994). *Jewish wisdom: Ethical, spiritual, and historical lessons from the great works and thinkers.* New York: Morrow, p. 200.

## Chapter Seven

1. Jacobson, S. (1995). *Toward a meaningful life: The wisdom of the Rebbe Menachem Mendel Schneerson.* New York: Morrow, p. 213.

2. Beach, S. R. H., Sandeen, E. E., & O'Leary, K. D. (1990). *Depression in marriage.* New York: Guilford Press.

3. Buber, M. (1974). (W. Kaufman, Trans.). *I and thou.* Old Tappan, NJ: Macmillan.

## Chapter Eight

1. Telushkin, J. (1994). *Jewish wisdom: Ethical, spiritual, and historical lessons from the great works and thinkers.* New York: Morrow, p. 279.

2. Sager, C. J. (1976). *Marriage contracts and couple therapy: Hidden forces in intimate relationships.* New York: Bruner/Mazel.

## Chapter Nine

1. Levenson, S. (1979). *You don't have to be in Who's Who to know what's what.* New York: Simon & Schuster.

2. Johnson, D. J., & Rusbult, C. E. (1989). "Resisting temptation: Devaluation of alternative partners as a means of maintaining commitment in close relationships." *Journal of Personality and Social Psychology, 57,* 967–980.

3. Kushner, H. R. (1987). *When all you ever wanted wasn't enough*. New York: Pocket Books.

4. Jacobson, S. (1995). *Toward a meaningful life: The wisdom of the Rebbe Menachem Mendel Schneerson*. New York: Morrow, p. 62.

5. Perls, F. (1969). *Gestalt therapy verbatim*. Lafayette, CA: Real People Press, p. 4.

## Chapter Ten

1. Cowan, P., & Cowan, R. (1989). *Mixed blessings: Overcoming the stumbling blocks in interfaith marriage*. New York: Penguin Books.

2. Fishman, S. B. (1994). *The changing American Jewish family faces the 1990s*. In S. Bayme & G. Rosen (Eds.), *The Jewish family and Jewish continuity* (pp. 3–52). Hoboken, NJ: KTAV Publishing, p. 26.

3. Burchinal, L., & Chancellor, L. E. (1963). "Survival rates among religiously homogamous and interreligious marriages." *Social Forces*, *41*, 353–362.

4. Pargament, K. I., Tyler, F. B., & Steele, R. E. (1979). "Is fit it? The relationship between the church/synagogue member fit and the psycho-social competence of the member." *Journal of Community Psychology*, *7*, 243–252.

## Chapter Eleven

1. Ariel, D. (1995). *What do Jews believe: The spiritual foundations of Judaism*. New York: Schocken Books, p. 95.

## Chapter Twelve

1. Buber, M. (1973). *Meetings*. (M. Friedman, Ed.). LaSallee, IL: Open Court, p. 61.

2. Peres, S., quoted in Telushkin, J. (1994). *Jewish wisdom: Ethical, spiritual, and historical lessons from the great works and thinkers*. New York: Morrow, p. 553.

## Chapter Thirteen

1. Halberstam, J. (1997). *Schmoozing*. New York: Perigee Books, p. 159.

2. Ibid., p. 157.

3. Ibid., p. 159.

## Chapter Fourteen

1. Westheimer, R. K., & Mark, J. (1996). *Heavenly sex: Sexuality in the Jewish tradition*. New York: Continuum, p. 3. "Dr. Ruth," the popular expert on sexuality, lost her entire family to the Nazis in the Holocaust. She found in Judaism and Jewish tradition an affirmation of life, and she writes compellingly about the life-affirming importance of pleasure in sexuality.

2. Singer, I. B. (1985). *Conversations with Isaac Bashevis Singer and Richard Burgin*. Garden City, NY: Doubleday.

# Resources

## Publications

Abramowitz, Y. I., & Silverman, S. (1997). *Jewish family and life: Traditions, holidays, and values for today's parents and children*. New York: Golden Books.

Biale, D. (1997). *Eros and the Jews: A review of Eros and the Jews: From biblical Israel to contemporary America*. Berkeley: University of California Press.

Cowan, P., & Cowan, R. (1989). *Mixed blessings: Overcoming the stumbling blocks in an interfaith marriage*. New York: Penguin.

Crohn, J. (1985). *Ethnic identity and marital conflict: Jews, Italians, and WASPs*. New York: The American Jewish Committee.

Crohn, J. (1995). *Mixed matches: How to create successful interracial, interethnic, and interfaith relationships*. New York: Fawcett.

Diamant, A. (1986). *The new Jewish wedding*. New York: Summit Books.

Jaffe, A. (2000). *Two Jews can still be a mixed marriage: Reconciling differences over Judaism in your marriage*. Franklin Lakes, NJ: Career Press.

King, A. (1994). *If I'm Jewish and you're Christian, What are the children?* New York: UAHC Press.

Kushner, H. (1997). *How good do we have to be? A new understanding of guilt and forgiveness*. New York: Little, Brown.

Levin, S. (1991). *Mingled roots: A guide for Jewish grandparents of interfaith grandchildren*. Washington, DC: B'nai B'rith Women.

Markman, H., Stanley, S., & Blumberg, S. (1994). *Fighting for your marriage: Positive steps for preventing divorce and preserving a lasting love*. San Francisco: Jossey-Bass.

Schulweis, H. (1994). *For those who can't believe: Overcoming the obstacles to faith*. New York: HarperPerennial.

Telushkin, J. (1998). *Words that heal, Words that hurt: How to choose words wisely and well*. New York: Morrow.

Wallerstein, J. S., & Blakeslee, S. (1996). *The good marriage: How and why love lasts*. New York: Warner Books.

Westheimer, R., & Mark, J. (1995). *Heavenly sex: Sexuality in the Jewish tradition*. New York: NYU Press.

## Web Sites

www.Jewish.com or AOL keyword: Jewish
*Jewish Community Online*
Popular site on the Web and AOL that brings together a tremendous collection of Jewish news, views, and resources.

www.Jewishfamily.com
The on-line Jewish community of *Jewish Family & Life!* Composed of over twenty-five different sites and 'zines, JFL! is committed to "changing the face of world Jewry one person at a time."

www.jta.org
Jewish Telegraphic Agency.
Jewish news the world over.

www.aish.com
Jewish outreach, discussion, and issues.

## Jewish Organizations

American Jewish Committee
165 E. 5th St.
New York, NY 10022
(212) 751–4000

Jewish Community Centers of North America
15 E. 26th St.
New York, NY 10010
(212) 532–4949
www.jcca.org

Jewish Book Council
15 East 26th St.
New York, NY 10010
www.Jewishbooks.org
(212) 532–4949, ext. 297
Sponsors Jewish book month and Jewish book fairs.

## Synagogue Offices

Aleph: The Alliance for Jewish Renewal
7318 Germantown Rd.
Philadelphia, PA 19919–1793
(215) 242–4074

Union of American Hebrew Congregations
(The Reform Movement)
838 Fifth Ave.
New York, NY 10021
(212) 249–0100

United Synagogue of Conservative Judaism
155 Fifth Ave.
New York, NY 10010
(212) 533–7800

Union of Orthodox Jewish Congregations
333 Seventh Ave.
New York, NY 10001
(212) 563–4000

Federation of Reconstructionist Congregations and Havurot
Church Rd. and Greenwood Ave.
Wyncote, PA 19095
(215) 887–1988

## Domestic Violence Resources

Jewish Women International
1828 L Street, NW, Suite 250,
Washington, DC 20036
(202) 857–1300
*www.jewishwomen.org/AWAKEN.htm*
Extensive resources for concerns about domestic violence, sexual
abuse, and child abuse in the Jewish community.
Jewish Domestic Abuse and Agunah Problem Page
www.users.aol.com/Agunah/index.htm
Includes links to other resources on Jewish domestic and sexual violence.

Shalom Task Force
P.O. Box 3028
Grand Central Station
New York, NY 10163
(718) 337-37OO (hotline)
Bibliography of sources on sexual and domestic violence
in the Jewish community.
*www.mincava.umn.edu/bibs/jewish.htm*

## Jewish Counseling

Association of Jewish Family and Children's Agencies
557 Cranbury Rd., Suite 2
East Brunswick, NJ 08816–5419
(800) 634–7346
www.ajfca.org

Jewish Family and Children's Services of
San Francisco, the Peninsula, Marin, and Sonoma
1710 Scott St.
San Francisco, CA 94115–3004
(415) 567–8860
www.jfcs.org

University of Judaism
Making Marriage Work
15600 Mulholland Dr.
Bel Air, CA 90077
(310) 440–1233

## Interfaith Support and Outreach

Jewish Outreach Institute
Center for Jewish Studies
365 Fifth Avenue
New York, NY 10016
(212) 817–1952
www.joi.org

## Jewish Adoption

Stars of David International, Inc.
Susan Katz, National Chapter Coordinator
3175 Commercial Ave., Suite 100
Northbrook, IL 60062–1915
(800) STAR–349
www.starsofdavid.org

# More Information on
# the PREP Approach

We conduct workshops for couples and train people as leaders for a variety of Prevention and Relationship Enhancement Programs (PREP). We maintain a directory of people who have been trained in each of these programs and who offer workshops or counseling using our methods. You can obtain a directory by writing us requesting a referral directory or by visiting our Web site.

We also have *Fighting for Your Marriage* audiotapes—a six-hour set covering the basic PREP content—and a four videotape series that covers the key communication and conflict management information. We plan to continue to create new ways to help couples learn from this material.

You can contact us at:

PREP, Inc.
P.O. Box 102530
Denver, CO 80250
(303) 759–9931

You can also e-mail us (info@PREPinc.com) or visit our Web site (www.members.aol.com/prepinc).

For more information on workshops for Jewish and interfaith couples and clinical training for therapists interested in Jewish identity issues, contact us at:

Jewish Relationship Seminars
817 D Street
San Rafael, CA 94901
(415) 456–1166

You can also visit us at www.jewishcouples.com or send e-mail to
jcrohn@aol.com.

# About the Authors

JOEL CROHN, PH.D., is a psychologist in private practice in San Rafael and Berkeley, California, and a research associate for Jewish Family and Children's Services of San Francisco. Dr. Crohn is a graduate of the University of California, Berkeley, and the Wright Institute. He has conducted research, written, and given lectures nationally to mental health professionals, Jewish and Family Service clinicians, and general audiences on Jewish identity, marriage, and intermarriage for over fifteen years. He is the author of *Mixed Matches: How to Create Successful Interracial, Interethnic, and Interfaith Relationships*, a book on the problems and possibilities of intermarriage that was the outgrowth of research he conducted for the American Jewish Committee. His work has been featured frequently in print and the broadcast media, including on the *Leeza* show and on the Arts and Entertainment Network.

HOWARD J. MARKMAN, PH.D., is a professor of psychology and co-director of the Center for Marital and Family Studies at the University of Denver. He received his Ph.D. degree (1977) in clinical psychology from Indiana University. He is internationally known for his work on the prediction and prevention of divorce and marital distress. Among his many published works on the subject is *We Can Work It Out: Making Sense of Marital Conflict*, which he co-authored with Clifford Notarious. Markman has often appeared in the media, including on *20/20*, *The Oprah Winfrey Show*, and *48 Hours*, in segments on the PREP approach.

SUSAN L. BLUMBERG, PH.D., is a psychologist in private practice who specializes in working with couples, families, and children. She received her Ph.D. degree in clinical psychology from the University of Denver. Dr. Blumberg is co-director of Interpersonal Communication Options, which provides *Fighting for Your Marriage* seminars for couples in the Denver area. She has been involved in doing research on PREP and developing professional training materials for PREP workshops. She also consults with businesses and organizations about providing PREP in corporate settings. Dr. Blumberg has also been a teacher in the Denver Jewish community since 1982.

JANICE R. LEVINE, PH.D., is a clinical and developmental psychologist who lives with her husband and two children in Lexington, Massachusetts. A graduate of Yale and Harvard Universities, she is currently Clinical Instructor in Psychiatry at Harvard Medical School. Dr. Levine is the author of *The Couples Health Program*, a nationally known psycho-educational program that teaches couples how to communicate and resolve conflicts to achieve greater intimacy. She has won many professional honors and awards, appeared in newspapers, in magazines, and on TV, hosted her own Parent Education Series, and lectured throughout the United States on various aspects of couples' relationships.

# Index

and, 178–195; escalation interactions in, 27–31; impact of Jewish psychology on, 25–26; impact of negative patterns on, 44–48; impact of religion on, 201–202; interactions patterns listed, 26; invalidation interactions in, 31–33; negative interpretations interactions in, 38–44; relationship dynamics scale on, 49–51; sexuality and, 265–282; wisdom of Jewish traditions and successful, 283–284; withdrawal and avoidance interactions in, 34–38. *See also* Interfaith marriages; Marriage; Relationships

Jewish men: affective disorders of, 286n.6; attitudes toward rules by, 65–66; of the boomer generation, 57–58; emotional response to conflict by, 63–66; examining complaints of, 59–61; intimacy as defined by, 61–62; new American role changes for, 56; satisfaction with sacrifice by, 184–185; spiritual resistance and nonviolence by, 55–56; transition generation of, 56–57. *See also* Gender roles

*The Jewish Mind* (Patai), 8

Jewish psyche: conditional acceptance/self-hatred of, 7–8; dilemmas of assimilation and, 8–10; impact of admiration on, 4–5; impact of hatred on, 5–7; impact of history on, 3–4; unfulfilled expectations of, 157–159

Jewish relationships. *See* Relationships

Jewish self-hatred: basis of, 12; conditional acceptance and, 7–8

Jewish Sephardic society, 56

Jewish shtetl society, 55

Jewish society: from patriarchy to modern American roles, 55–56; gender roles in shtetl, 55. *See also* Gender roles

Jewish stereotypes: of controlling Jewish mother, 57; domestic violence and, 37; projection on opposite sex

of, 285n.5; self-hatred and, 12–13. *See also* Anti-Semitism

Jewish women: attitudes toward rules by, 65–66; of the boomer generation, 57–58; comfort with verbal intimacy, 64–65; examining complaints of, 59–61; intimacy as defined by, 61–62; satisfaction with sacrifice by, 184–185; traditional roles of, 55–56; transition generation of, 56–57; view of conflict by, 63–66. *See also* Gender roles

*Jewish Women/Jewish Men* (Cantor), 55–56

Johnson, V., 269, 280

Judaism: conversion to, 207–210; as dimension of Jewish identity, 19; successful marriages and wisdom of, 283; teachings on repentance by, 221–222. *See also* Core belief systems

**K**

Ken ahora (against the evil eye), 260

*Kiddush hashem* (holy martyrs), 8

Klein, J. W., 12, 13, 15, 57

Kushner, Rabbi H., 27, 188

**L**

*La'da'at* (to know/having sex), 276

Levenson, S., 69, 177

*Life Is with People*, 55

Listening: exercises to enhance, 255–256; like a friend, 252–253. *See also* Speaker-Listener Technique

**M**

Markman, H., 26, 105

Marriage: impact of religion on, 201–202; interfaith, 202–207; sexuality and, 265–282. *See also* Interfaith marriages; Jewish marriages

Martyr/suffering patterns, 43

Masters, W., 269, 280

Memory and communication filters, 82–84